Principles of Productive Software Management

Principles of Productive Software Management

Michael W. Evans
Pamela H. Piazza
James B. Dolkas

A Wiley-Interscience Publication

JOHN WILEY & SONS
New York Chichester Brisbane Toronto Singapore

Library of Congress Cataloging in Publication Data:

Evans, Michael W.
Principles of productive software management.

"A Wiley-Interscience publication."
Includes bibliographical references and index.
1. Computer programming management. I. Piazza, Pamela.
II. Dolkas, James B. III. Title.

QA76.6.E978 1983 658.4'0388 83-6815
ISBN 0-471-89796-5

Printed in the United States of America

10 9 8 7 6 5 4

Preface

In recent years, industry emphasis has dealt with the technical aspects of software development, and very little work has been accomplished in the area of software management. Effective research in management techniques and controls has taken a backseat to technology, and as a result, development problems persist despite the industry's commitments to software development solutions. It is obvious that technology alone will not solve the development problem. Unless effective management techniques are used to harness the technical aspects of software development, problems in development, performance, and reliability will continue to have a devastating overall effect on system implementation, integration, and application.

In short, the software industry will continue to experience severe development problems until effective management techniques are not only developed but also used.

This book is an attempt to resolve the management problem. The methodology described herein is an integration of software management and control techniques for the total software development process. This methodology is applicable to small-, medium-, and large-scale development efforts.

The process of software development is an integration of many diverse technologies, management, and administrative techniques integrated through project control and management practices. The key to development success is management application of how and when these practices are to be applied, what resources are required, and the ability to anticipate development crises. This book describes how individual techniques are integrated into the software project and how each phase of the project is monitored, controlled, and integrated with other phases to ensure a smooth, controlled flow of work as the development proceeds. It also describes various project problems that are generic to software development and may be anticipated by software management.

MICHAEL W. EVANS
PAMELA H. PIAZZA
JAMES B. DOLKAS

Morgan Hill, California
Los Altos, California
Columbia, Maryland
July 1983

Acknowledgments

This book is based to a large degree on the authors' combined experiences, gathered through progressive experience in a variety of technical and management situations. The knowledge gained during these years has proven invaluable and, it is hoped, is usefully portrayed in the chapters that follow.

Many individuals, too many to mention singly, contributed ideas that have been used by the authors in project situations and, as a result, have indirectly contributed to the book. Several corporations and individuals deserve special thanks.

First, we thank Ford Aerospace and Communications Corporation, Western Development Laboratories (WDL) Division, The Small Business Systems Consultants Company, and the Integrated Computer Engineering Corporation for their patience, understanding, and support without which this book would not have been possible.

Secondly, we acknowledge and thank Clell Gladson of Gladson Associates, Robert Ligouri of WDL, and Michael Murphy of Boeing Computer Services for their manuscript reviews and offerings of constructive encouragement and criticism, which improved the quality of the resultant manuscript.

We would like to give special recognition to Richard Baker of Litton Industries, Mellonics Division, who reviewed both the preliminary and final manuscripts and without whose encouragement the book might never have been completed. We also thank Colonel John Marciniak of the Rome Air Development Command, whose thorough and professional review greatly enhanced the quality of the manuscript, and Jack Munson of SDC, who reviewed the final manuscript.

Two sources deserve special recognition: Paul MacDonald of Procurement Associates, Inc., provided the basic information from which the program interface chapter was extracted, and Raymond Zachary of Ford Aerospace and Communications Corporation supplied several of the principles upon which the chapters were based.

We also thank those who supported production of the early manuscripts: Bud Porter Roth of Tandem Computers, who edited the early raw ideas into readable prose, and all others who directly or indirectly assisted in the production of the final manuscript.

We thank three other individuals without whose help, understanding, and encouragement this book would never have happened. Richard Piazza's encouragement, optimism, and understanding bolstered us all when the road seemed endless. Charlotte Evans (Mrs. Michael) provided encouragement and support and had the patience and fortitude to type the final manuscript. Finally, we give special thanks to our editor, Jim Gaughan, who supported us and provided the encouragement to complete this book.

M.W.E.
P.H.P.
J.B.D.

Contents

1 The Trouble with Software

Industrial and commercial firms continue to make a significant investment on data processing and software development activities. Despite these expenditures, software continues to be the "problem child" and provides much anguish to the program manager.

The software development problem has many symptoms evident throughout the development period:

1. Inability of development personnel to understand development requirements and organization responsibilities.
2. Inability of design personnel to design a technically acceptable system responsive to the user's needs and requirements.
3. Inability of program management to control the development within schedule or cost constraints.
4. Inability of implementers to build an executable system and successfully complete predefined test cases.

As significant as these problems appear, they are only symptoms of a far more fundamental issue: software development is treated not as an engineering discipline but rather as a technical art form.

Many technical solutions have been heralded as panaceas for development. Structured design and development, top-down testing, automated development aids, software quality assurance, and many other tools and techniques all have assumed important roles in the development process; none by itself, however, has solved the fundamental software problems. We still do not know how to develop quality software consistently within cost and schedule.

System failures caused by poor software development practices or performance are commonplace. The problem with software development projects cannot be solved by the introduction of new design methodologies or programming languages or techniques alone; it can be solved only by applying basic management skills that have long been applied in other areas of business.

A building contractor begins from a set of blueprints and a list of materials that are needed to accomplish the task of building a house. These are documents agreed to by the customer before work begins. The contractor knows the order in which events have to take place; one cannot put up walls until the foundation is laid. He hires different groups of people to perform the various tasks involved and gives each group written plans and specifications as to what work they are supposed to accomplish. The contractor stays in contact with the customer throughout the process, and if changes are requested after work begins, he evaluates the cost of the changes (both in materials and labor) and revises the blueprints accordingly. The contractor knows that if walls are positioned according to last week's blueprints he will have to pay for tearing them down and putting them in the proper place.

How many software development projects are begun without first defining on paper what the product is going to look like to the customer? How often does work proceed without having formulated firm specifications? How many times have programmers been given work to code and test without being given written specifications of what they are supposed to produce? How many times have specifications changed daily through discussions or rumors so that no one knows the latest decisions that have been made, and, worse, programmers are proceeding to produce code against outdated assumptions? In other disciplines these practices would not be tolerated.

Configuration management has only recently been recognized as a necessary process in the development of software and is even regarded by many as a new discipline. It is being followed in many projects as a superfluous process that can quickly be abandoned in order to save time when the project gets into trouble. Few software personnel realize that configuration management is the process of defining the current state of a changing set of conditions on paper instead of trusting it to memory. These people would never think of writing a personal check without recording the amount and subtracting it from the balance, because they know they would not be able to remember the transaction in a week. But they do not see that keeping a current document describing file layouts is necessary.

The preceding paragraphs are not meant to underestimate the complexities of software engineering. Indeed, software is difficult to develop. There are several intrinsic attributes of software that make its development more complex than that of an average product.

THE END PRODUCT IS DIFFICULT TO EVALUATE

The product of a programmer's work cannot be examined by eye for correctness. The most tangible product is a listing of lines of code that have been written by a programmer to solve a data manipulation problem, and it is not possible even to tell what the original problem was by looking at program instructions alone. With a great deal of time and effort a skilled programmer can determine what kind of data are input to a program and what happens to that data as a result of the program's execution. Without any further information, however, he cannot determine if this is really what was required.

The only way to evaluate a software product is to test it on the basis of specifications. Specifications detail what the software is supposed to do. Testing the software to determine performance is very complex because of the difficulty in defining all the possible combinations of inputs and what should occur in each case. Defining a thorough set of tests to evaluate a piece of software can take longer than coding the instructions.

A LARGE NUMBER OF CHANGES ARE INEVITABLE

Another difficulty of software development is the inevitability of a large number of changes. No matter how much time is spent on the specification and how carefully the design is considered, better ways to do things will always be exposed as the project progresses. Unfortunately, the nuances of a set of requirements can be discovered only by getting more deeply involved in the design and implementation.

To compound the problem, most software development projects are of a size that requires the work to be split into a number of separate pieces, all of which must eventually work together. Any change in the system may affect the work of others. Even the slightest change of software code produces a new and different system, which must be thoroughly tested to ensure that no side effects have rippled throughout.

As an example of the problems that changes can cause, a thoroughly tested and documented system was shipped to a user who encountered a strange problem immediately after compiling and loading the system for the first time. Programmers looked at the source listings and scratched their heads for days. They even obtained the exact input data and ran the system at the development site with no problems. The mystery was finally solved when it was discovered that the conscientious chief programmer, just before shipping the system, decided to add a comment to one of the programs. The comment line contained an error that caused several lines of code to be considered comment, so the system had compiled correctly, but the programmers were looking at source code that did not match that which produced the running system.

PROGRAMMING IS AN ACTIVITY WHICH IS DIFFICULT TO MEASURE

Further, the development of program logic is something that cannot be measured accurately from the time the programmer begins until he finishes coding the instructions. When a programmer says the program is 50% coded, he is merely creating a figure to satisfy management. Getting the instructions on paper is not a measurable end product. The code must compile without errors and then be tested and modified until it does what is required under all conditions.

These intrinsic qualities of software have caused many managers to throw up their hands in despair, assuming that developing software is an intellectual process that cannot be categorized or controlled as can other processes leading to a product. They have also despaired of being able to test the product thoroughly, for the combinations of logic paths are seemingly infinite. Finally, they feel it is useless to document design decisions until the system is complete, because the design is constantly changing. In short, software development has been looked on as an art form, and programmers have been treated as temperamental artists whose work is an abstract intellectual struggle.

The key to software development lies in recognizing that software can be developed successfully by taking development as a series of small tasks, each resulting in a tangible product. These tasks, properly allocated to personnel and executed within a controlled environment, can lead to a system that works. Software managers must borrow basic management principles from other disciplines and apply them instead of using the excuse that "software is different." Keeping current versions of plans and products used during the development process, for example, is not a methodology or tool to aid the development, but is a requirement of getting the job done.

The following chapters describe what is involved in making the software development process an orderly set of tasks leading to the production of a quality system that meets customer requirements.

When discussing the role of the software manager and staff the assumed project organizational structure is a centralized software project. The manager has responsibility for software requirements specification, design, code, integration and test of multiple software subsystems. These subsystems are loadable, executable entities and may be software or firmware. Although the disciplines, project management and control techniques, and testing requirements and methodologies are described in the context of this project structure, when scaled to a project with a single subsystem they work equally well.

2 The Software Development Process: An Overview

The development of software is a rigorous process of integrating technical, administrative, and management disciplines into a cohesive, well-planned, and controlled structure.

The effective software project is characterized by a smooth flow of data and project responsibility as the software development proceeds and as data products are developed and reviewed. The software manager orchestrates the process by applying resources to the project. The manager also plans, schedules, and reviews the development activities. Also, as required, to avoid unanticipated project crises and to ensure a smooth, controlled development flow, he coordinates and infuses energy and a sense of urgency into the project.

Although the requirements of the software development life cycle are generic, the development environment and structure is specific to each project and must be defined, documented, and implemented accordingly.

This chapter discusses the general process of software development, identifying the major activities and products involved in creating a software system. Also discussed are management tasks that must be executed in order to ensure that a quality system is produced within the time and cost allocated to the project.

As illustrated in Figure 2.1, the software development flow most often perceived by management has five serial stages. The first stage, project planning, consists of those tasks that define specific software project requirements and tailor these requirements to characteristics of the application. The project budget and schedule parameters are developed during this period, and a viable software technical, organizational, and control environment is established.

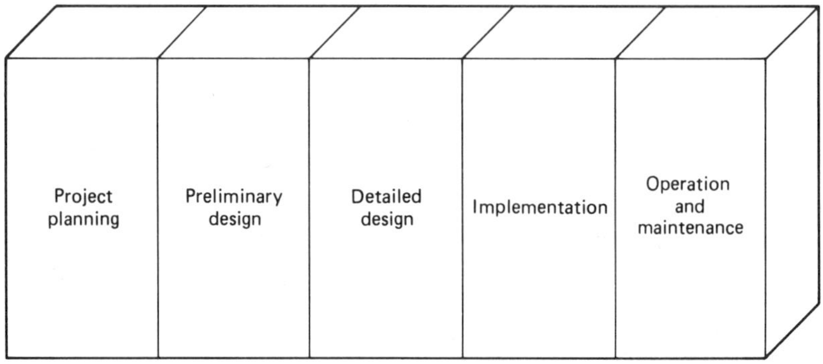

Figure 2.1. Software development phases.

The second development stage, preliminary design, defines the software system's functions and allocates the software requirements to specific software components.

The third stage, detailed design, produces a viable design by which the software can accomplish the required functions.

The fourth stage, implementation, translates the design into software source code, which is tested and corrected until it performs the desired functions.

During the fifth stage, operation and maintenance, the software is used in the field environment and modified in response to actual operational experience. The quality, maintainability, and adherence to actual user requirements built into the software determine how effective or chaotic the operation and maintenance period will be.

Although this view of software development is an accurate portrait of the main processes that must take place, it does not reflect the important management tasks that must be involved throughout the process. Each development phase is actually an amalgamation of many tasks spanning the artificial boundaries imposed by the standard development flow. The software development process is, in reality, an integrated grouping of several interdependent categories of tasks linked together through the development schedule, project configuration management requirements, test requirements, internal and external software project reviews, and customer requirements.

As illustrated in Figure 2.2, nine general categories of software management tasks form the foundation on which the project rests and must be continuously integrated into the project throughout the five stages of development previously described.

A commitment to configuration management principles, for example, must be made from the first day in order to have any decisions involving the project written on paper, disseminated to each current project member, and filed for availability to new project members as they become involved.

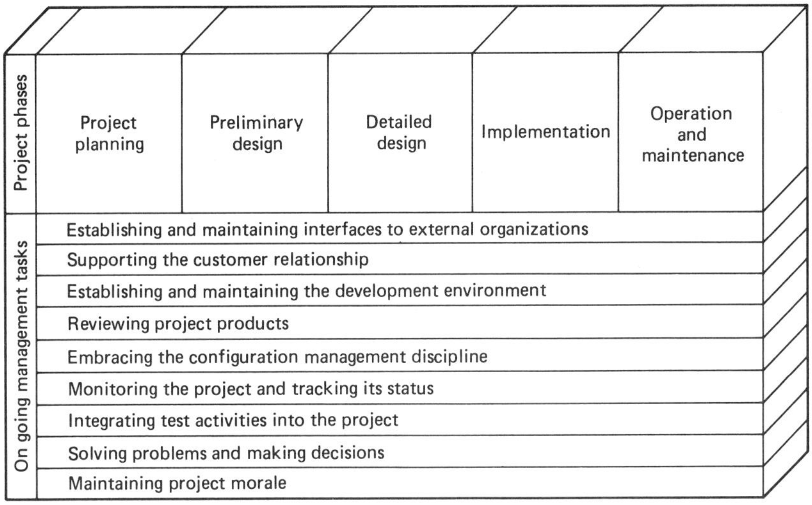

Figure 2.2. Relationship between software development phases and management tasks.

The five stages of software development will result in a quality system only if:

1. The important management tasks shown in Figure 2.2 are continually and faithfully administered.
2. Each stage of development is defined as a series of tasks, each of which results in a product that serves as a stepping stone, or baseline, for the next.

THE IMPORTANT MANAGEMENT TASKS

The success of the project depends as much on the proper execution of the nine interrelated management tasks pictured in Figure 2.2 as it does on the definition of project stages and products. As we shall see, the execution of these tasks imposes a basic structure and organization on the project and influences the definition of the stages and products of development.

Establishing and maintaining interfaces to external organizations involves identifying the organizations with which the software group must interact during the project. It also involves determining the type of relationship that will be involved and establishing and maintaining communications with these organizations.

In order to be effective, the software manager must understand the environment in which his organization must function. He must understand the immediate environment, which may include various program organizations, such as systems engineering, as well as the total company environment, which will involve interfaces with personnel, procurement, facilities, and other organizations. The manager must work within the company structure and be aware of company policy in order to get the software job done. During the life of the project, he will need to interface to many company organizations in order to acquire and install facilities and equipment, staff the project and deal with personnel issues, provide training courses and materials for the staff, and arrange for travel as necessary. The manager must also determine what is required of the software organization by higher management and understand the specific relationship his or her project has to long-term company goals.

Supporting the customer relationship involves cultivating and maintaining a mutually beneficial interface with the customer throughout the project. This means establishing unambiguously what the customer wants so that he is getting what was requested and what is being paid for. Supporting the customer means obtaining his concurrence on a written set of requirements and specifications that define the work and making it known that any requested changes will have to be analyzed with regard to cost and schedule. It means establishing the interfaces between customer and project personnel to allow customer visibility without disrupting the work that is performed. Supporting the customer also means establishing the extent to which the customer will be allowed to dictate contractor development and management procedures.

Chaos can result if firm customer relationships are not established early or are ignored. For example, if the customer does not approve a written set of requirements and documentation, he can request changes constantly, expecting no extra schedule and cost impact. Conversely, if the customer is not involved in the process of establishing requirements for the system and in the development process, he may end up with a system that has no value to him. Although the customer may have no legal recourse in this case, it is not good business practice to play on the naiveté of the customer. It is in everyone's best interest to keep the customer involved throughout the project through a controlled interface.

Establishing and maintaining the development environment means setting up the facilities and the atmosphere under which software will be developed. It includes acquiring and/or developing the:

1. Equipment
2. Operating system, software tools, and utilities
3. Facilities (computer room, terminal placement)
4. Operating procedures
5. Organization
6. Documentation production services necessary to document, develop, and test the software

These items must be considered early in the project because equipment procurement and installation can involve lengthy waiting periods. It is very disruptive to project members to be ready to code and test and have no facilities to do so. Operating procedures must be clearly defined, for without them, people are bound to fight over computer or terminal time. A word processing system is necessary for document production, as specifications change so often. A graphics facility is necessary for drawing figures and diagrams. An editor is essential to ensure consistency of format and grammatical correctness. Someone must be responsible for coordinating each document's production through its many trips from author to data entry and graphics to editing personnel until it is published. If a smoothly running facility is not already in place for document production, its creation is very time consuming.

Reviewing project products involves including appropriate personnel in the review of each intermediate and end product developed during the project. Such reviews will allow early detection of problems and will help to ensure that a quality system is being developed. Each document produced should be reviewed internally before release to the customer. Software code should also be reviewed against development standards and for technical soundness against design documentation.

Embracing the configuration management discipline means making a continuous, firm commitment to the principle of keeping track of the current status of a set of information that is constantly changing. The need for the configuration management discipline is clearly recognized in any business, no matter how small. It is clear that a business that does not attempt to perform bookkeeping and accounting activities will not last very long. It is also universally recognized that a business needs a staff just to attend to these activities. Why does the software business not realize that bookkeeping activities must be done and that a system must be devised and personnel hired to do this work?

Even in a small system with very little code produced, the need for managing specification documents and source and executable code exists. When there are no facilities available to match executable code with the source code from which it originated, keeping track of a developing software system becomes at least as large a problem as an accounts payable/accounts receivable system. The problem, of course, is compounded in proportion to the size of the software system.

Much emphasis has been placed on describing software configuration management policies and procedures in great detail. Often when people read this type of literature, they get so bogged down in the complexity of the procedures that they abandon the configuration management discipline. What is important is that the reason for configuration management is understood and that the goals are clearly seen. Once the need for the process is understood, there will be no question that it is required and that there are hundreds of ways configuration management can be implemented for a particular system to meet the goals.

What are the goals of configuration management with regard to a developing software system? An organization should be able to respond to the following requests:

1. I want a copy of the latest ——— (document name) and a list of all changes that have been approved since the last time it was officially published
2. I want a copy of the latest version of the executable system with a list of all outstanding problems and a list of features that are not yet implemented
3. I want the source listing for module x, version y
4. I want to know when this change was made to the ——— (document name), who approved it, and why it was implemented

Project monitoring and status tracking involves breaking large pieces of work into a series of tasks, each of which results in a tangible end product, so that the status of the project can be clearly assessed. It requires maintaining a detailed schedule for all tasks clearly showing the interrelationships among the tasks and what effect a problem encountered in completing a particular task will have on total project status. It involves defining and implementing a system for collecting and updating status data on a timely basis, so that problems can be quickly recognized and resolved.

Integrating test activities into the project must be done continuously from the beginning of the project. Two types of testing are required in a system composed of interfacing pieces of software. First, each software module should be tested by the programmer to ensure that the lowest level functions it is designed to perform are in fact supported by the module. Because the module will receive data from other modules instead of from the user or external sources directly, module tests will require that software be written to produce input data according to design specifications that detail the format of internally generated data. These tests are extended to include tests of several interfacing modules that form a unit and perform the next level of functions. All tests up to this point are tests of the software against the detailed design specifications.

At the point where software is integrated into subsystems that provide the high-level system functions required by the user, the testing becomes functional testing and should be performed by a team separate from the personnel who code the system in order to eliminate any bias resulting from intimacy with the internal design of program logic. Testing should be done against known requirements and specifications of how the user interfaces with the system. Functional testing is, therefore, a separate process that must be planned, documented, and executed in parallel with, but running just behind, the development process.

Test requirements must be considered from the project's beginning, for a test may require specific equipment to be procured and/or simulators to be developed. Test cases must be developed and test data created and documented so that errors can be reproduced for the development team to correct.

Tests cannot be executed until the software is developed. The most time efficient way to test is to plan for partial system capabilities to be produced and tested early, adding more functions to the system for the next test phase until the entire system is developed. The planning for what capabilities will be added and at what stages requires cooperation from both test and development team members.

Problem solving and decision making will occur daily if management has created a controlled, organized, production-oriented environment. Communication of technical, procedural, and personnel problems must be encouraged and effectively acted on within a reasonable amount of time, or the staff will cease to communicate problems. Decisions will be better decisions if those who are involved are able to participate in making them. If an unpopular decision must be made, it will be respected if it is made firmly but with an explanation of why it was made.

Maintaining project morale involves management's relationship with personnel. Morale will be high if the project is well organized, if each person knows his or her responsibilities and the organizational relationships involved, and if people feel in control of their work. Feeling in control of one's work is one of the most important contributors to employee satisfaction. Each employee is to have as much responsibility and authority as he can handle, and each person knows that if a problem arises over which he has no direct authority, superiors will provide necessary action.

Morale is also high if the project members work as a team. If management communicates the feeling that the team is trying to develop the best product possible and that cooperation is a valued goal, the staff will generate peer pressure to cooperate with one another. People will also tend to make decisions on the basis of the project good rather than on the basis of individual convenience. For example, when a technical problem arises during the design phase affecting the layout of a file that interfaces to several modules, if those whose modules are affected are involved in the problem and its solution, the best solution for the problem will often be agreed to by the person whose code is most seriously affected. When such changes are made without involving the affected personnel, they are justly angry at having to rework their modules.

Management's level of commitment to the eight other categories of tasks already described has a great effect on the morale of a project. Chaos is not satisfying to any good employee. When chaos becomes a way of life, personnel become very individualistic and are concerned only with finding the least amount of frustration in doing their own jobs.

DEFINING THE TASKS AND PRODUCTS OF SOFTWARE DEVELOPMENT

A high-level software life cycle, showing the stages and major products of software development and the relationships among the products and tasks, is shown in Figures 2-3 through 2-7. Definition of this life cycle is strongly influenced by the implications of the previous discussion of the nine categories of management tasks. Several features distinguish this life cycle from the traditional software project work flow. These features will be pointed out in the following discussion of each stage.

There are three major categories of activities spanning the entire development process: technical development, configuration management, and test. These activities are carried on concurrently, and each activity provides data and feedback to activities within the other two categories in order to produce a quality software system.

This view of software development implies an organization composed of three functional groups of personnel, one for each of the three types of activities, so that the activities can be carried out in parallel. Although in a small project configuration management activities can be performed by the combined efforts of development personnel and the software manager, neither typically has the time to perform these duties in a larger project, for these activities become more complex, more numerous, and more critical as project size increases. As we have advocated previously, the functional test program should always be executed by personnel who are not involved in the development of the software code.

The Planning Stage

As illustrated in Figure 2.3, during the planning stage the requirements for the software system are defined, the configuration management program is established, the test program is begun, the project schedule and budget are forumlated, and official, detailed plans for the way the project will be run are formally documented.

Laying the Foundation for Success

The software manager establishes the tone of the project, whether by conscious action or by default, within the first few days and weeks of the project. If he does not immediately assign to the staff work that is focused toward clear goals scheduled, controlled, and reviewed by management he will have trouble executing any project plans that may later be generated, no matter how complete, efficient, or elaborate they may be.

The configuration management activity begins immediately, as all project documentation is identified, collected, and analyzed as to its current status. Are some of the documents already out of date? Exactly what does each mean to the project? A list of all existing documentation, its official

Activity Category	*Task*	*Product*
Technical Development	Analyze requirements	Requirements baseline: Requirements document
	Allocate requirements to software components	Preliminary software architecture
	Size software components	Software sizing sheets
Configuration Management	Collect, identify, baseline all project data	Product inventory
	Establish change control procedures	Preliminary: CM plan
	Develop standards for development	Preliminary: Development standards
	Establish support tool requirements	
	Develop outlines for user's manual, preliminary design document, format for file/interface specifications	Documentation outlines
Ongoing Activity	Establish baseline for products, record change requests, problem reports, issue monthly summary of problems, update and release new versions of products	
Functional Test	Analyze test requirements	Input to requirements document, software plans
	Establish test philosophy	Preliminary test plan
	Establish requirements for test support tools	Test tool specifications
Software Management	Analyze requirements	Input to requirements document
	Estimate project size, cost, schedule	Budget; Schedule
	Establish project structure	Software development plan
	Expand into detailed plans as required	QA plan; Staffing plan; Security plan
Ongoing Activity	Review products, report status, obtain & apply resources, solve problems	

(Software requirements review)

Figure 2.3. Software Development Lifecycle. Stage I—Planning.

Activity Category	*Task*	*Product*
Technical Development		Functional baseline
	Establish system functions	Users manual
	Design file/interface formats	File/interface specifications
		Design baseline
	Establish software architecture, module, unit design requirements	Preliminary design document
	Allocate software functions to major system builds	Preliminary build test plan
Configuration Management	Analyze software file and build procedure requirements	Final CM plan
		Final development standards
	Develop support tools	
	Develop outline for detailed design specification	Detailed design specification outline
Ongoing Activity	Establish baseline for products, record change requests, problem reports, issue monthly summary of problems, update and release new versions of products	
Functional Test	Analyze test program requirements	Final test plan
	Analyze system functionality, ease of use	Input to user's manual, build plans
	Develop test tools	
Software Management	Produce detailed schedule for next stage (detailed design to module level) Recost & reschedule	
Ongoing Activity	Review products, report status, obtain & apply resources, solve problems	

Preliminary design review

Figure 2.4. Software Development Lifecycle. Stage II—Preliminary Design.

Activity Category	*Task*	*Product*
Technical Development	Design units, modules	Code baseline; Detailed design specification
	Finalize build plans	Final build test plan
	Identify test requirements	Module, unit test plans
Configuration Management	Set up build procedures, software version control procedures	CM procedures
	Develop support tools	
Ongoing Activity	Establish baseline for products, record change requests, problem reports, issue monthly summary of problems, update and release new versions of products	
Functional Test	Develop test cases for each build	Test procedures
	Identify environmental conditions for each test case	Test scenarios
	Develop test input data	Test data
	Develop test tools	
Software Management	Produce detailed schedule for next stage (code + unit test to module level, schedule builds) Recost & reschedule	
Ongoing Activity	Review products, report status, obtain & apply resources, solve problems	

Critical design review

Figure 2.5. Software Development Lifecycle. Stage III—Detailed Design.

Activity Category	*Task*	*Product*
Technical Development	Code and test modules Integrate into units and test Deliver to configuration management Receive official build 1 from configuration management Correct problems from build tests	Build 1 . . . Build N
Configuration Management	Establish source baseline Build executable system Release system to test and development groups Release system to customer	Source library Executable system — Build 1 Version description document Product baseline . . . Build N Includes latest version of all documents forming previous baselines.
Ongoing Activity	Establish baseline for products, record change requests, problem reports, issue monthly summary of problems, update and release new versions of products	
Functional Test	Execute test procedures Record problems Summarize test results	Problem reports — Build 1 . . . Test reports — Build N
Software Management	Plan o + m support Plan installations Recost & reschedule	Support plan Installation plan
Ongoing Activity	Review products, report status, obtain & apply resources, solve problems	

Figure 2.6. Software Development Lifecycle. Stage IV—Implementation.

Activity Category	*Tasks*
Technical Development	Install system in field Support customer questions, problems
Configuration Management	Apply updates to documentation Keep track of problems Release new systems to customer sites
Ongoing Activity	Establish baseline for products, record change requests, problem reports, issue monthly summary of problems, update and release new versions of products
Functional Test	Analyze test requirements for enhancements to system Test corrections to customer problems
Software Management	Plan for implementing enhancements to system
Ongoing Activity	Review products, report status, obtain & apply resources, solve problems

Figure 2.7. Software Development Lifecycle. Stage V—Operations and Maintenance.

identification (title, control number, etc.), and a short description of the information it contains should be prepared, and notification of its existence should be communicated to all project members, specifying where the materials are and how they can be accessed.

Change control procedures for all project products should be designed and instituted. These procedures should specify how changes are requested and problems reported, what approval is necessary to implement changes, how the changes will be implemented, and what method will be used to identify the latest version of each product.

The requirements documentation must be examined to determine the extent of the work needed to produce a document that details an expanded and clarified set of requirements from which budgets and schedules can be prepared and design can proceed. A detailed outline and guidelines for the generation of this document should be generated, as this will be the first product developed.

The software manager must determine how documentation will be produced and maintained. The facilities for the preparation of text and figures must be identified. The method by which the document is pulled together for printing and publication must be established.

As the first major technical task, the requirements for the software to be developed are analyzed, clarified, documented, and approved by the customer as the basis for preparing project budget and schedules. In order to estimate how long a job will take and how much it will cost, it must be known what the job is. This simple principle is often forgotten or ignored in software development projects.

The problem arises because a large part of the act of developing software is determining exactly what the job is. We really do not know exactly what we are building until we have analyzed the requirements and broken them down into a specific software design—which steps will not occur until late in the project. Clearly, neither customers nor the company nor the software organization itself can wait that long before having some idea of how much the process will cost, how long it will take, and how many people must be applied to the project. Instead of abandoning any attempt to pin down project parameters, we should at least do a thorough job of specifying the basic requirements, knowing that we should recost and reschedule as more information becomes available.

The Requirements Document

The requirements document, as normally provided by the customer, is a specification of the basic functions the user wants the system to perform and the environment in which it is to be employed. This document can serve only as a starting point from which software engineers can begin to amplify and clarify the requirements for the software system. The customer either does not have the expertise required to expand his or her basic system goals into a software architecture or has chosen to give the job to an outside vendor. The first step in the software development process is, then, to take the narrative description of basic requirements and analyze it thoroughly to identify requirements that are implied but not clearly specified, high-level requirements for which there are options left open to the customer as to how to proceed, and ambiguous or conflicting requirements that must be clarified and resolved. As a result of negotiations with the customer on these areas, a complete set of clear, crisp software requirements must be produced and approved as the basis on which to estimate the job and produce the system. These requirements must provide:

1. A clear definition of what the software must do to support the operational requirements of the system.
2. A description of the system environment and the relationship of the software application to the system architecture.
3. An identification of system interfaces that impact software requirements or design.
4. A definition of those system operational characteristics that provide the basis for selection of software design and architecture.
5. An identification of the specific development, delivery, production, and support requirements that are essential components of the software development.

The software requirements defined at this stage of the program are the basis for all planning decisions and provide the basic input for all technical development. As such, the requirements must be clear and nonambiguous, defined in a manner that is traceable through the design, expressed in a manner that is testable, and agreed to by customer, program, and project personnel. There are many techniques, procedures, and facilities available that may support the software manager in defining and documenting software technical requirements. These techniques are based on various technical criteria and must be selected based on satisfaction of several fundamental short- and long-term project objectives:

1. To bridge the gap between user-specified operational requirements and the software design and implementation specifications.
2. To provide a basis for controlling and monitoring the correspondence and allocation of user requirements to software architecture.
3. To provide up-front criteria for definition of software test requirements and a basis for evaluating and accepting software products.
4. To provide a basis for defining, by engineering judgment, what specific project management and control practices are to be followed and how these are to be integrated into an effective software development environment.

Reviews and Baselines

Before the requirements document is issued to the customer for review and approval, it should undergo a thorough internal review to ensure that it reflects the understandings of the entire software staff as well as higher management.

At this point the customer may require a formal requirements review, called the software requirements review, prior to approval of the requirements. The approved document establishes the first software baseline, the requirements baseline. Any proposed changes to this baseline must be carefully evaluated with respect to their impact on cost and schedule parameters before they are applied.

Software Budget and Schedule

The approved requirements must then be translated into a preliminary software architecture, which can be used as a basis for estimating the cost of the project, producing the schedule, and determining labor requirements. An attempt must also be made to allocate the functions to major software builds which divide the system functionally for test and integration purposes.

Planning Documentation

The next step in the software life cycle is to plan the project in detail. Notice that the plans for project development are formal documents. These documents are baselined and disseminated to the entire staff.

The major planning document is the software development plan, which is written by the software manager and states his plans for how the entire job will be run. This document details the project organization, the major products to be produced and the flow of work from product to product, test and configuration management philosophy, and the reviews and management control that will be applied during the software development process.

The configuration management organization will produce a separate, more detailed plan, which will spell out how products are to be stored, how changes to the products will be controlled, and how project information will be disseminated to the staff. At a later time, this document will be expanded to include detailed procedures for the building of the software itself.

Configuration management planning also includes the setting of standards for the design and coding of the software. A preliminary document that specifies the design techniques to be applied, the standards for documentation, and the general rules for the development of software code will be generated. Later, these standards will be amplified to lay out detailed software coding conventions specific to the operating system and language chosen for each source module.

Simultaneously, test personnel will produce a preliminary software test plan. This document will describe software test and acceptance procedures. It provides the framework for the entire testing process and serves as the basis for all subsequent test planning and development.

Other areas of the software development plan may require expansion in separate, more detailed plans, depending on the complexity of the project and the manager's judgment. A separate staffing plan, quality assurance plan, or security plan may be warranted by project conditions and should be produced at this time if necessary.

The software manager will support these plans immediately and will see that they are kept current as changes occur throughout the life of the project. The advantages of formalizing and communicating detailed information about how the project is to be run are that project personnel are introduced into a controlled environment from the beginning and that management has thought out these matters in detail. The plans will be of no use unless they are accurate at all times and the standards and policies set forth are consistently enforced.

Preparing for the Next Stage

In preparation for the next stage of development, the software manager must schedule the preliminary design tasks in detail and assign the work. The detailed outline for each document to be produced must be prepared.

The Preliminary Design Stage

As illustrated in Figure 2.4, the preliminary design stage results in a definition of functional requirements in order to start development. A radical departure from the traditional software development schedule is made by moving the production of the user's manual to the front of the project, just after the requirements for the software are established. Typically, the user's manual is the last document produced.

The User's Manual

The user's manual is the only document that describes the system from the customer's point of view—exactly what data are input to the system and exactly what is produced by the system for the customer to see. Examining such a document is the only way the customer can tell how easy the system will be to use and whether it indeed meets his needs.

It is a great mystery of the software industry that customers do not demand to see this document before any design or coding is begun. It is analogous to asking a contractor to build a house with three bedrooms, two baths, a kitchen, and a family room and not demanding a blueprint until the house is built.

It is also a mystery that software developers do not produce this document as a basis from which to proceed with design and implementation. The production of this document will indeed involve design considerations, such as what kinds of data should be grouped together on a terminal display (directly influencing file structures) and how cursor positioning and errors should be handled. These factors should be considered up front to ensure consistency in display and report formats, error messages, cursor positioning, and the like, because these are the most visible products of software development and are quite often the main criteria for accepting the system.

It is only when the user interface is completely specified that all the underlying functions of the system can be determined. Often, the functions of the system are determined first, and the user interface is constructed to fit these functions. The problem that arises with this approach is that the user interface, although known in the minds of the designers, is not formally specified, reviewed, and controlled and inconsistencies in these important areas arise. The user does not see the interface until the testing activity begins, and then is bound to want changes, which at this point are very costly to effect, for they may suggest new functions requiring design modifications.

When this document is written in the beginning of the project, all developers know what they are trying to build, and many ambiguities can be uncovered early in the project. Moreover, test personnel can begin to create specific test cases on the basis of a document stating exactly how the user makes the system perform its functions. Without this document, testers are forced to glean this information from coders who are too busy to talk to them and who are probably establishing the way the user interfaces with the system as they code. As these parameters are not formalized, the testers can only guess whether the system is working properly at any point in time. We have heard discussions between testers and developers in which the developers say, "If that's the way the system works, then that's the way it's supposed to be!" If this is true, then what are the testers really testing? Acceptance of this kind of logic means that there is really no use in testing at all, because the system is to be assumed correct, no matter how it is implemented.

Moving the production of the user's manual to the beginning of the project puts the software development process into the category of a business, where it belongs. Software professionals often forget about the user entirely, looking upon a computer program as an end in itself, an artistic exercise in producing an elegant algorithm. The software industry must come to the realization that a computer program's only value comes from its use to a human being. If a program is difficult to use or does not produce what is desired by the user, it is a useless program, no matter how sophisticated or efficient the code happens to be.

The user's manual itself should be written in a manner that addresses its intended audience—the user community. It should not go into design detail or describe anything the user does not need to know. It should state the purpose of the system and guide the user through all the functions it performs in terms of what inputs are required of the user and what outputs result. A detailed description of the inputs required of the user should include detailed cathod-ray tube (CRT) display formats, in which each request for input is described with regard to purpose, format, valid user responses, and system reaction to invalid input. Outputs should also be detailed, whether they appear on a CRT display or on a printed report. For each output, the manual should describe what the output means to the user and what format is being used, if it is not obvious. A summary of each possible error message, its causes, and corrective measures must be supplied. In short, the document should provide a guide showing the user how to make the system perform all its possible functions.

The user's manual should be written by a small team of senior-level software engineers, and test-team members should provide input as it is being written. Test personnel are hired primarily to act as users in ensuring that the system performs what is required. They will spend their entire project time planning for and actually using the system as built. They will naturally notice ambiguities and features that are inconvenient, and they can contribute to the quality of the user interface as it is being specified. The software development team members are specifying the system with an eye toward what is feasible to implement. Both views are needed, and the software manager must arbitrate disputes that arise as members of these two groups provide checks and balances on each other.

Reviews and Baselines

After the first draft of the user's manual is produced, it should undergo a thorough internal review by all project members. It should then be submitted to the customer and approved, or reworked until it can be approved, before further work proceeds. This document provides the next major baseline, which we have called the functional baseline. Changes to this document should be made only after customer concurrence, whether or not it is formally required.

Final Test Plan

The test plan can be finalized during this period, as the system environment is being determined in detail. Test personnel can then begin to produce detailed test procedures and scenarios that specify the exact input data required and the expected results.

File and Interface Specifications

A natural part of the process of constructing the user's manual is the determination of what functions the system must perform and what major data must be carried through the system. Another important aspect of the preliminary design stage as depicted in our life cycle is that major files and external interfaces are designed in detail before any other design is begun. The files and external system interfaces are the skeleton of the software product and should be designed and documented so that the substance of the system can be placed on this skeleton.

In many cases, the software organization must rely on other organizations to supply information concerning external interfaces, especially if hardware currently under development is involved. This situation, adding another level of data that will change throughout the development process, should prompt the software manager to establish the interfaces to these external organizations early in the project and to allocate extra time to the project for the complexity these interfaces will impose.

The Preliminary Design Specification

The functions required by the specification of what the system is supposed to perform are then identified, and a software architecture that will support them is designed. A few more senior software engineers may be added to the project at this point. The preliminary design document is then produced from the act of breaking the software that must be coded into smaller and smaller pieces, until all the modules of the system are identified. The preliminary design document is the specification of how the software will be constructed to produce the system described in the user's manual. It will be used as the basis for designing each system module in detail during the next phase, and the detailed design of each module will be added to it. The software file and interface formats will be added to produce the detailed design specification.

The preliminary design document should include an overview of the entire system, naming and introducing each major subsystem to be developed and including a high-level interface block diagram of the relationships between subsystems and any external interfaces. There should be a section for each subsystem in which the major units (groups of modules) that support each subsystem function are identified. The diagram in the first section will be expanded for each subsystem to show the units involved and their relationships. Within each subsystem section will appear a description of each unit's functions and an identification of all the modules that must be written in order to build the unit. Many low-level functions that are required by several of the units may be identified. These may be grouped as a unit of support routines.

Within each unit section there should be a hierarchical chart showing the calling relationships between the modules of the unit, and for each module a specification must be made as to the data that will be input to the module, the processing that must be performed, and the output required of the module. Although the design document is only preliminary at this point, it serves as the basic software system architecture upon which the detailed design will be built and should be reviewed internally and baselined for the next phase. We have called this baseline the design baseline.

PRELIMINARY BUILD TEST PLAN

During this phase, the development group will also determine how the software identified in the preliminary design document will be integrated into major system builds. The specific modules and units that must be coded in order to support each build will be specified, as well as what instrumentation will be required to simulate the missing functions. The test team should be involved with this effort, as it directly influences the order in which the functions will be tested, what kinds of data will be needed for each build, and where the input data for a build will originate. This analysis results in a preliminary build test plan.

PREPARATION FOR THE NEXT STAGE

At this point, the software manager should reschedule the design and implementation stages, because there now is enough information to determine the order in which the units should be designed and coded to support the build process that has been defined. The remainder of the effort can now be broken down into small tasks and brought back together for integration, with many units being designed and developed in parallel. At this point there also is a better idea of the size and complexity of each module to be coded, and the schedule produced at this time can be much more accurate than previous schedules.

The outlines for the documentation to be produced during the detailed design stage must be prepared, and the development standards document is finalized by adding detailed coding standards. The configuration management plan is also finalized, as detailed procedures for building and controlling the software system are included.

FORMAL PRELIMINARY DESIGN REVIEW

It is at this stage that a formal preliminary design review may be required by the customer. This review will concern all the products that have been developed up to this point.

The Detailed Design Stage

As illustrated in Figure 2.5, during this phase the system is specified in enough detail for more junior-level software engineers to be brought on board to design and code the units that must be produced. Detailed design of software at the module level should be performed by the programmer who will be responsible for coding and testing it. Each developer should be assigned modules and units that are related to each other, so that interface design can be handled without consulting other staff.

For each module, the documentation that should be supplied for the detailed design specification will be the following, at a minimum:

1. Official module identification (name and control number)
2. Purpose of the module
3. Language in which the module is written
4. The call line necessary to invoke the module
5. Description of each parameter passed to and from the module
6. List of all constants and variables used by the module and for each, its purpose, format, and value or range of values
7. List of all files or data base structures used
8. Graphic or structured English representation of the main logic flow
9. Narrative description of the detailed logic flow

Development Test Planning

During this phase, the development group will also document a plan for testing each unit and demonstrating its functions in a standalone environment. Instrumentation software, which simulates the passing of data from one unit to another, must be identified during this analysis and developed prior to the unit test.

The programmer responsible for the detailed design of a module will also produce a plan for testing the logic paths in the module. The module and unit test plans detail the methods by which the software will be tested before integration with other units into builds, which will be tested by the functional test team.

Tests at this level are made against the design specifications. Future functional tests are made by the test team against the user's manual.

Incremental Internal Design Reviews

As each group of related modules is documented in the preceding manner, a design review is held to determine the soundness of the design. Once reviewed and approved, the detailed design for each unit is baselined and released to the document coordinator and to configuration management for inclusion in the detailed design specification. Changes to these unit specifications are controlled even before the entire design document is assembled.

Detailed Design Specification

The detailed design specification is produced by adding the module specifications and the file and interface formats previously produced to the preliminary design document.

REVIEWS AND BASELINES

Once assembled, the entire design document should be reviewed internally. It is at this time that project members are first able to explore the design of all other units in depth. This document is not usually officially approved by the customer until final delivery of the system; however, it does represent the baseline against which all source code is developed. We have called this baseline the code baseline.

TEST PROCEDURES, SCENARIOS, AND TEST DATA

Meanwhile, the test team is producing the test procedures document, which details the test cases to be run against each build of the software. Detailed test scenarios must then be designed, identifying the exact conditions under which each test case is to be run, the data to be input, and the results expected from the test case execution. Production of the test data is planned and begun.

FORMAL CRITICAL DESIGN REVIEW

At this point, the customer may wish to hold a formal review, often called the critical design review, in which the system design and test procedures are discussed before coding proceeds.

PREPARATION FOR THE NEXT STAGE

The schedule for the implementation period should now be reviewed and changed as necessary to produce a detailed plan for coordinating the code, test, and system build testing activities that will be required during the implementation phase. Depending on the number of changes that have become necessary during the detailed design phase, the software manager may need to recost and reschedule at this point.

Configuration management activities are those that prepare for the actual building of systems from source code.

The Implementation Stage

As shown in Figure 2.6, coding of modules, integration of modules into units, build testing, and correction of problems found are activities that are carried on in parallel.

INCREMENTAL REVIEWS AND BASELINES

As a unit is coded, it undergoes a review in which source code is examined against the detailed design specification before module and unit tests are begun. After a unit is tested, a test review is held to ensure that the unit is ready to be integrated into the next build, at which time the source code is baselined. When all the software necessary for the next build has been baselined, the system is built by the configuration management group and released for functional testing. The latest released system build forms the current test baseline.

A programmer may proceed to code another unit after the unit on which he has been working is baselined. He must, however, correct any problems found in the build testing process for that unit as a first priority.

During this stage, many pieces of information are produced and must be rigorously controlled. Problem reports are produced by the test team and must be tracked with regard to which system build and what test case resulted in the problem, who is responsible for correction, and what is the status of the problem. Problems to be corrected in the next system build must be easily identifiable so that the test team can rerun previous tests to ascertain whether the correction solved the problem.

For each system build, a version description document must be produced that details the exact system configuration, the outstanding problems, and the functional capabilities of the system. A version description document is necessary because of the many iterations of system builds. Quality software cannot be developed unless attention to these details is maintained throughout the development phase.

Test reports are generated by the test team upon execution of the tests for that build.

It is at this stage that the unstructured project literally falls apart. All the misunderstandings and ambiguities resulting from unspecified or uncontrolled design interfaces are uncovered as the system is integrated, causing much chaotic activity as software is hurriedly patched and redesigned to resolve these conflicts in time to meet the rapidly approaching delivery date. An uncontrolled environment for system integration and testing results in spending much time trying to reconstruct test cases and finding the versions of each module which was used in the system at the time the error was detected.

In an environment in which the development has been planned and executed in a structured fashion, the pace will be hectic as problem reports are generated, the problems are analyzed and corrected, and new systems are built and tested, but the structure that has been imposed upon the project from the beginning will result in few, if any, interface conflicts. Problems that arise within this environment can be resolved quickly.

When all the software has been added at the final build, all attention is placed upon testing and correcting the system until it is accepted by the customer and delivered.

Final Reviews and Baselines

Formal acceptance tests are normally run and the results approved by the customer before the system is delivered. The delivered documentation and software forms the product baseline, against which all future modifications will be made at the customer's request.

Preparation for the Next Stage

Development staff may begin to leave the project as their units undergo build testing successfully. The software manager must plan for enough remaining staff to support the operations and maintenance phase, in which the field environment will uncover previously undetected errors that must be corrected and that may affect the released documentation as well.

Plans for the installation of the software must be made, and any requirements for user training must be analyzed, scheduled, and staffed.

The Operations and Maintenance Stage

As illustrated in Figure 2.7, this stage of the project starts upon completion of the acceptance tests and extends throughout the operational life of the software. Installation of the software at customer sites must be supported, and often user training classes are requested.

Sound configuration management procedures used during development will be sufficient to support the software in the field environment. The major difference between configuration management activities in the operation and maintenance stage and those carried on during development is that software is released to and problems are originated from customer sites instead of the development site. The situation may arise in which different customer sites require different versions of configurations of the software developed. The configuration management program must keep track of what versions are released to what sites, and all problems must be reported and future modifications and releases keyed to the particular site.

The benefits of standardized coding practices, detailed design documentation, and solid configuration management practices come to light during this stage.

As this brief trip through the software development process has shown, there is a myriad of activities that must be carried out in order to produce a software system. In order to do a good job, the software manager must be cognizant of all the parameters affecting software development from the beginning of the project. He must create a smoothly running organization of people with the required skills, talents, and experience necessary to carry on these diverse activities. He must identify and acquire all the other resources needed to support the staff in the execution of these activities.

Often, software managers are appointed on the basis of the excellent technical work they have accomplished and are not given any training or guidance in undertaking the very new and different job of managing the project. This amounts to what was called "trial by fire" in colonial New

England. Unprepared and unassisted, many potentially excellent software managers find themselves overwhelmed by the software development crisis and are either branded as failures or request to be placed back in the technical ranks.

The remaining chapters of this book present basic management principles that apply to software development, in the hope that the information can be used to forewarn and forearm a potential or current software manager with an awareness of the many special processes and problems associated with the software engineering business.

3 The Configuration Management Discipline

Whenever two or more people are involved in producing a single product, the configuration of the resulting product must be carefully managed in order for the separate pieces to be brought together into a coherent whole.

Any product that is produced from the work of two or more people runs the risk of becoming an amalgamation of ill-fitting partial products. A desk built by three people with no configuration management might result in a frame with drawers of differing sizes and styles, none of which fit into the slots constructed for them.

In order to ensure that a cohesive unit is produced, the configuration of the end product must be planned before the work of separate producers is begun, and the current configuration must be known to all producers at all times during the development of the product. This requirement means that changes to the configuration must be applied in an orderly fashion and communicated to all producers.

THE SOFTWARE CONFIGURATION MANAGEMENT PROBLEM

In software development there is an extreme configuration management problem, in that there are many people developing a series of products, each of which builds upon previous products and all of which are constantly undergoing change by the very nature of the work involved in producing the final system. To make matters worse, a change to one of the products may require that changes be applied to any number of the products that currently exist. Figure 3.1 shows the relationships among the software products within the project structure advocated in this book. As shown in the figure, a change to any of the products must be evaluated for its impact on all products produced thus far.

The final product of the software development process consists of the entire set of products shown in Figure 3.1, all of which must agree in content, or the software system is not valid. A collection of tapes and disks containing executable software is of no use without information as to what functions it performs and how it can be made to perform those functions.

With regard to the software development process, the configuration management discipline must be rigorous in order to ensure that all personnel are working toward the same goal. It must consist of a set of plans and procedures designed to keep constant track of all the software products being developed, so that at any point in time the system can be thoroughly described with regard to the following:

1. What is the ultimate system supposed to do?
2. What are the products that will comprise the ultimate system?
3. What is the purpose of each product to be developed, and what is the content and format of each product?
4. What does the current system do?
5. How does one use the system?
6. What problems are associated with the current system?
7. What is the history of the system?

In order to accomplish the major goal of describing the current and planned system, the procedures developed must ensure that:

1. The configuration of each product is specified with regard to the content and format before work is begun on that product
2. The products that comprise the system are known by name and latest version number
3. Changes to products are controlled and the reasons for the changes recorded
4. Records of current problems with system products are maintained

Importance of Formalized Standards for the Development of Software Products

Because there are so many products, each being developed by more than one person, there is a double requirement for ensuring consistency throughout the system. Each intermediate product must be consistent within itself as well as consistent with all other intermediate products that comprise the final system.

Documentation produced by several people must be written against a predefined outline that specifies the form and content of each section. Consistent formatting conventions must be used throughout each individual document as well as across all system documents. As much as possible, the format and contents of the document should be specified in enough detail to minimize the noticeability of highly differing writing styles among the authors. For example, if the outline for the design specification merely specifies that a section will be written describing each software module in the system, the authors will choose to present the information in differing levels of detail and in a variety of styles. However, if the section itself is outlined in detail, the content of the section and the order in which the information is presented will be consistent from one such section to the next, and the reader can find information easily.

Just as documentation must be consistent, source code should also be written in a standardized format to permit ease of reading and maintainability. No matter how much some programmers think that their code is their personal property, it is an absolute fact that in a software system of any size each programmer's work will have to be accessed and read by other people. Gone are the days when a programmer can hide his program listings under his coat. There are too many interfaces among programs and too much turnover during the life of a long project to hope that programmers will not need to read one another's codes. Much maintenance time will be saved if the format for source modules is standardized. For example, the version number and programmer name should appear at the same place in every source module, and all variables should be defined and commented as to purpose, possible range, and so on, in a place near the beginning of the module.

The outline for each document should be formulated and distributed to all project members before work is assigned to them, and the standards for code development should be documented well before any module design or coding is begun.

Importance of Change Approval and Change Impact Analysis

Because the products of software development are so highly interdependent, and because many people are involved in producing them, almost any one proposed change will be controversial within the staff. Changes should not, therefore, be applied unless there is an analysis of the change considering system goals as a whole. Also, there must be a legislator who has the final authority for change approval, which means that all requests for changes should be written and submitted for review and evaluation. The software manager should be the final authority for all changes, for he is responsible for the final product and must ultimately answer for the acceptability of the final system. He can and should use the available technical staff to help with decisions regarding proposed changes and should consult with all those whose work is affected in order to keep the morale of the staff high and to keep the staff project oriented rather than area oriented.

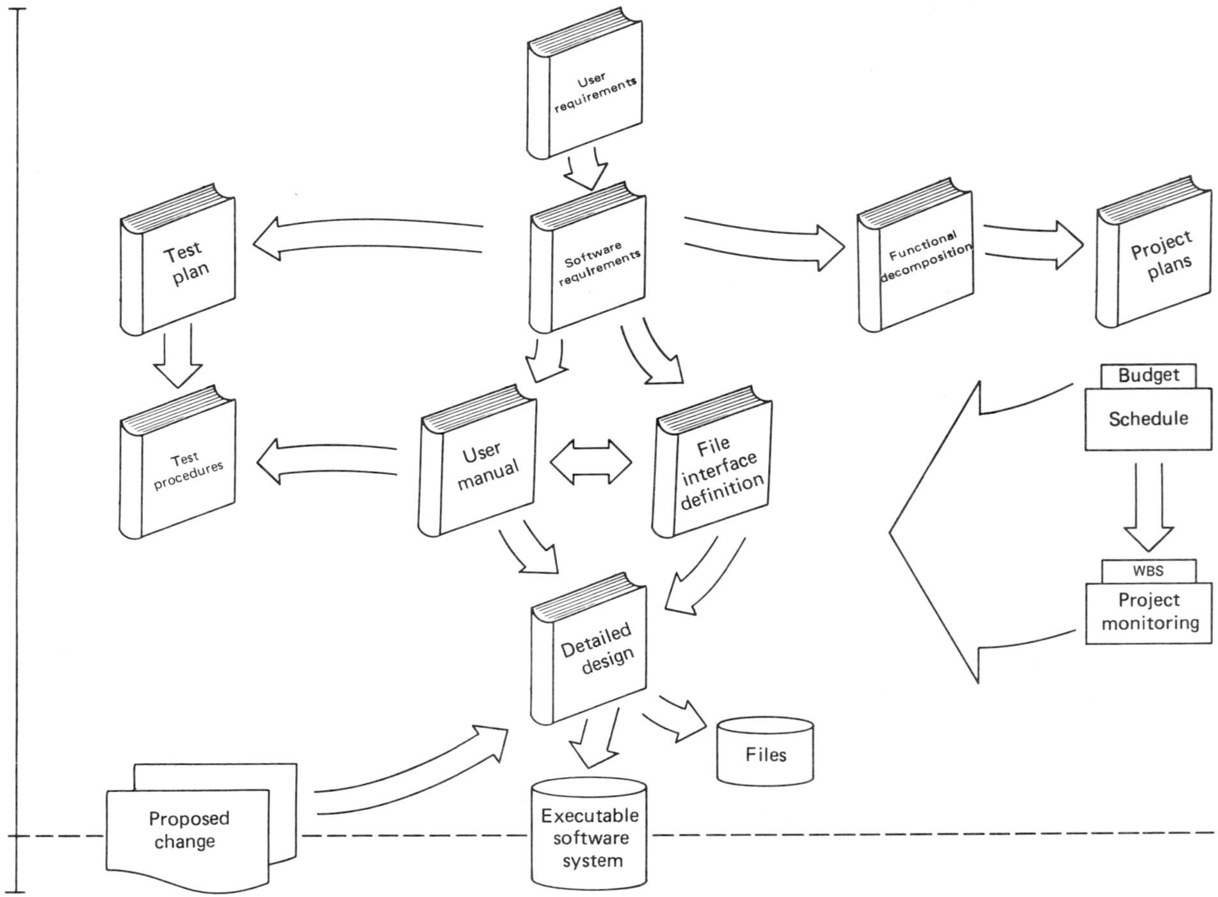

Figure 3.1. Software development products.

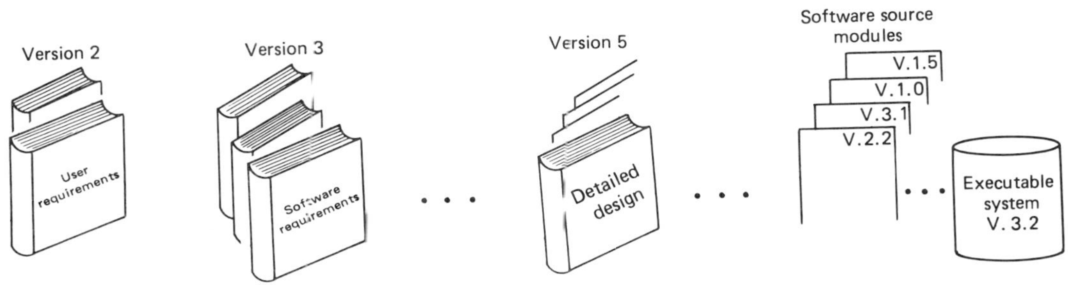

Figure 3.2. Latest system products and version levels.

Each change must be evaluated with respect to its effect on all current products. The impact of each change on schedules and budgets must also be evaluated. Any change that affects customer-approved products must be discussed with the customer as well.

Lack of such change-control principles can easily result in project chaos. A bleak picture can be painted in which people are developing separate products, each of which is being created to satisfy different requirements, making it practically impossible that the product will work in a predictable way when integrated from its parts. In such an environment, it may not even be known what the requirements of the final system are by any project member.

Problems in Identifying the Latest System Products

Even if changes are carefully controlled and applied, the task of keeping track of these changes and the resulting products is not easy. In order to keep track of a single product that changes often, we must be able to identify each successive product resulting from a change. The typical way to do this is to apply a version-numbering scheme to successive products, so that the original product is labeled version 1, and successive changes result in versions 2, 3, and so on. Since a change to one product may impact any number of the products comprising the system, it is typical to have a situation in which the products are at differing version numbers. Figure 3.2 shows a possible snapshot of the latest system products. Thus, it is necessary not only to keep track of the latest version for each product but also to maintain an inventory of each product's latest version number in order to be able to assemble the current system.

The problem of keeping track of all system products gets progressively worse as more products and more people are involved and increases dramatically at the point where software itself is introduced to the set of system products. Not only is an executable software system composed of many individual modules, each of which is literally changing by the minute during the code and test phases, but also each module can exist in several different intermediate states, none of which exists in human readable form. Figure 3.3 explodes the product labeled "Executable software system" in Figure 3.1 into its worst-case number of intermediate products and associated physical representations. That a single piece of software can exist in several intermediate forms increases the likelihood that all the pieces do not match one another unless rigorous control procedures are applied.

Philosophy for Control of Software Products

It is literally impossible and actually undesirable to control all the changes that occur to software modules during initial development. Part of the

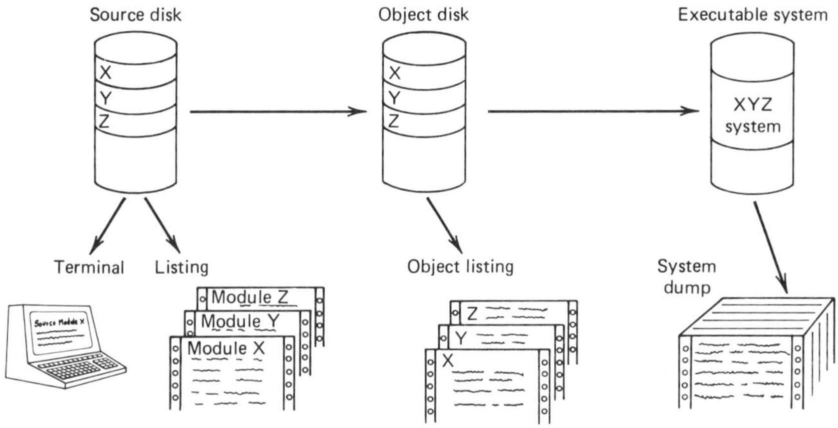

Figure 3.3. Software intermediate products and physical representations.

process of coding a module is the testing of all possible logic paths to find coding errors, which inevitably are numerous. Programmers must feel free to correct their programs and make changes until they are satisfied that the programs work according to the design specifications using test data that are simulated to agree with the formats expected to be received from external files and modules. It is at the point when modules created by different individuals are brought together for test that it is important to baseline the executable system so that tests made against the system can be rerun against the same system when problems are found.

Interfaces between pieces of software should be tested as early as possible so that problems can be isolated and corrected before the addition of more interfaces. The testing philosophy advocated in this book is one in which the system is developed and tested in stages. Functions are added to the system incrementally, and at the point where the module testing is complete for all the individual modules that accomplish the functions called for, they are brought together to create an executable system, called a system build, that will test the interfaces among these modules.

It is at the point where a source module first enters a system build that it should be baselined for control, for other programmers are using source listings of this work in order to identify problems that have arisen in the newly tested interfaces with their modules.

Likewise, when a problem is found in a module as included in a system build, the programmer should be able to apply the change and correct the code informally until he is convinced the problem is solved. At this point the software configuration can be updated for the next build. In this way, the configuration management function is taking a snapshot of the integrated system at specified points in time instead of burdening programmers and the configuration management staff with tracking all the changes that occur inbetween the official builds.

Once Is Not Enough

Unfortunately, during the development of a software system it is not enough to have available the latest version of each product. We must be able to trace the products through all their previous versions and know why and when each change was applied. For example, the customer late in the project may request a change that seems easy enough to implement. At some point in the design process, this change may have been considered, but when analyzed thoroughly, it was found to have unacceptable effects on the system. If this fact is not documented, much time can be lost reanalyzing the situation. Worse yet, the change can be partially implemented, affecting several documents and much software before it is realized that it causes unresolvable problems in some other part of the system.

Another example of the necessity for keeping all versions of all products occurs during test and integration. Often, when testing a set of software to which changes have been applied, it is found that functions that worked in previous versions no longer work, even though they themselves have not been changed. It is invaluable in finding the root of such a problem to be able to go back to previously working versions of the system and analyze the effects of changes that have been made one at a time.

Importance of Management Support

Once the major goals of configuration management are realized, there are many ways detailed procedures can be developed to implement them. In order for any set of configuration management procedures to work, however, it is necessary that they be made known to the entire staff and that they are firmly and rigorously supported by the solftware manager. Although the amount of record-keeping required on a software project is expensive and time-consuming, a price cannot be placed on the amount of wasted effort expended when control of the many software products is lost. Documentation written by several people without guidelines on content and format must be reworked until it is consistent within itself as well as consistent with other documents produced. Code developed against outdated design assumptions will have to be thrown away and redone. Analysis of software problems against outdated source code listings is also wasted effort. It is amazing how quickly schedule and budget can be overrun when several project members spend time on what turns out to be fruitless work. A cost of ineffective or nonexistent configuration management procedures that is less obvious and harder to quantify is the effect on project morale when people are constantly forced to revise their work for reasons they do not know or understand.

CREATING A CONFIGURATION MANAGEMENT PROGRAM

Because the configuration management discipline requires definition of the configuration of all system components such that consistency is maintained throughout the system, it can be thought of as a quality control function. The architect of the configuration management program should be someone who knows software, who can create content and format guidelines for documentation and source code, who can design a logical structure for the storage and updating of computer-resident files, and who can build a software system from source input, troubleshooting problems experienced during the building process.

This position requires a senior software engineer who has designed and implemented software and is of the caliber to evaluate the content of all project products. This person should be the software manager's right hand in ensuring that the configuration of the system is sound.

As we will see in the following sections, the configuration manager may well need to supervise a staff of assistants to support the procedures that will be devised. The following sections describe basic configuration management principles and examples of procedure that must be tailored to the particular project environment.

Guidelines for Developing Configuration Management Procedures

In order to implement the configuration management discipline, it is necessary to answer the questions described in the following subsections. These questions will be presented and discussed in such an order that when answered, they may be used to produce a viable plan for the execution of the configuration management program.

It is important to remember that before any configuration management procedure can be implemented, the contractual requirements for the project must be researched thoroughly. In some cases, the customer may dictate the types of records that must be kept and the exact format in which they are required. The outline and format of each document may be specified in detail. The guidelines presented in the following subsections show the minimum informational requirements for each record-keeping activity. Even if the activities described are not required by the customer, they should be supported in order to ensure that current project status is available.

Question 1: What Are the Software Products to be Developed?

The first step in setting up a program for the configuration management of software products is to identify the products that will be controlled. In the beginning we do not know the names of all the software modules that will be developed, but we should know the major subsystem names. At the

XYZ Software Product Inventory					
Product Name	Control no.	Version no.	Release date	Approval	Baseline
XYZ software requirements	02000-01	1.0	10/08/82	Customer	Requirements
XYZ software development plan	02000-02	1.0	10/28/82	Internal	
XYZ standards and conventions	02000-03			Internal	
. . .	. . .	. . .	. . .	. . .	. . .
XYZ user's manual				Customer	Functional
XYZ preliminary design document				Internal	Design

Figure 3.4. Sample software product inventory table.

very least, we know that each source module and each executable software system created for test and integration purposes must be uniquely identified and controlled.

It is necessary to determine which products will serve as baselines for the next phase of development and for each product, whether initial product acceptability and change approval authority lies with the customer or within the software staff.

All this information can be presented in a tabular form, as illustrated in Figure 3.4, which shows the beginning of such an inventory using the products and baselines advocated in this book. This figure will form the basis for the official product inventory that will be maintained throughout the project and will include other information necessary to track the status of each product, such as a unique control number assigned to each product, the correct version number of the product, and the date of the product's last release, as it becomes available.

Question 2: Where Will the Official Versions of the Software Products Be Stored, and How Do Project Personnel Access Them?

The most efficient way to keep track of all project products and associated records is to locate the data in a centralized site and place its maintenance and distribution under the control of a single individual. In all but the smallest software efforts, the amount of record-keeping and physical control of products is too much for the software manager or configuration manager to handle. A concept that works very well is to establish a project support library (PSL), or a single location in which all project products are kept under the control of an official librarian.

The librarian should possess exceptional organizational skills, know enough or learn enough about software to execute the procedures necessary to build a system from its component parts given the procedure or command files, and have the capability to supervise others, in case the procedures developed require additional clerical staff.

In the project support library environment, the librarian identifies each product by name and version number and determines where each physical product will be stored. In the case of documentation, the librarian keeps the original of each version under lock and key and keeps copies available for project members on request. The librarian also keeps a current list of all project personnel who must be notified when new products are distributed from the library or changes are made.

In the case of software, the librarian keeps a set of source listings for current system modules, a source listing of the build procedure necessary to create the executable system, and backups of all source and build files as well as a backup of the official executable system. The source and build procedures on tape or portable disk media can be used to rebuild the system if necessary, and the executable system backup can be loaded quickly for testing purposes.

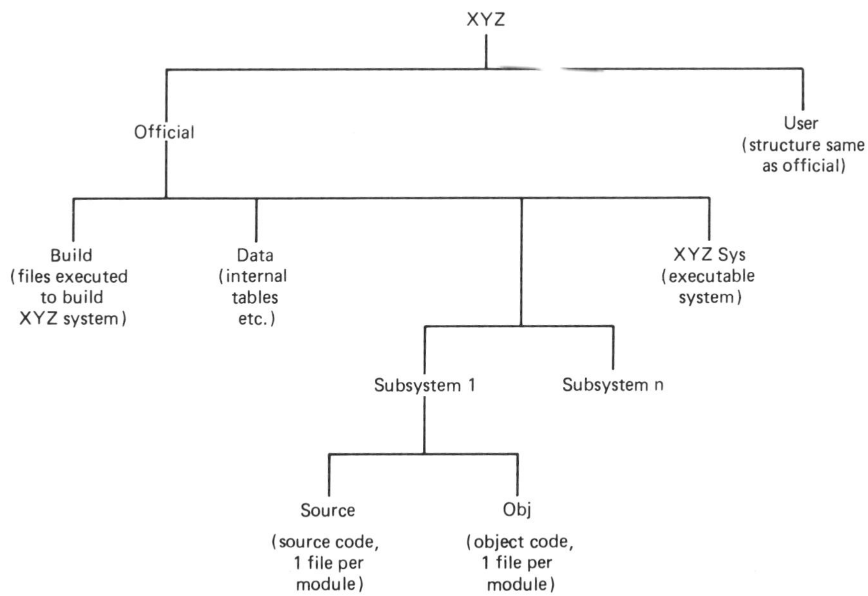

Figure 3.5. Sample software file naming structure (directory-oriented operating system).

For computer-resident software files, the location must also be identified. Working and official versions should be kept in different sections of computer storage, and the official versions should be protected against change by anyone but the librarian or configuration management staff.

Laying out the locations of computer files for source code and executable systems should be done by the configuration manager and is easier on some operating systems than on others. In a directory-oriented system, the purpose and type of each computer file can be identified through construction of the directory tree to each file. Figure 3.5 shows a sample file layout in which all computer files relating to a single module can possess the same name, whereas the use, type, and location of each file is identified through the names of the hierarchical directory structure. Locations for supporting files, such as build procedures and data files, should also be planned.

In a less desirable environment, these pieces of information may be stored by devising file naming conventions for each file type. For example, the official source module X in subsystem ABC of project XYZ can be named XYZ.ABC.X.SOURCE.

Question 3: How Will Products Be Initially Submitted to the Library for Storage and Control?

The procedures for submitting a new product to the library should address the following:

1. What approval is necessary in order for the product to be placed into the library?
2. In what form should the product be submitted, and what additional information must be supplied with the product?
3. How will the original version be numbered, and where will the version identification appear?

Because the nature of documentation and software products is so different, the discussion for each product type is treated separately in the following subsections.

Initial Submission: Documentation. For documents, one requirement may be a release sheet in the front of the document containing signatures of all people whose approval is necessary in order to release the product. With this method, the approval is attached to the product itself and thus does not have to be tracked separately. Figure 3.6 shows a sample cover sheet for documentation.

The document should be delivered to the library in its original hardcopy form, including the originals of all artwork. Information on where the text is located if it resides on a word processing system should also be supplied and filed for future reference.

ABCD Corporation **Document Release Sheet**

Title: ______________________________
Control no.: ______________________________
Version: ______________________________
Release date: ______________________________

Approved by: Date:

Originator: ______________________________ ____________
Software manager: ______________________________ ____________

Figure 3.6. Sample documentation release sheet.

There should be a project documentation format guide that dictates format rules to be followed by all documents, such as paragraph and page-numbering conventions. The configuration management procedures should reference this document and state that documentation submitted for release will be checked for this basic style before storage in the library, although the primary responsibility for conformance to format requirements will rest with the technical editor, and for the approval of the content, the approval signature team.

The original version number for the product should be identified in the configuration management procedures (whether it is 1, 1.0, A, etc.), and it should be stipulated where the version number will appear. The version number should at least appear on the release sheet, and it is helpful for it to appear on each printed page for the purpose of tracking future changes.

Initial Submission: Software. In the case of software, the first products submitted will be the source code files that have been approved and go into the production of the first system build. Each individual source code module exists in a computer file. Its baselining will consist of moving a copy of the file from the working area to the official area and adding its name and version number to the product inventory. The name of the working module should already be known, as these were identified in the procedures developed to answer question 2, earlier.

XYZ Module Release Form

Subsystem: ______________________ Module name: ______________
Programmer: ______________________

Detailed design walkthrough (DDW)

Detailed design approval: ______________ Date: ______________
PSL design acceptance: ______________ Date: ______________
DDW comments:

Code walkthrough (CW)

Code approval: ______________ Date: ______________
CW comments: ______________ Date: ______________

Test walkthrough (TW)

Test approval: ______________ Date: ______________
PSL code acceptance: ______________ Date: ______________
TW comments:

Figure 3.7. Sample module release form.

The point at which source modules will be submitted for initial baselining is after they have undergone module and perhaps unit testing, and thus changes made will mainly be those found in the integration testing process. A module release form can be used as the vehicle to track approval of the source module for initial baselining. Figure 3.7 shows a sample module release form and the required approval process verifying its readiness for baselining.

All source modules should be required to contain a version number located in the same relative place within the code. If possible, the first line of source code should be a comment line containing the initial version number and date of approval. For the purpose of tracking changes later, with every version a comment on what this version represents must be included. At initial submission, this comment line may read "initial baseline."

The initial submission for baselining the executable system will most likely occur after changes to the original versions of the source modules are required. For that reason, the procedures involved with baselining the first and all subsequent system builds will be discussed after change control procedures are introduced.

Question 4: How Will Changes to Products Be Handled?

As we have discussed previously, there will be many changes to each of the products of the software system throughout its development. All changes must be documented, evaluated, and approved before applied, and the resulting changed products must be kept track of with regard to version number. Changes may be classified in several different ways during the life of the software project. Changes may be desired because of system design considerations or be necessary due to errors in the products. They may require customer approval, or they may be administered at the discretion of the software staff. They may be those changes considered "nice to have," or enhancements to baselined design, or design changes necessary to meet the requirements of the system. The different kinds of changes require different tracking information and different updating and approval procedures.

One method that can be used to handle all changes in a similar manner is to employ the concept of the Software Configuration Review Board (SCRB). The SCRB is a group of people who meet regularly to consider current system problems, which are submitted on a single form often called a software problem report (SPR).

Under this concept, all project members are made aware that the software problem reports are available from the PSL and may be submitted at any time to report any problem perceived with the system and to request a change in any product as a result of the problem. A sample SPR form is shown in Figure 3.8. Project members should also be made aware that the SCRB meets regularly to consider each problem submitted and will take

XYZ Software Problem Report

Title:	SPR Number:

Priority:	Immediate Urgent Routine	Class:	Class I Class II Internal	Area:	Hardware Software Documentation

Subsystem/document: ______________________ Originator: ____________

SW version: ______________________ Date: ____________

Problem description:

Proposed solution:

Actual solution:

Impact:

Consequence if not corrected:

Review date	Assignee	Due date	Action

Resolved by:	Date:	Change required
Concur by:	Date:	Other products
SCRB approval:	Date:	
PSL acceptance:	Date:	

(continued)

Field	Description	Responsibility
Title	Brief phrase identifying problem	Originator
SPR number	Unique ID of SPR, assigned on receipt	SCRB recorder
Priority	Relative importance of SPR	Originator
class	I = involves baseline and requires PMD approval II = involves baselined documentation but requires only PMD concurrence (not approval); these are usually nontechnical changes Internal = affects nonbaselined items that are under only internal control	Originator
Area	Categorization of problem type	Originator
Subsystem/ documentation	Identification of affected subsystem or document	Originator
SW version	Identification of SW version if SW effort	Originator
Originator	Name of person originating SPR	Originator
Date	Date SPR was originated	Originator
Problem description	Describe problem or question, using attachments if required	Originator
Proposed solution	Provide suggested resolution to problem or answer to question	Originator
Actual solution	Final resolution to problem or answer to question	Resolution assignee
Impact	Effect on cost, schedule, or performance	Originator
Consequence	Classification of problem as being necessary or "nice to have"	Originator
Review date	Date of review of SPR by SCRB	SCRB recorder
Assignee	Name of person assigned responsibility by SCRB for resolution	SCRB recorder
Due date	Date by which a response is expected	SCRB recorder
Action	Type of action requested (study, resolve, etc.)	SCRB recorder
Resolved by	Signature of person resolving problem	Resolution assignee
Concur by	Signature of originator of problem	Originator
SCRB approval	Signature of SCRB chairman	SCRB chairman
PSL acceptance	Signature of PSL librarian	PSL librarian
Change required Other products	List of other products requiring change because of this problem	

Figure 3.8. Sample software problem report.

action on the problems in a timely fashion, that the results of the problem evaluation will be available to them, and that they may attend the meetings if they desire. The software configuration review board should not take the place of management informally listening to problems. This should not be the only way that the staff can communicate problems, but it should provide a formal means to identify and track issues within the project.

The software configuration review board should be composed of responsible representatives of all project areas. The software manager should chair the board and hold final approval authority. A sample SCRB membership might include:

1. Software manager, chairman
2. Software technical task leaders
3. Software configuration management
4. Software test leader
5. Systems engineering representative
6. Program office representative
7. Quality assurance representatives
8. PSL librarian, recorder

The SCRB should routinely meet weekly to discuss each SPR that has been submitted and to call in other project members as needed to obtain information concerning a particular problem. The problem may be solved during the discussion and thus will be marked "closed" and signed off immediately. An SPR requiring further work or research in order to solve the problem will be assigned to the appropriate individual(s), and the action to be taken and date due will be recorded on the form. Such SPRs will be considered "open" until the action is taken, a written solution is delivered to the librarian for inclusion on the form, and the solution is approved.

The PSL librarian will be in charge of keeping these forms up to date and of scheduling and coordinating these meetings. The librarian's duties regarding the tracking of these forms are many. Blank SPR forms must be available from the PSL in a designated location so that project members can retrieve them, fill them out, and submit them for consideration. Each submitted form must be reviewed for completeness of information and assigned a number for future tracking purposes. To prepare for the SCRB meeting, the librarian must:

1. Pull all newly submitted SPRs
2. Pull all SPRs that are due for review at this meeting, along with solutions that have been delivered in response to the SPR
3. Contact assignees who have not responded with solutions to due SPRs for a status report on their activities
4. Provide copies of all this material for each SCRB member

At the meeting, the librarian must:

1. Record results of each discussion on the form
2. Mark any SPRs determined to be closed

After the meeting, the librarian must:

Notify each assignee of the SPR assigned, action required, and date due
Collect approval signatures for all closed SPRs
Pull all SPRs due at the next meeting and send reminders to assignees
Prepare minutes of the meeting and distribute to all project members

The SPRs will be important in describing current system status and thus must be maintained in a fashion that allows easy access in a number of different ways. The information will need to be accessed in the following ways:

1. All SPRs assigned a particular person for action
2. All SPRs concerning a particular product
3. All open SPRs
4. All closed SPRs
5. All SPRs against a particular software build

The existence of these kinds of access requirements makes the collection of SPRs a data base storage and retrieval application, and if possible, automated procedures should be implemented to support the SPR collection as such a data base.

Once the procedures for the documentation, evaluation, and approval of changes are decided, we must develop procedures for the actual updating of the products involved. The methods required for documentation and software are different and therefore are discussed separately in the following subsections.

Update Procedures: Documentation. An SPR that requires a change in a document should not be approved until the actual change is supplied in the form of photocopies of the latest version of the affected pages marked to reflect the change. As the official release of the new version of the document will require time spent in data entry, editing, and rerelease, it is important that staff members be notified of each change immediately so that their documents can be kept current. It is seldom feasible to issue a new release of a document for each change required, therefore changes will normally be saved and incorporated into a new release as time permits or as the magnitude or importance of the particular changes dictate. Thus, the PSL librarian must keep the library copy of the document current at all times so that the changes can be identified easily and submitted to the responsible documentation production facilities for incorporation into a new version of the document.

The customer will often dictate the exact procedures to be followed in the reissuing of documents. It is much easier to keep track of changes to documentation if the entire document is rereleased. The expense involved in this practice is sometimes prohibitive, however, and only the changed pages are released, along with a summary of the changes to be applied. The recipients of the document must then update their copies according to the summary, for the changes may have required that new pages be added or old ones deleted. When changed pages only are released, these pages must be marked with the new version number in order to distinguish them from the old pages of the document. When the entire document is rereleased, sometimes the new version number is imprinted on every page, and sometimes the new version number is used only on pages that have been changed. Whether the entire document is reprinted or whether changed pages only are published, change bars may be placed on the side of the page to indicate where each change was applied since the last version. Whatever update scheme is used, it is the responsibility of the technical editor to enforce and the data entry personnel to apply. The updated document is delivered to the PSL in the form of the entire document or the changed pages and a change summary.

The PSL librarian then files the original of the updated pages, incorporating them with the old document original, and releases either the changed pages or the new document to the project immediately. An SPR written against the document should not be marked closed and signed off until the actual update has been applied and the resulting document issued.

Update Procedures: Software. An update to a software source module should be applied to the working version of the module and tested before submittal of the change to the PSL. At that time, the librarian should receive notification that the source module is to be updated, and the new module should be checked for a properly updated version number. A comment on the reason for the change should be recorded in the form of the number of the SPR authorizing the change before transferral of the module to its "official" file location.

This procedure raises the question of what to do with the "old" official source module and, ultimately, how many old versions to keep on line. One plan might be to rename the old module with version number placed into the name, for example, XYZ.ABC.X.SOURCE.1. The latest version thus is always named XYZ.ABC.X.SOURCE, so that when building the system, the build procedures will not have to be modified for name changes each time a module changes.

There are configuration-management-oriented programming tools available in which version numbering is automatically updated with each change applied. Some of these actually save all previous versions so that the problem is reduced. It is valuable to investigate the possibility of using such tools when planning for software configuration management.

Without a set of configuration management programming tools, the best way to solve the problem of the number of old versions to keep on-line is to collect official changes to source modules only as often as necessary, which is just before each build of the system is performed. The corrections to software may be verified only at the time of the next build. Proper backup of the source modules producing a build will allow access to previous versions without storing all versions on-line.

The software build process is described below in terms of what must be done in order to baseline each software build, whether it is the first or a subsequent build. Before a system build can take place, all source modules that are required must have been released to the library and baselined. In addition, the following products must be submitted to the library:

1. Any command files necessary to be run in order to produce the executable system
2. Any data files necessary for the system to run
3. Documentation delineating step-by-step procedures to be followed in order to build the system
4. Documentation describing how to initiate the system
5. Documentation describing system functions supported by the build

The build procedure files will be baselined in the same manner as the source modules, and their names and locations will have been determined in answering question 2, described earlier. Documentation for the build procedure must also be baselined. The documentation for how to initiate the system should be included in the existing User's Manual, but if the nature of the system functions available in this partial system make these procedures different from what they will be for the final system, this must be a separate, baselined document. The system functions supported by this build should be delineated in the appropriate test plan document.

The build is initiated on the submittal of a request from the appropriate technical staff member. The request should be in writing and supply all the information needed for the build. A sample build request form is shown in Figure 3.9. This form is designed so as to handle the first as well as subsequent builds. For the initial build, however, all modules will be "added" modules, and the comment for each will be "initial build."

The librarian checks to see that all sources modules listed on the build have been baselined, and if any modules are marked for update, the old version is replaced with its new version, and it is checked to ensure that the appropriate version number and change comment are correct and in the

XYZ Build Request Form

Update to (release, version) ______________________________

Module	Update/Add/Delete	File Location	Comment

Authorizing
signature ______________________ Date ______________________

Figure 3.9. Sample build request form.

proper location. The executable system should be required to display the system title, version number, and release date. One designated source module should provide the code necessary to display this information, and the librarian should be able to locate this code and check it or apply the proper information.

The build procedures are then followed, producing an executable system. Errors occurring during the build process are corrected until a successful build occurs. Errors may result from missing files, which will then have to be submitted and baselined before the build can be attempted again. Errors may also result from the source code itself. In this case, the changes and updates should take place in the normal fashion before the build is attempted again.

The version numbers for executable systems should track with the planned major build numbers—1, 2, 3, and so on. Often, however, an error in testing is uncovered and must be corrected before testing of the system capabilities can proceed. Interim builds constructed to allow further testing should be numbered so as to distinguish error-driven builds from builds resulting in new system functions. For example, build 1.0 may require that build 1.1, 1.2, and 1.3 be constructed and tested prior to construction of build 2.0.

XYZ Version Description Document

Version number: ____________________ Release date: ____________________

System inventory

Media type	Media identification	Description of contents

Installation instructions:

Source code summary

Module name	Version number	Date last changed	Reason for change (SPR number)

Applicable documentation

Document name	Document number	Version number

System capabilities

Open problem reports

Figure 3.10. Sample version description document.

Once the building is successful, the official executable system is ready for release. Release of the system requires the following tracking procedures:

1. Backup of all source files, including modules, build procedures files, and data files necessary to build the system onto tape or other physically maneuverable media
2. Backup of the executable system
3. Preparation of documentation on how to reinstall the system from backups if necessary
4. Preparation of a version description document, delineating exactly what comprises the system, what the system does, and how to initiate it

A sample version description document is shown in Figure 3.10.

The staff should then be notified of the system delivery and the system is released to the test manager for official testing. No SPR on software should be closed until the test team has verified that the problem has been corrected, and the SPR should be marked with the build number in which the problem was determined to be corrected.

Completion of the Configuration Management Procedures

Once the basic questions raised in the preceding sections have been thought through in detail, it will be necessary to go back and add details and procedures discovered to be missing in order to tailor the software to the project environment. It is valuable to consider developing or acquiring tools to aid in the tracking, updating, and backing up of software products.

Once the procedures are thus detailed, what personnel will be required to support these activities must be analyzed. The PSL librarian may need clerical personnel to assist in the duties delineated in the plans. One section of the plans and procedures must be written to address the size, organization, and duties of the configuration management staff.

The resulting procedural documentation should be published, baselined, and disseminated to each staff member as he comes on board. The PSL should be set up as soon as possible, and the mechanics involved in starting the SCRB process should be initiated. All existing project documentation should be gathered, baselined, and situated in the library according to the plan, and an inventory should be prepared of existing products that will be maintained throughout the software development process.

The configuration management plan and procedures resulting from the analysis done thus far will undoubtedly change as the project progresses, and the details of building the system and storing computer software files will probably need to be augmented as the exact nature of the system being built becomes better known.

CONFIGURATION MANAGEMENT PROCEDURES: FINAL NOTE

The results of the analysis detailed in this chapter may identify a requirement for more staff to execute the procedures, more schedule time for development personnel to produce software tracking tools, or more money to purchase existing tools—requirements not considered during the scheduling and budgeting phase of the project. Higher management and/or the customer may not see the need for expending extra funds to support these activities. Let us here reemphasize that no matter how expensive this kind of activity seems, it is vital to the timely release of a quality system. The software manager must be able to convince everyone involved in the project of this point, for when schedules and budgets are overrun, the first area that is threatened with cutbacks is likely to be the configuration management area. If configuration management is implemented with the attitude that it is "nice to have" rather than with the conviction that it is absolutely necessary, the time and money invested in the activities will indeed be wasted, for if it is not rigorously followed and constantly enforced, it may as well not exist. If it does not exist, however, wasted time and money in development is guaranteed, and the amount will increase exponentially with the number of products and people involved on the project.

4 Documentation Development and Production

The most critical aspect of software development is the creation of excellent documentation, not the production of elegant code.

Project documentation developed during the software development life cycle described in Chapter 2 is of three main types:

1. Those documents that form the primary baselines for the development of the software.
2. Those documents that specify the procedural bases for all aspects of the development process.
3. Those documents that provide the basis for the major supporting activities that must be carried out in order to develop the software and are dependent on the specific software design and implementation decisions made.

The documents that form the primary baselines are the requirements document, the users manual and the file and interface specifications, the preliminary design document, and the detailed design specification. These documents are the most important ones produced, for they set forth the major design commitments that are made to the project and the customer concerning the construction of the software system. They specify the system from the highest to lowest level of design necessary to implement the software. The user's manual and the detailed design specification specify for those who will be concerned with the system throughout its operational life how it can be used and how it can be maintained and enhanced. It is of vital importance that these documents be technically sound, consistent throughout with regard to content, and at the appropriate level of design to ensure an orderly progression of design decisions throughout the pre-coding phases.

The major document specifying the procedures to be followed in the development of the software is the software development plan, which is written by the software manager in order to set forth the basic project organization and the main criteria to be satisfied by each element of the project structure. A series of lower-level plans specify the exact responsibilities and methodologies to be followed for each area of the project. For example, the standards and conventions document details the design methodology to be employed and the coding standards to be enforced during implementation. Documentation in the form of memoranda may be required during the project to spell out procedures to be followed by personnel in the daily execution of their duties. For example, a document describing procedures for computer operation and usage may be required, depending on the particular project environment established.

Documents that provide the basis for the major supporting activities include the test and configuration management documents, which must be based on the specific software development requirements. The details of the test program, for example, are directly derived from the specification of what the software system is to perform. The lowest-level details of the configuration management program depend on the configuration of the computer equipment and operating systems chosen for development and test.

It should be apparent that the requirements for developing the different types of documentation to be produced vary from very informal to highly formal and that the number of people involved in the writing of a document may range from one person to a large number of people. Some of these documents are required by the customer, and some are required so that the software development organization may function properly.

The most stringent requirements for documentation production are imposed on those documents that are formally delivered to the customer, those that form the baselines for software development, and those that involve the largest number of separate authors. This chapter focuses on the problems associated with the production of the major developmental baseline documents, for they usually reflect all three of these characteristics at the same time. If the software manager plans for the efficient production of excellent documentation based on the most stringent requirements, the project will be prepared to produce any document in this manner.

THE DOCUMENTATION DEVELOPMENT PROBLEM

A large part of the software development effort is rooted in the production, review, delivery, and acceptance of project documentation. In a typical project, this support may constitute well over 50% of the available resources, and, to compound the problem, the support requirements are heavily front-loaded. The manager must have an effective procedure for developing documentation in place from the very beginning of the project, for a requirements document must be produced before any cost estimation, scheduling, or definition of project structure can begin.

Unfortunately, the effective production of quality documentation is inhibited by three familiar project conditions:

1. *Staff reluctance to write*—the reluctance of technical personnel to document their work.
2. *Unacceptability of the documentation produced*—an inability on the part of the project to produce acceptable documentation consistent with the requirements of the contract and the needs and expectations of the customer and technical staff personnel.
3. *Difficulty in acquiring adequate documentation production resources*—a consistent lack of the essential resources necessary to produce, publish, and update documentation within schedule constraints.

All three of these problems stem from management unawareness of the importance of documentation and the complicated set of factors influencing the quality and timeliness of its production.

Documentation is the most important portion of the software development process. During the life of the project, documentation should be the only type of product developed for over half the elapsed project time. Thus, it is the only representation of the work that is being performed and provides the sole vehicle by which the manager, the staff, and the customer can evaluate the current and future software system. It remains the most visible product of the system after delivery, for no matter how sophisticated or appropriate to the user requirements the software may be, it cannot be employed until the documentation that describes its use is read and understood. Any corrections or enhancements that are required or desired for the life of the system cannot easily be made without adequate documentation describing the architecture of the software components, for the reading of software code alone is needlessly time-consuming and therefore makes the system needlessly expensive to maintain.

Software management must realize that the entire company's software development reputation is largely dependent on the quality of the documentation it produces. Through the years, the industry has promoted an attitude toward documentation that is damaging to the software development business and must be changed. Software management has seen the problems that engineers have with writing and has reacted by assigning documentation duties to junior-level programmers as part of their training in learning about a system, or by hiring professional technical writers to take the writing responsibility, and hence the involvement in documentation production, away from the key software engineers on a project. Therefore, software engineers have come to believe that documentation is not a requirement of their jobs, that documentation is not important and does not have a direct relationship to the work they are hired to do, and even that writing is work that is beneath their skill level and should be done by others less experienced or talented in the "technical" aspects of the job than they are.

When technical personnel are not directly involved in the production of a document, they do not feel responsible for its quality or accuracy. They feel that it cannot truly be an important part of the work of software development or they, as the architects and implementers of the system, would have been assigned the job directly.

Progressive software managers must recognize the fallacies in such thinking and discourage it rather than encourage it by their actions. Bad writing should not be condoned or accepted as a characteristic trait of the technically brilliant. Software engineers who are not able to express themselves clearly in written communication should be enrolled in technical writing courses, and the skill should be required to be developed through training and experience. It is incorrect to assume that an employee who excels in the technical arena is not capable of improving his or her writing abilities, or that it is unimportant to do so. It must be stressed that documentation is the physical representation of the technical ideas and processes that lead to the implementation of the software system and that technical personnel must produce and maintain this documentation as the accurate description of their current and future work.

In order to minimize the effects of these problems on software productivity, the software manager must, from the very outset of the project, understand and give proper emphasis to the problems of software documentation development. The manager must be aware of the impact on productivity of poor documentation support and a consistent, well-defined set of technical, procedural, and support facilities upon which development of the documentation products may be based.

Technical Reluctance to Document

An almost universal complaint of software managers is that they cannot force technical personnel to document their work. In many cases, this reluctance arises because coding and debugging activities are given first priority and documentation of the design and use of the system is done as an afterthought, so that software engineers look on the job as a "cleanup" operation. If the documentation effort is started during the hectic debugging period in order to finish it as well as the testing of the system by the delivery date, the software engineers are justifiably resentful of the added work of documentation duties. This separate, very different responsibility is in this case being imposed on them while they are being pressured to complete what has been regarded as their main commitment. In essence, the documentation work is now a burden added to what is already a full-time job. Moreover, at this stage of the project, the staff is psychologically "burned out" on this particular application, having given their all during the code and test phase and feeling that they should be finished with the project. It is very demoralizing to feel that the end of a period of hard work is near, then being asked to embark on another large-scale effort in order to complete the job. In this atmosphere, documentation cannot help being considered anticlimactic by the staff and will not be given the commitment and enthusiasm necessary to a good job.

In the software development life cycle advocated in Chapter 2, documentation is regarded as a series of stepwise products, each of which represents the design activities that are to take place during the particular stage of development. The job of software development is broken into a series of design tasks, starting at a high level and working toward the detailed definition of the system to be built. Changes to each document must be made as they are required, so there is no large cleanup operation to be attacked at the project's end. The production of a document is the only task required of the technical staff during each precoding stage, so that the documentation task is a fresh one at all times. The code and test activities can then be given the full attention of all project members, and coding changes that affect the documentation are proposed, approved, and ready to be incorporated into the document before they are implemented in the code.

Unacceptability of the Documentation Produced

Even if the documentation is performed before code and test are begun, technical personnel may have problems in executing their assignments. The manager often provides the staff with firm direction on the production of documentation, schedules the process in great detail, and provides the required resources, only to find that the data produced are of unacceptable quality and are inconsistent with project requirements.

Software engineers are often assigned writing responsibility for a section of sections of a document to be integrated into the deliverable format by an editor assigned to the project. The engineers are not given clear direction on the level of detail, acceptable writing style, or expected content. In this situation, project productivity is often impacted by the "blank paper syndrome." Uncertain of how to express their ideas in an acceptable fashion and afraid of writing documentation of marginal or inferior quality, the engineers spend long hours composing inappropriate prose or, worse still, deciding how best to attack the problem. Eventually, some text is produced; however, it is often so unclear and of such poor quality that it must be redone. Often this writing-review-rejection cycle repeats several times, ultimately affecting documentation delivery schedules. This documentation development cycle is doubly destructive, for it not only impacts the project's ability to meet critical documentation schedules but also affects the quality and integrity of the remainder of the project because each major document provides the baseline for further technical work.

One common project response to this situation is to proceed with the technical tasks despite the lateness or poor quality of the document currently being produced. This response comes from the natural staff desire to keep the project moving. *However, a high price is paid later, when the technical work is found to be based on incomplete information and/or conflicting design assumptions.*

This inappropriate response is clearly a management planning problem, for whenever a product is to be produced, it is important that the specifications for the product be defined as the first step. Just as coding should not begin before the design specifications are produced, no major document should be written for which the purpose and information it is to contain is not first defined. As suggested in the previous chapter, a detailed outline for each document should be prepared by a staff member who has an understanding of the technical task and also knows how to specify the required contents for a particular document and judge the quality of the resulting product. The configuration manager will ideally be the person who meets these qualifications.

The outlines should be created in enough detail to minimize the ambiguities in what information is required of each section and also to minimize the degree of organization required of the writer. This kind of outline removes much of the "blank paper syndrome," as it sparks the writer to provide specific information rather than to produce all the information he feels is necessary for a particular topic and to organize it as he sees fit. It also documents in advance the requirements of the technical task that is physically represented by the document. This factor is important in ensuring that the proper level of design has been achieved in order to proceed with the project and that the document will indeed be acceptable technically.

Often, the customer provides a detailed outline for a required document. Many times such an outline has been developed as a standard to be applied for the particular document type for any software project funded by the customer. As in any area of software development, no "standard" can be blindly accepted without evaluation of its suitability to the particular application. The configuration manager must analyze any externally provided outline, with regard to not only its applicability to the project at hand but also the clarity of the definition of what is required in each section. The configuration manager must pinpoint areas of concern and discuss the outline with the software manager. The customer should be involved in this process, and the result should be an outline that is restructured if necessary, that is reworded in order to leave no area open to differing interpretations, and that provides specific examples where they are needed to clarify the requirement. Such an annotated outline may be called a style guide, for it specifies the style expected to be used in writing the document.

Figure 4.1a and 4.1b show a portion of a customer-provided outline for a software requirements document and a sample style guide to be used in writing the document according to the outline. As can be seen from the example, there are many ways that a documenter may interpret the customer-provided outline. The structure of the section, the organization of the requirements, the narrative style, and the technical depth are all left to the writer to define. If the selected approach is not consistent with the expectations or nonspecified requirements of the customer, the documentation will be unacceptable, requiring reworking and restructuring before the document is acceptable. The sample style guide interprets the intent of the section, provides a standard introductory sentence, and details the exact information required of section 3.1.1.

If a document is required by the customer, whether the style guide is based on a customer-provided outline or has been created originally from within the project, it must be approved by the customer before the writing is begun. Once approved, such a guide provides clear, agreed-on instructions on exactly how to produce the specification and what constitutes document acceptability.

During the assignment and scheduling of the writing of document sections, it should be realized that one person must be responsible for the document as a whole. Separate pieces of a document produced by different authors are unlikely to fit together into a coherent whole without the attention of one good writer who can smooth the transition from one section to another and identify and resolve inconsistencies in content and style. For

---

Section 3: Requirements. This section shall define and specify all functional, operational, and performance requirements, plus all design constraints and standards necessary to ensure proper development and maintenance of the computer program.

Paragraph 3.1: Introduction. This paragraph shall contain a general discussion of the digital system within which the program will operate. It shall show the relationships of each component, such as radars, displays, and converters, with the computer program. In particular, the role assigned to the computer program should be stressed to delineate the functions it must accomplish. This paragraph shall include the following subparagraphs:

a. Paragraph 3.1.1: General description. This program shall provide a general discussion of the computer system and make reference to other component performance specifications that will further clarify the performance requirements of the subject system.
b. Paragraph 3.1.2: Peripheral equipment identification. This paragraph shall provide an identification of the peripheral equipment with which the specified program will interface.
c. Paragraph 3.1.3: Interface identification. This paragraph shall provide an identification of any computer programs or computer systems with which the specified program will interface.

Paragraph 3.2: Functional description. This paragraph shall provide a detailed description of the functions of the computer program and shall describe the functional relationships of the computer program with interfacing equipments and with other computer programs. This paragraph shall include the following:

Figure 4.1a. Typical contract specification requirements.

Section 3.1 Introduction

The following format shall be used in the makeup of section 3.1:

3.1 Introduction. This paragraph and its subparagraphs describe the computer system within which the CPCI will operate. They also specify the interface to peripherals and other equipments and other computer programs with which the CPCI and its host computer must interface.

Section 3.1.1 General description

The following format shall be used as the makeup of section 3.1.1:

3.1.1 General description. The [name] CPCI shall be designed to operate within the characteristics of the [computer name]. The major characteristics of the [name] computer are listed [either below or in an associated table].

1. In a table or text, indicate the official designations and the main characteristics of the CPU and memories (unless memories are to be described in separate subparagraphs under peripherals) that are to be used to implement the CPCI. Unless reference is made to documentation included in the applicable documents section, the minimum characteristic description should also include:

   —Available memory capacity
   —Available cycle times
   —Access times
   —Transfer rates
   —Number and type of interructs
   —Time required for representative instructions
   —Special features (e.g., parity, memory protect, OMA capability.

2. Present a block diagram showing the relationships of the CPCI, the computer, and the I/O peripherals.

Section 3.1.2 Peripheral equipment identification
The following format shall be used for section 3.1.2:

Figure 4.1b. Sample style definition.

each document produced, one of the writers should be appointed as the "document coordinator," responsible for the technical integrity and professionalism of the end product. This person must have proven talent in producing written communication and be able to resolve conflicts in technical approaches among the authors.

The next important step in ensuring the acceptability of documentation is to provide for formal internal reviews of the draft copy of each document before its final release to the customer and the project. The authors have not yet seen the entire document, and the technical content on which further system work will be based must be given careful attention by the authors as well as qualified outside parties in order to ensure that the level of design the document represents is appropriate for this stage of development and is technically sound.

The review must be organized so that it can lead to quick action in areas

Preparer: ____________

Date: ____________

Document Review Sheet

Document Name: ____ Control number: ____________ Version: ____________

Page number	Comment

Figure 4.2. Sample documentation review sheet.

found to need revision and quick incorporation into the final document. Each reviewer should be given a copy of the document to read and comment on, and he should be given enough time to give the review the attention it deserves. Each reviewer also should be given a formal review sheet, such as Figure 4.2, to complete before the review is held. The review should be chaired by the software manager, who must be intimately familiar with the document and the requirements under which it was written. The document should be covered from front to back, taking review comments as they arise in page order. As each comment is discussed, the action to be taken must be decided, assigned to the responsible author, scheduled for completion, and recorded so that the corrected document can be produced in an efficient and orderly manner. All decisions should be approved by the software manager at this time, but they should be made in the main by the engineers involved, with the manager stepping in only as a resolver of conflicts and enforcer of standards.

A document that is written and reviewed following these steps runs a very small risk of being technically unacceptable.

Difficulty in Acquiring Documentation Production Services

Many software managers do not realize the requirements for producing a document for publication that exist from the time the words are first penned. The publication process requires personnel trained in several different disciplines, all of which are totally unrelated to the software development discipline. The separate sections of the document must be typed in the same format, checked for typographical errors and any changes that are desired, and retyped until the section is satisfactory as typed. The figures drawn by the authors must be redrawn by professional graphic artists, corrected, and redrawn until the authors are satisfied with them. The entire document must be checked for grammatical correctness, compliance with publication standards such as acceptable labeling of headings, figures, and tables, basic readability, proper usage of footnotes, references to other documents, copyrights and trademarks, and consistency in nomenclature and format throughout. The final document must be assembled in the proper order with figures and tables inserted, and it must be paginated properly (with small letters for front matter and either consecutive page numbers throughout or renumbered for each section). Front matter such as table of contents and lists of illustrations must be supplied. The document must be numbered by versions according to the requirements of the configuration management procedures established for the project. The type of reproduction to be used must be decided on, and the document must be produced in the physical form that is suitable for that type of reproduction. It must be reproduced in the numbers required for publication and must be bound and covered in some fashion. It must be baselined by the project support library and sent to the proper locations in the numbers required. All concerned parties must be notified of its publication and availability.

It should be apparent that the services of several different groups of professional publication specialists must be involved in this process and that the publication of a document will take much time and coordination. Unless the software organization plans for the acquisition of the resources required and defines a detailed set of procedures for routing each individual piece of the document through the many functional groups required and bringing them together for publication of the final document, confusion, chaos, and slipped schedules will be the only logical consequences.

The responsibilities required by the process must first be understood and delegated to the proper personnel. The requirement for typists, graphic artists, and a professional print shop, if printing is required, is straightforward.

A professional editor must be provided to handle the enforcement of detailed publication standards, as described earlier. Even the best writers are not aware of the many rules governing the production of an excellent publication and certainly are not cognizant of the professional tools and procedures for producing camera-ready copy from the text and figures provided.

Detailed formatting conventions for the project documents must be decided on before any work, including work on the style guide, on any document is begun. If detailed formatting requirements are provided by the customer, they should be made available to the staff, the editor, and the data entry and graphic arts managers. The configuration manager should be responsible for locating customer formatting requirements and disseminating them to the proper personnel. If there are none, the editor should provide detailed formatting requirements in the form of a specification that can be used by all personnel involved in documentation production.

Someone must be responsible for the technical content of the document as a whole and serve as the source of resolution of questions that arise from each of the major areas concerned. This person logically should be the document coordinator for the particular document.

There must also be someone in charge of maintaining the latest version of each piece of the document during its creation, disseminating each piece to the next group in the chain of events, and providing a copy of the latest version of any section or the entire document on request.

The software manager must then acquire the services of any external organizations required. The text production support chosen for the project demands special attention. The manager must realize that the text is the bulk of the material to be produced, that it will be changed many times between the first handwritten draft and the final document, and that the "final" document will also change many times during the life of the project. Unless the project is minuscule, typing without the aid of word processing equipment and experienced operators will be very costly and time-consuming, as entire sections will have to be retyped repeatedly in order for the text to be formatted properly after changes are applied.

The mere availability of word processing equipment and experienced data entry operators does not solve the problem. The word processor itself adds a new requirement for careful management planning. Because the data are stored on a separate medium, the location of the data must be known at all times, and changes must always be applied to the latest version of the text. It is required that someone be responsible for allocating the data entry work, for setting standards for storage and update of the text produced, and for establishing the formats for the document to be used by the operators. It is wise for the software manager to locate a word processing shop that is well managed, well staffed, and able to handle the volume of documentation that will be required of the project, even when it is busy with other customers' jobs. It is necessary to realize that the facility to be used for text production should be established and used throughout the project. Data are not easily transferable from one type of word processing system to another, and unless all pieces of project documentation are located on the same type of word processing system, and preferably in the same machine area, the potential for problems in updating and incorporating separate sections into a consistent document is enormous. Moreover, if the same group of data entry personnel are consistently used throughout the project, they will become familiar with the project-specific terminology, the format required, and even the authors' styles and handwriting. *The time savings that can be realized through this familiarity is sizable, yet this factor is often unrecognized and not exploited.*

The editor chosen for the project should be an extremely organized person, capable of seeing a document in its entirety even while working on separate sections. The same editor should be used throughout the project, for the "familiarity" factor applies to this area as well as to the text production area.

The graphic arts facility must be chosen with the same general guidelines used for the text processing facility, and the importance placed on the choice of this facility depends on the amount of artwork that will be required throughout the project.

If the procedures to be followed during the development of a document are laid out in detail before any document is begun, much time will be saved in the project, and key responsibilities will not be omitted. Nor will there be any confusion as to the chain of events that must occur.

The organization proposed in Figure 4.3 for handling the documentation production activity must be studied and tailored to fit the needs and availability of resources for the particular project. Under this organization, the procedures derived would consist of those described in the following paragraphs.

Each author receives an assignment for a section of the document he is to write. Through discussion with the creator of the style guide and, if necessary, with the software manager and even the customer, the document coordinator resolves any questions that arise with regard to the content required.

Each author delivers his written text to the document coordinator, who checks it briefly for adherence to the style guide. If there are serious problems, the document coordinator discusses them with the author and has the

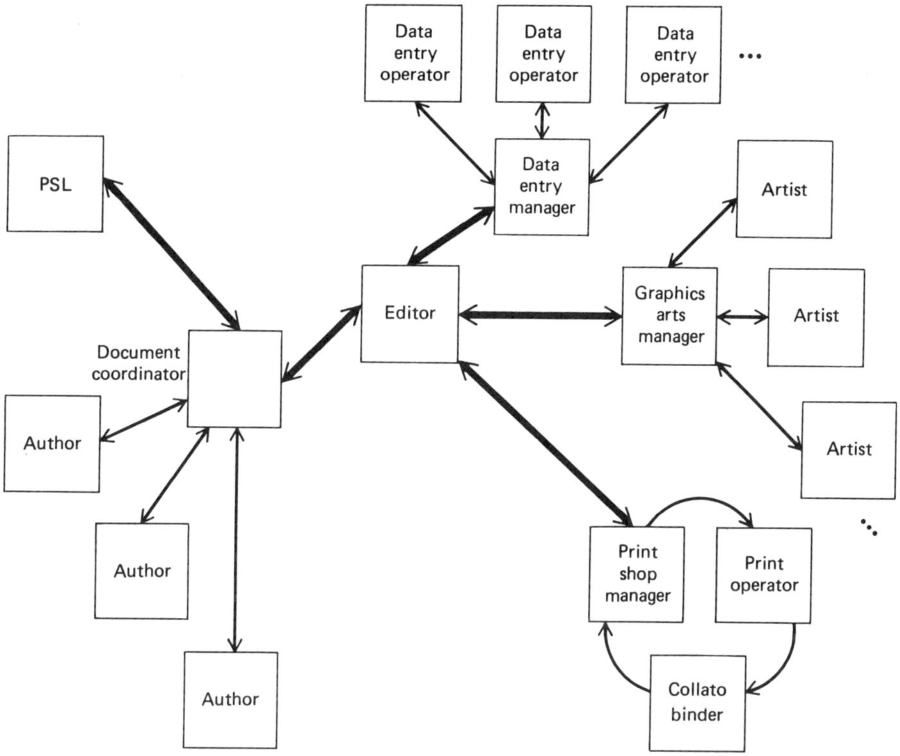

Figure 4.3. Sample documentation production organization.

problem areas rewritten. The section is then delivered to the editor, who separates the text from the figures, delivers the text to the data entry manager, communicating a need date, and the figures to the graphic arts manager. The data entry and graphic arts managers assign the incoming work to their employees and keep track of the status of all work done by their staffs. The completed work is returned to the editor, who proofs the data for typographical errors, grammatical errors, inconsistencies, and areas in which the ideas the author is trying to express are unclear. The marked document is returned to the document coordinator, who resolves with the author any questions that have arisen, provides any rewording, additions, or deletions on the copy, and returns it to the editor. The editor then reroutes the corrected copy to its proper production facility for incorporation of the corrections. The editor proofs the returned copy against the input and returns it to the document coordinator for approval to be reentered as marked or to make any further corrections required. This cycle is repeated until the document coordinator and the authors are satisfied with the text.

The editor then assembles a draft copy of the document, adding the figures and the appropriate front matter and numbering the pages. The document coordinator then schedules and executes the internal review and marks the results of all completed action items on one copy of the draft. The updated material is then delivered to the editor for review and dissemination to the data entry and graphics arts managers. The correction cycle is repeated until all the comments are incorporated.

At this point, the document coordinator routes a copy of the final document to each person on the approval list prepared by the PSL, collects all signatures on the release sheet, and delivers the release sheet to the editor. The editor prepares the camera-ready copy and delivers it to the printer for production. The document coordinator delivers the original and all copies to the PSL for baselining and dissemination of the copies to the customer. The PSL also prepares an official notification of the publication of the document and its availability to all project members.

This basic organization has the advantage that the lines of communication are simple, and the work is split so that each group is managed, each person is busy, but no one person is overloaded. The detailed procedures to be followed, like the organization itself, must be tailored to meet the requirements of the project and may even need to be modified for particular documents. The documentation production procedures must be designed to comply with the particular configuration management procedures implemented and to support the reviews and approval cycles planned by the software manager. The detailed design document, for example, will be developed over a long period of time, and each detailed module specification will be baselined by the PSL after its design walkthrough is held. This process will occur for some modules long before the entire document can be assembled. The detailed design specification is assembled by adding the module specifications and internal file layouts to the previously produced preliminary design document; therefore, a separate procedure is required to support the production and maintenance of this document.

The level of detail presented here in describing typical documentation production events is necessary because this area is the least understood by software management. A lack of knowledge of what is involved in this important area can effect the entire project, especially if no company-wide facility is already established with procedures for submittal and publication in place. Company facilities are often overloaded, and the incoming work is prioritized by higher management, who will most likely rank proposals first. As a result, it may seem to the project manager that he can easily circumvent such problems by acquiring data entry services from various groups as needed, borrowing an editor, or having software engineers hastily pasting pieces of a document together in order to "get it out," not realizing the problems that will result in trying to update that document. He may even decide to establish his own documentation production facility. This decision is sometimes valid but can be disastrous unless the expense, personnel requirements, requirements for the establishment of data entry procedures, the requirement for technical editing services, and the management of the entire process are not clearly understood. The documentation production and publication area is a separate business requiring skills, talents, and training different from those of software engineering or even technical writing, and the software manager should beware when expanding his or her responsibilities to include a possibly unfamiliar business area.

DOCUMENTATION PRODUCTION PLANNING

An understanding of the problems of documentation production, publication, and maintenance levies a requirement on the software manager for early planning of this area of the project in great detail. As described earlier, the problems are not only those concerned with composing written communication reflecting technical excellence but also those concerned with the mechanics of publishing a document. An understanding of the complicated and interdependent set of factors affecting documentation production even levies a requirement for additional documents—formatting guides, style guides, and documentation production procedures. It has implications that touch the scheduling, organization, staffing requirements, and cost of the project and that must be addressed at the very beginning in order to avert major project problems.

5 Project Data Flow

The smooth flow of data and responsibility within the software project during the period of implementation has a greater effect on productivity than do the technical methodologies used or automated aids applied.

The process of software development is an integration of several methodologies, each supporting a different phase of the project. In a typical project, individual methodologies support the following project areas:

1. Project planning includes the specific techniques, procedures, data and control requirements for planning the software project. The techniques and procedures are supported by a methodology that takes basic project, technical, contractual, administrative, and development requirements, translating these into a project structure that supports the productive development of software.
2. Requirements definition is the process by which user technical and operational requirements are defined in a traceable, testable form that serves as the technical basis for functional decomposition and software design.
3. Software design is the specific procedure techniques, technical requirements, and data required to decompose the software functional requirements and derive the software design.
4. Software code and test includes the procedures, techniques, data, and supporting environments that are applied to support and control the development of software code and conduct preliminary software testing.
5. Test and integration includes the specific technical procedures and techniques applied to integrate the software into an operational configuration and the management policies and practices implemented to control the process.
6. Configuration management and control includes policies, practices,

and techniques implemented to coordinate and control the flow of data within the project and control all data baselined by the project or approved through a project review.

7. Automated support includes the tools and automated support facilities developed or installed in support of the project methodologies.

The degree to which these methodologies "play" together is the measure of a productive development activity. The data compatibility between each of the individual methodologies and the smoothness and control of the data flow (between each of the individual methodologies and the various components of the project) is the measure of how efficient the project implementation is proceeding.

A smooth data flow must be built into the project as a base premise of the planning activity. Although a data plan is not one of the basic documents developed as part of the project planning tasks, the requirements for planning this flow are fundamental to all planning within the project.

The manager must anticipate the way data will flow through the project during the development period. He must incorporate an effective review structure for evaluating data quality as it passes through the project. The manager must also plan for the controls that ensure that all pieces of data used by more than one organizational component are controlled and, more importantly, that only one approved version is being used within the project.

As illustrated in Figure 5.1, there is a hierarchical relationship between each of the primary development activities of the project and the data products developed by each. The software manager must ensure that the specific methodologies selected and applied in support of each phase of the project are compatible and that the data that result from one methodology are compatible with the requirements of related methodologies and the requirements of the contract. This principle may seem fundamental; however, it is a common, and often catastrophic, oversight on the part of managers when selecting or implementing the technical structure of the project.

When selecting the methodologies to be used on a project in support of each development area, the manager may define a general set of requirements for each technical area and assign these to the organizational staff for technical planning and methodology selection. These methodologies typically are very specific to the segment of the project they support. For example, the methodologies used for requirements definition do not necessarily support the functional decomposition process; those used for functional decomposition are not effective when specifying requirements or designing the software. The data requirements and products produced by each of the methodologies are specific and, as a result, may not be compatible with the requirements of other project areas.

This linking of methodologies is not the primary consideration of the technical groups in defining or selecting a procedure for use in a particular

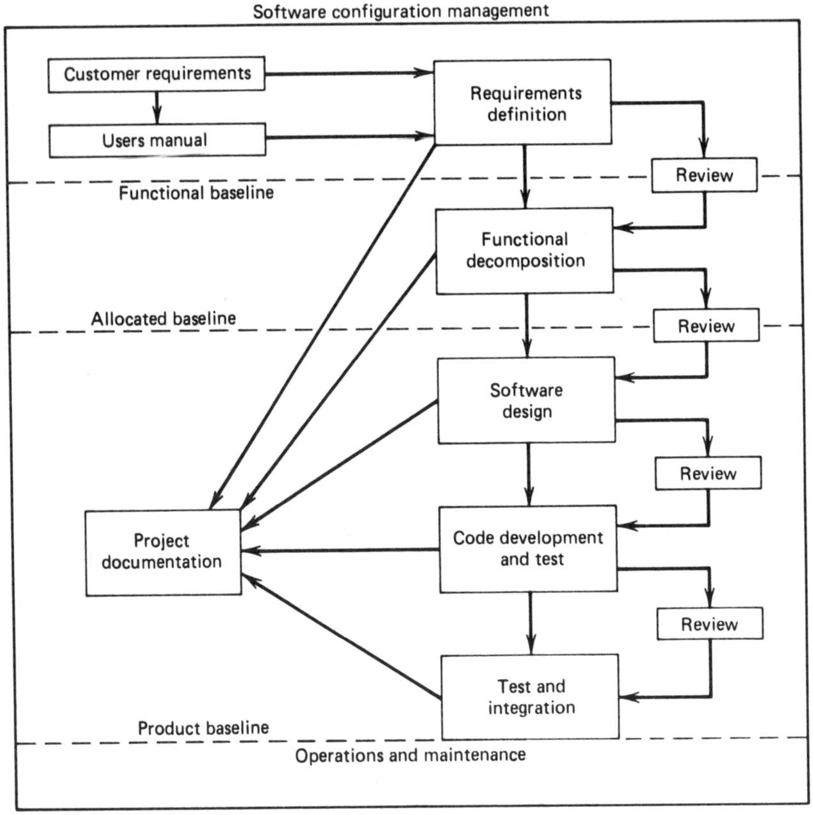

Figure 5.1. Data flow for primary development activities.

area of the project. Criteria used in making the selection range from the experience of the manager to the currency and technical acceptability of the methodology in the industry community. As a result, the transition of data between differing segments and phases of the project becomes muddled, and much rework is required to maintain data compatibility.

The problem of methodology compatibility and selection may be minimized by planning the selection of methodologies first at the management level through definition of the standards and conventions document.

SOFTWARE STANDARDS AND CONVENTIONS

Project standards and conventions spell out, in detail, rules for development of project documentation and data products.

Development and dissemination of a complete set of project standards and conventions early in the project avoids three problems that impact software productivity and product acceptability:

1. Development of documentation and data by the technical staff in differing formats and in varying degrees of detail.
2. Iterative reviews of project documentation resulting from unclear specifications of document and data requirements and inadequate definition of project criteria for content and acceptability.
3. Software that is difficult to maintain when the original coder is no longer with the project, and software difficult for others to understand when debugging software that interfaces to it.

The standards and conventions should describe specifically how products are to be developed and what criteria the products are to be measured against. The standards and conventions to be defined are in four categories:

1. Technical project methodologies include the specific techniques to be used in defining and allocating software requirements and interfaces, functionally decomposing the requirements into a software architecture, synthesizing all software design from the functional definition, and coding and ensuring the adequacy and acceptability of implemented software source.

2. Documentation standards and conventions include the specific content and format requirements by section for each deliverable document identified in the software development plan and nondeliverable documentation requirements such as unit development folders and programmer notebooks. The description should be amplified and extended in style guides to be developed for each primary document.

3. Coding standards and conventions describe the specific rules for developing code and criteria for commenting variable usage, formatting, naming and size. These criteria provide the basic review and acceptance criteria for evaluation at project walkthroughs and reviews.

4. Review and reporting requirements describe specifically what is required at each project review and acceptability criteria for each data component required for the review.

In addition, the requirements for each internal and external project report and the format and content requirements of each are defined.

The specification of an integrated set of standards and project conventions consistent with the needs and characteristics of the project is an essential element of project success. Too often, however, decisions such as methodology selection, documentation format content and delivery requirements, and coding standards evolve as the project proceeds, or, worse still, they are defined in an ad hoc manner by technical staff members without an understanding of the development needs or requirements or the objectives of the project.

During the planning phase of the project the software manager and his staff are inundated with short-term project support requirements demanding immediate attention. Long-term project requirements do not always appear critical. These longer-term project parameters are, however, what define how the project is to be designed, implemented, and integrated and what specific technical techniques and procedures are to be applied to the project. All planning and project requirements and definition of tools, techniques, and project control procedures are keyed to the methodologies, standards, and conventions selected and applied. *Early definition, documentation, review, and project acceptance of the data provided in the standards and conventions document is essential for the ultimate success of the project. Without this acceptance on the part of project personnel, the development stands little chance for success.*

The specific technique or techniques selected by a software project has a critical effect on the success of the development. As the project transitions through the various phases of the development cycle, the integrity, responsiveness, and acceptability of the software product will become questionable in the context of contractual, technical, administrative, and control environments if the development techniques are not well defined.

A software manager must consider five factors when selecting or reviewing the selection of a methodology set for application to the project:

1. Have the proposed technical techniques been proven in development applications of similar size and complexity with similar environments and characteristics?
2. Do the techniques produce data products consistent with the documentation and review requirements of the contract? Can these products be used without modification in other phases of the development?
3. Is there clear traceability between requirements specified by the methodology and those needed by related methodology? Are the individual requirements definable, testable, and demonstrable in the context of overall project requirements?
4. Is it possible to plan the overall flow of the project, interfaces, and relationships among project segments and define a schedule that integrates specific requirements of the selected methodologies into a consistent and effective project structure?
5. Are the resources and proposed requirements of the methodologies consistent with project budget and schedule constraints? Is it possible to labor or configure the application of the methodology to the characteristics of the project?

These five factors must be addressed by a manager as part of the decision-making process leading to selection and implementation of a set of specific methodologies for the project. More often than not, the manager finds that the latest technical solution to the software development program does not match his or her requirements and must be discarded in lieu of a less esoteric but more effective method of development.

Unless this effectiveness analysis is done up front, methodologies may be applied to the project that result in confusion and poor performance as the development proceeds.

The software project has available a myriad of tools, techniques, and methodologies from which a project environment may be defined. These are different for each phase of the project and must be integrated through the software development plan, project standards and conventions, and the implemented project management and control structure.

The specification of user requirements and system interfaces is a structured application of analytical techniques toward provision of a nonambiguous, traceable definition of system requirements.

Requirements Definition

Decomposition of the baselined user requirements for use in the system design proceeds is a two-step process:

1. **Specification Analysis.** The requirements specification is decomposed into several components, which include system requirements, environmental considerations, performance requirements, interface requirements, operational and support requirements, and narrative. These requirements are then synopsized and become the basis for design implementation and test activities.

2. **Requirements Amplification.** The requirements set is an ordered set of user requirements. These requirements must be extended to include derived requirements that adapt the system to the applications configuration, performance constraints, system control requirements that control and schedule system execution, and reliability, fault isolation, and recovery requirements that ensure acceptable system performance in anomalous environments.

There are a variety of available automated and manual techniques for defining, documenting, and controlling the specification of user requirements. Examples of these follow:

1. PSL/PSA is a computer-aided technique for defining and documenting system requirements and providing a traceable baseline for use in the design phases of the project.

2. SREM is a computer-aided technique for specifying and analyzing basic software requirements and describing the required flow of processing to satisfy system objectives.
3. HDM is a computer-based methodology that provides facilities for the on-line definition of a set of user requirements and the translation of these into a set of design specifications that integrate user needs with environmental characteristics and constraints.
4. ICEPAC provides CAD (computer-aided design) support to automate the top-down structured development of software and also supports requirements analysis and definition by prompting requirement specification completion, tracking the allocation of requirements, and automatically generating requirement traceability matrices. The ICEPAC also automatically generates the requirement segments specification document.
5. Special purpose or company proprietary tools have been developed to provide traceability and testability of a set of basic user requirements.

The software manager should research the methodologies available for application to the requirements specification and, based on analysis of project effectiveness, select a single methodology or blend of various components to satisfy his or her particular requirements.

Functional Design

Functional design is an orderly process that decomposes the functional definition of the system into lower and lower levels until the final level is reached and the software systems design process can proceed. There are several key elements that must be considered in the definition and allocation of functional requirements to system design components:

1. **Requirements Traceability.** By decomposing system functional requirements from the requirements inventory and interface definitions, complete and clear traceability must be maintained back to the specified needs of the user.

2. **Functional Allocation.** By defining a top-level flow of systems support and vigorously decomposing each of the elements that comprise this support interactively to lower functional levels, a systems designer ensures that what he specifies as functional system requirements accurately reflects the top-level design of the system as well as the needs and requirements of the user.

3. **Data Collection and Control.** By maintaining a dictionary of system data elements keyed to the functional allocation and decomposition

process, a complete definition of internal system data requirements is maintained as the design progresses.

Several methodologies have been developed and are available to support the functional software decomposition process. Examples of these follow:

1. Structured Analysis and Design Technique (SADT) is an automated graphic data flow structure that uses a graphic language to define a hierarchical decomposition of functional and data requirements.
2. USEIT is an automated, graphic technique for decomposing functional requirements into a software structure that, when taken to its lowest level supported by the methodology, supports the automated development of code.
3. ICEPAC performs automatic checks to see that all requirements and designs have been allocated downward during the decomposition process. It also flags modules that do not have requirements or design allocated to them. A structured design language with full-screen prompting automates the detail design process.
4. Project and company methodologies and techniques have been developed by companies to support the process of functional design and should be identified, analyzed, and considered when defining specifically how functional requirements are to be identified and allocated to software components.

These methodologies are the precursor to the software design. The output of the methodologies selected for use must be clear, concise, complete, and consistent with the technical needs and requirements of the project.

Software Design

When the functional design has been integrated with user requirements, it is decomposed until the lowest level is reached. At this point, software system design begins. This means that the preliminary design is expanded to a level that enables code to be generated as the next development activity.

Routines within each module are designed, with all outputs and the processing steps defined. Timing and memory budgets are allocated to each routine; sources and destinations for data are defined; the hierarchy of interfaces among modules is defined down to the routine level; and restrictions on each routine are specified.

Internal and external data inputs and outputs are specified. The minimum and maximum data values are determined precisely, and the location of each data field is prescribed. Factors such as the protocol between software and communications hardware are described in detail following the definition of functional interfaces during preliminary design.

As with the other segments of the project development, several methodologies have been developed that may be relevant in the context of the project development environment:

1. Structured design is a process by which the data structures of a particular coding object are defined, and then a program structure that will produce the required data is synthesized.
2. USEIT generates software design as an integrated part of the USEIT functional decomposition process.
3. Transform analysis is a method of defining and transforming specific software design from the requirements specified from the functional decomposition process.
4. ICEPAC supports traceability of detailed design for compilation and module debugging. ICEPAC simplifies testing by providing skeletal test documents and by ensuring that all requirements and data have been allocated during the design process.

The design synthesis defines what software constructs are required to satisfy effectively requirements, goals, and objectives.

The design problem requires that functional requirements be translated into design constraints. The designer works with a predefined data component, ordered and structured in accordance with the hierarchical functional architecture through the functional specifications, summarizes the requirements, and resolves design issues prior to satisfaction of the design requirements.

When the process of defining functional design is complete, the designer then defines tasks that assign specific design structures to the lowest level of functional definition. These structures define the specific constructs that, when implemented, satisfy the requirements of the system. These structures are the lowest level of system design and serve as the basis for software design.

Coding Development

The methodologies to be followed in developing and testing code implemented in accordance with the functional and architectural requirements of the design may be less rigorous than those used during the decomposition and design process. This flexibility is due to tight coupling between the software development environment, specified project and contract standards and conventions for code readability, and in-process reviews of the coding process conducted through an integrated set of walkthroughs. Also, the code represents a physical and tangible commodity that may be reviewed and evaluated, unlike the design process, which in the review deals with data products that are difficult to evaluate.

The coding methodology must, however, satisfy several basic software development requirements:

1. The implemented code must be readable, understandable, and traceable to the requirements of the software design.
2. The code must be maintained in the software architecture, data base components, and the requirements for coding specified in the coding standards and conventions segment of this document.
3. The code must be sufficiently modular to facilitate the development and testing of several software segments while providing elements when executing in an integrated configuration.

The structured coding techniques support the three preceding project areas. Before accepting this methodology for project use, however, the manager must evaluate three aspects of the application that may impact or preclude its use. First, requirements of the software application must be evaluated to determine whether the overhead associated with code is developed in accordance with the application characteristics. Second, support and language constraints implicit in the development environment may make the application of structured constructs difficult or impossible. Third, limitations in personnel experience make development of quality structured code impossible.

If structured coding techniques are not applied, the manager must define a consistent methodology that addresses the coding needs of the project as well as the customer requirements for production, documentation, and reliability.

Documentation Development

The documentation methodology has five component parts that must be planned and integrated:

1. How the program, customer, and contractual contents and format requirements are to be defined, documented, reviewed, and approved.
2. How the data required for the production and evaluation of documentation are to be developed, used by the technical organizations.
3. How the technical writing and integration of the technical data into the document is to be accomplished and reviewed during the development of each specific document.
4. How the documentation development is to be supported, administered, and controlled; how technical data are to be converted into a form consistent with established document standards for the quality

of the documentation to be ensured; and how the project is to respond if documentation is of unacceptable quality.

5. How the software project is to deal with document revisions, and how the updates are to be developed.

By documenting early in the project specifically how documentation is to be produced, the software manager ensures that minimal confusion will be experienced in the production of project documentation, and cost and schedule risks will be minimized.

As described in the previous chapter, the software manager may anticipate and plan the documentation development process, avoiding the significant impacts on project productivity caused by ineffective or inefficient document development practices. Through the use of style guides, the specific requirements for individual documents are defined and communicated to the staff. Through the project reviews, evolving data and documentation are evaluated early enough to correct problems before the document is released. Through the organizational support provided by the document coordinator, all documentation is entered in a single organizational entity responsible for the development and production of all documentation, and the quality and acceptability of end products is ensured. These factors, coupled with the controlled flow of data within the project as the development proceeds, minimize the impacts associated with software documentation and production.

Design and Coding Standards and Conventions

An early definition of a set of coding standards and conventions consistent with the characteristics and needs of the other methodologies used to support the development of software is an important component of the productive management of software.

The standards and conventions have a material effect on the techniques used in other methodologies as well as the tools used or developed to support the project. *The way that the coding is blocked affects the file structure used to control the source code and the review procedures used to evaluate software quality.* The commenting and internal source code documentation procedures affect how the software documentation is defined and developed. The definition and implementation standards and conventions for development of data base components affect the definition and implementation of the design methodologies selected. And the software design practices and standards for representation (through graphic techniques or through a design language) have a major impact on the coding and methodology selected as well as on the documentation, review, and testing methodologies applied to the project.

The definition of coding standards and conventions should not, or could not, be a precursor to the selection or definition of specified methodologies to be used to support the development process. They should follow this definition and serve to expand and provide detail on how the various aspects and requirements of the methodologies are to be translated into standard code consistent both throughout all of the software and with the requirements of the software project.

The coding standards and conventions to be defined are in seven categories:

1. Module and unit sizing describes how the software is to be blocked in a system configuration and provides architectural rules for the functional allocation to the design of the software.
2. Design-to-code translation describes how to determine how much code is represented by each component of the low-level design specifications and the standards for translation of design to code.
3. Module form and structure defines the module to be structured, the prologue requirements to be used, and the commenting, labeling, and formatting standards.
4. Coding conventions identify specific coding techniques, procedures, and forms to be followed in the implementation of all project codes.
5. Documentation defines the standards for modules and unit documentation and the convention for development during and after the development.
6. Design and coding evaluation procedures describe standards for defining and evaluating specific module and unit characteristics, such as cohesion, coupling, and design heuristics, and for evaluating code against design requirements.
7. Software interface requirements define the design and coding requirements for calling sequences between software components and the access and update procedures for data components.

Definition of design and coding standards provides a clear definition of how designers and developers are to standardize the form, structure, and documentation of all software design and code.

REVIEW AND REPORTING REQUIREMENTS

Reporting requirements define the checks and balances implicit in the project; the reporting requirements establish from the project outset how the quality requirements of the project are to be evaluated and how implementation of the various methodologies are to be accessed. *The disciplines associated with the software development methodologies, implementation, and application are complex. If they are to prove effective, they must be tightly coupled and carefully coordinated and controlled.*

Problems in the application of the methodologies to the project environment are subtle. Serious project problems occur throughout the almost imperceptible occurrence of many small events and conditions; often a point is reached beyond which meaningful or effective progress toward the production of an acceptable product is impossible.

The role of the project review and reporting methodologies is to define project monitoring procedures to provide visibility and recognition of small slips in software development progress early enough to facilitate correction or reassignment of resources to the project to alleviate the situation.

The five areas that must be continually evaluated through formal and informal project review and reporting procedures are:

1. Schedule and budget performance, to provide continuous low-level monitoring of resource expenditures in relation to projected project progress and performance.
2. Standards adherence, to evaluate continuously the compliance of software data products with documented and established standards and conventions.
3. Quality characteristics, to identify and evaluate specific quality characteristics of development products prior to delivery to the customer or user.
4. Baseline and requirements correspondence, to ensure correspondence of definition and development of software products as they are produced with related essential basic requirements or constraints.
5. Personnel effectiveness, to evaluate continuously the effectiveness and performance of the management systems and staff in controlling and orchestrating the development of software.

The reviews must be defined by the standards and conventions documents. The reviews are the window through which the manager views project performance and development progress. The rules for each review must also be identified in the standards and conventions document. The reviews fall into four categories:

1. Formal project reviews are held for either the customer or the program, require defined agendas and structured presentations, and provide the forum for project decisions and approvals.

2. Informal project reviews are held with the customer or program but do not have a predefined structure. These reviews are required to communicate project plans or to present technical decisions. Definition of the organizations and personnel commit the project; how commitments are made is a key in ensuring management control and project adherents to contractual and technical baselines.

3. Internal project reviews, walkthroughs, and audits provide ongoing assessments of technical and quality characteristics of the development products.

4. Resource expenditure and progress reviews are held either for the customer or internally with the software project to identify the expenditures of resources and problems with project performance in relation to schedule and budget projections.

In order to report the results of the project reviews internally within the software project and externally to customer and program offices and organizations, a standard set of project reports and reporting requirements is essential. These requirements should provide:

1. Formal reports developed in accordance with program or customer schedules with fixed, predefined content.
2. Informal reports developed by the project to communicate product progress, performance, and experience.
3. Red-flag reports that communicate to management and project personnel issues of concern or conditions requiring action or resolution.

The reporting standards define the specific format and content requirements for each report identified in the software development plan. These reporting standards also describe how and by whom the reports are to be developed and what internal reviews are to be employed in ensuring the quality of the report prior to release from the project.

The software project standards and conventions document specifies how the general requirements in the software development plan are to be translated into a consistent, ordered, and standard set of quality software products. The standards and conventions provide clear guidelines to technical personnel and describe the structure and techniques to be used to develop software products. These techniques help ensure compatibility among project elements and communicate to all levels of the program and project specific descriptions of products to be developed. The structure also helps determine how the development will proceed and define the reviews, audits, and reporting requirements that will maintain and ensure management visibility into the development process.

Definition, documentation, and implementation of standards and conventions ensure that project requirements are assigned from the software manager throughout the organization and do not evolve from the project in response to crises or catastrophic system conditions.

Specific Project Reviews

As the data moves through the various stages of development, the software manager must ensure that there is a structure of reviews for evaluating the quality of the data and adherence to project standards.

The project reviews fall into two general categories: (1) formal project reviews that evaluate the status and quality of the major project baselines as they are produced; and (2) internal walkthroughs and reviews that assess the integrity of data being developed by the technical organizations within the project.

Formal Reviews

Through the project planning, the software manager establishes, with customer and program participation, a means for evaluating and approving each of the baselines as they are developed. Formal reviews should be defined to evaluate the technical integrity of the project.

1. **Software Requirements Review.** This review evaluates interpretation that the software staff has made of the specified user requirements. It also analyzes the trade-off and system analyses conducted to evaluate the requirements and define an architecture and support configuration.

2. **Software Design Review.** This review presents and evaluates the overall software architecture and the preliminary definition and allocation of function requirements. It is the first purely software technical review and should consider:
   - (a) Quality and technical integrity of documentation presented and reviewed.
   - (b) Stability and integrity of requirements presented.
   - (c) Completeness and adequacy of software interface definitions and specifications.
   - (d) Program languages used and the rationale leading to the selection.
   - (e) Software standards and conventions and technical methodology selection.
   - (f) Project complexity evaluation.
   - (g) Operating system and support software selection.
   - (h) Data management selection.
   - (i) Personnel selection, application, and qualifications.
   - (j) Development facility selection and planned application.
   - (k) Project management plans and procedures.

3. **Preliminary Design Review (PDR).** This review provides a means for evaluation and approval of the progress, consistency, and technical adequacy of the selected design approach to satisfy the allocated performance requirements contained in the functional specifications. A PDR will be held for each major component of software. At the PDR, the following actions should be performed:
   - (a) Review all detailed functional interfaces between the software subsystem and other subsystems and between the software and related equipment. Action should be taken to ensure that interface design requirements are adequately identified and solutions documented.

(b) Ensure that the software processes or tasks and their functions have been identified, and review the functional interfaces between the processes.
(c) Review word lengths, message formats, available storage, memory maps, and other considerations included in the functional specification.
(d) Review critical timing requirements and estimated run times.
(e) Ensure that the design meets the functional, performance, interface, and design requirements in the requirement specifications, interface specifications, data base specification, and the software/software interface specifications.
(f) Review the human interaction aspects of the software, and ensure that the requirements of the user's manual are supported by the design.
(g) Review the qualification test plan and all available test requirements, documentation, and tools. Ensure that the incremental builds provide for adequate testing of requirements.
(h) Review the project standards and conventions.
(i) Review the software development facility, including configuration and availability.
(j) Review the software development plan and the software project management, including detailed schedules, personnel requirements, manning, internal management milestones (e.g., unit test and releases), and resource allocation. Review status monitoring and reporting.
(k) Review any critical technical and contractual issues.

The PDR should be approved by the customer, with approval being the point at which design is baselined under configuration management. The PDR establishes that it is prudent to proceed with the detail designs.

4. Critical Design Review (CDR). This review establishes that it is prudent to proceed with the coding and software integration. During the CDR, the integrity of computer program logical design is established. Also during this review, the design language representation of the design, the unit development folders, and the "build-to" design specifications are scrutinized. These documents are made available to the review group and technical management prior to the review. At the CDR, the following actions are performed:

(a) Review the compatibility and traceability of design with the functional specification.
(b) Review the detailed design and other descriptive documentation to establish compatibility with the system design.
(c) Ensure that the interface requirements are satisfied and are specified in detail. Review the detailed user interface.

(d) Review interaction of the software with the data base.
(e) Review the test and analytical data such as logical diagrams, algorithms, and storage allocation charts.
(f) Review the design specification, with the exception of the program listings (which will be produced only after coding), and ensure that the softwarc is specified at a level of detail that permits the writing of code without further design.
(g) Review design changes affecting the preliminary design.
(h) Review the computer loading, interaction rates, processing rates, processing time, and memory estimates.
(i) Ensure that the design meets the functional, performance, interface, and design requirements in the segment requirement specifications, interface specifications, data base specifications, and the SW/SW interface specifications.
(j) Review the current detailed development and test plans. Ensure that the incremental builds plan for requirements to be tested, the modules to be included, and the test procedures to be used.
(k) Review the development facility capability to support full-scale code and integration.
(l) Review critical technical and contractual issues. The CDR will be approved by the customer.

The CDR is conducted on the software after the detail design is essentially complete. Its purpose is to establish the integrity of computer program design at the level of functional flow diagrams of computer program logical design prior to coding and testing. The "build-to" design specification is to be reviewed at CDR: it is subject to change and will not be baselined and controlled until after the development effort is complete.

Informal Reviews and Walkthroughs

The formal reviews provide a means by which the customer, program, and software management staff may evaluate the quality and integrity of baselines established by the program. Many managers limit the specification of project reviews to these, neglecting the more important problem of in-process evaluation of the evolving technical data. *Without a method for conducting these reviews, the manager will soon find that project personnel are working with data not consistent with project standards and, worse still, data that are technically unsound.*

By incorporating into the structure of the project a requirement for walkthroughs, the manager ensures that these reviews take place at key points in the schedule and that data products are evaluated before they are used by more than one organizational component within the project.

The walkthroughs differ from the formal reviews in that formal reviews are stand-up presentations of large segments of the system requirements of functional support or of design supported by a cast of thousands, whereas walkthroughs are small and informal and deal with a very small piece of design, code, or test data developed by an individual or small group within the project. The walkthroughs are peer reviews normally limited to the responsible programmer, his or her immediate technical supervisor, and a group of his or her peers. In an ideal situation there is no management involvement other than at the schedule or planning level.

These walkthroughs are very important in the project because they are the means by which the quality and integrity of software data products are evaluated as the products are being developed and they are the status points used by a manager to plan and measure schedule performance. There should be four walkthroughs planned for every unit of software, as follows:

1. **Design Analysis Review.** A walkthrough will be held for software component and detailed functional allocation prior to the date when process descriptions will be made available. The participants will include the responsible programmer, his or her immediate technical supervisor, and a group of his or her peers. The participants will review the material for completeness, compliance with standards, and interface requirements.

2. **Design Walkthrough (DW).** This walkthrough should occur on completion of the unit design and the unit test definition. This should be when the design is completed on paper and not coded beyond that level. The DW should concentrate on adherence to requirements, design, and interfaces and on the relationship of the module(s) to the software subsystem. A structured design walkthrough should be held for every unit to review the intended design. The Program Design Language (PDL) specification of the module, the module description specification, the related module structure charts, data dictionaries, and the module test plan should be reviewed during the walkthrough. These materials will be provided to the walkthrough participants prior to the walkthrough. The participants will include the responsible programmer, his or her immediate technical supervisor, and a group of his or her peers, particularly those responsible for other software that interfaces with the modules being examined. The design walkthrough should have the following approximate structure:

   (a) The walkthrough leader will open with a general discussion of how this module fits into the design hierarchy represented by the structure charts.
   (b) Following this discussion, the design and inputs/outputs will be presented by the responsible programmer and reviewed line by line by the walkthrough group.
   (c) After the general walkthrough, members of the reviewing audience may ask for a walkthrough of specific postulated input. This process continues as long as anyone can think of situations where the program's behavior is suspected.

(d) Next the responsible programmer maps the requirements to the design.
(e) Then he walks through the test plan.
(f) The last thing the walkthrough participants must decide is whether it will be necessary to review proposed corrections and changes to the design or test plan. If further review is required, the walkthrough is not signed off as completed, and the walkthrough process is repeated after the design is modified.

Completion of the DW will authorize the coding and initiate transfer of the module(s) design to the program support library. When completed, including necessary changes and corrections, the responsible programmer will transfer the updated design, which results in unit design release. The PSL librarian will review the design material in the user area (unit design, PDL, and test specification) for format and adherence to established standards. If the design material is acceptable, the PSL librarian will copy the design material from the specified user files to the corresponding controlled files. At this point the unit will have successfully completed the DW, the design phase, and the schedule milestone. The unit(s) design will now be under configuration control and require SCRB action via the SPR to change.

3. **Code Review (CR).** The CR will occur upon completion of coding. It will be conducted by a senior designer (normally the task leader) or the senior technical member of the staff. The CR will concentrate on acceptable coding techniques and adherence to standards. The design will be verified against the coding to identify any coding errors. Upon successful completion of the CR, the reviewing authority will indicate required changes and corrections. The code walkthrough will verify that this unit implementation meets project standards and implements the unit design accurately. The software to be reviewed must compile cleanly—that is, without errors—prior to the code walkthrough. A copy of the source code will be distributed to the walkthrough participants for review at least two working days prior to the walkthrough. The walkthrough will have the following structure:

(a) The walkthrough leader will open with a general discussion of how this unit fits into the system hierarchy.
(b) Following this, the responsible programmer will "step" through the code.
(c) Failure of this walkthrough requires the repetition of the walkthrough.
(d) The coding phase of the module is completed when the code walkthrough has been successfully completed and signed off.

If during the testing major code changes are required, the responsible programmer will request a new code walkthrough. The code walkthrough is used as a status point for the schedule. However, the review should not be used to transfer data into the PSL. Code should not be transferred until it has been established through unit testing.

4. **Test Walkthrough (TW).** The TW will occur on successful completion of unit testing. It will validate the final module source code, review the unit test scope, and test materials for completeness and correct results. The responsible programmer will make required changes and corrections and conduct any necessary retesting. This is the last informal review of the software prior to the start of integration testing. As such, the manager must ensure that TWs are conducted for each and every unit despite schedule and cost pressures and management assurances that sampling will be just as good. The responsible programmer transfers to the tested source code and the software documentation updates to the project library. The program walkthrough leader will independently review library copy of the code and documentation for compliance with standards and conventions and will place them under configuration management and sign off the unit as completed. The walkthrough establishes that it is prudent to proceed with software integration. The following items are evaluated:

(a) All interfaces have been incorporated and tested.
(b) The software has been coded and complies with design.
(c) The code meets the functional, performance, interface, and design requirements, and the unit tests verify compliance.
(d) The unit test plan identifies the requirements to be tested, the modules to be included, and the test procedures to be used and confirms that the unit tests have been completed.
(e) The code is consistent with the standards and conventions.

After completion of the TWs, the PSL librarian will review the unit materials in the user library and the units test material for proper format and incorporation of all required changes. Also, after completion of the TW, the librarian will transfer the unit code materials from the user library to the controlled library and store the unit test materials. At this point, the unit will have successfully completed the unit schedule milestone, and the unit will now be under configuration control. All further changes to the unit require SCRB action via the SPR.

5. **Build Review.** An additional informal review will be held to evaluate each build to be conducted to moderate and verify the software.

A build review will be conducted prior to the demonstration of a build to the software manager. The integration and test plan, the unit development folders, and the remaining contents of the build development folders will be reviewed. The participants will include the technical supervisors and key programmers involved with the build. Materials to be reviewed will be provided to the participants prior to the review.

Upon completion of the review, the integration test procedures and integration test results will be made available to the software manager prior to the build demonstration. The build demonstration must be brought under library control prior to the demonstration. The demonstration will be conducted in front of the software manager. If the demonstration is determined to be successful and is signed off by the software manager, the build is considered to be complete and will be internally frozen and configuration controlled by the SCRB. If the demonstration is not successful, the rework must be accomplished and a build review conducted on the reworked build prior to redemonstration for the software manager.

6 Test and Integration: The Basic Tasks

The rigor associated with software testing must be retained, especially in periods of technical cost or schedule difficulty.

The cornerstone of a successful software project is the effectiveness of the controls and technical tasks associated with the test and integration of the software. These tasks span the entire period of development. Because of the long lead times associated with the production of test materials and the close coupling between the various test phases and other project activities, these tasks must be started early in the project and supported throughout the development period.

The software manager must focus the project emphasis toward this most critical and difficult project area for the following reasons:

1. All project inadequacies and development difficulties become apparent during testing and must be resolved if the project is to proceed to a successful conclusion.
2. Any system or software design not resolved during the implementation period will require resolution during software testing.
3. The tools, techniques, planning, and test development required to support the software integration and test are extensive and require long lead times and effective project coordination for success.
4. Software integration and test is conducted late in a project when budgets and schedule constraints are most severe.

Software testing, traditionally the most frustrating, difficult, and tedious job in programming, should be performed under rigidly enforced standards of uniformity and tailored to the needs of the project.

By defining and then applying rigorous controls to test planning and early test execution, the software manager provides assurance that code

	Software Test Planning Documentation							
Basic test plan	Programmer's notebook	Unit development folders	Configuration control	Build test plan	Build test plan	Final build test plan	Software test review
Test detail	Module test specification	Unit test plan		Build integration plan	Build functional	Cumulative build integration plan	Procedures scenarios data
Test object	Module	Unit		System subset	Functional demonstration subset	System integration	Software functional demonstration
Test activity	Standards adherence	Module interfaciability		Unit interfaciability	Data interfaces	Build interfaciability	Data interfaces
	Design adherence	Unit integration		Data interfaces	Build support	Data interfaces	System support
		Unit functionality		Build integration / Build functionality	Build functionality	System integration / System functionality	System functionality

Test output	Completed module	Integrated unit	Integrated software build	Qualified software build	Integrated software system	Qualified software system
Test level	1	2	3	4	5	6
Reviews	Walkthrough	Walkthrough	Build test review	Build qualified subset	Software test plan	Software system acceptance
Test tools	Driver	Driver/ instrumentation	Simulation/ instrumentation	Simulation	Simulation instrumentation	Simulation/ hardware

Figure 6.1. Test flow.

matches the requirements of the design, that it is developed in accordance with project standards, and, at the lowest level, that it is tested in accordance with the requirements of the detailed software design.

It is during the software test activities that careful maintenance of requirements verification tools, the configuration management and quality assurance plans, unit development folders, and other documents pays enormous dividends. If significant problems are found during integration testing, they can be traced quite rapidly and inexpensively to their sources and corrected with minimum impact on the software schedules.

Formal documentation of each step during development does a great deal to prevent problems during integration. Major rework is increasingly rare at this stage for projects that have been managed according to the methods outlined.

THE SIX LEVELS OF TESTING

As illustrated in Figure 6.1, several stages of testing are required to validate the program design (i.e., determine if it meets the program requirements) and to verify that the implementation of the design is correct.

TEST ACTIVITIES

Testing activities begin during the planning phase and continue throughout the life of the system. The three major steps involved are: (1) gathering test requirements, (2) planning tests to meet these requirements, and (3) controlling specifications produced for each critical step. These steps are applicable to program development testing and to the activities involved in formally qualifying the program for operational use.

Establishing test requirements is the basis for determining the frequency of tests and scheduling these tests in the programming process.

Test requirements will provide the definition of technical requirements to a level of detail sufficient to enable the various organizations to plan and carry out the testing tasks. These requirements will define:

1. Objectives of the various tests.
2. Conditions and limitations under which the tests will be conducted.
3. Success criteria for all tests.
4. The required resources, such as the support programs, equipment, personnel, and customer-furnished items.
5. Any special or unique hardware needed to perform the test.
6. Source of specific hardware needed for the test.
7. All special test software needed.
8. Any new software required.

9. Need dates for all special or new software.
10. All preventive maintenance tools.
11. Data format of each test pattern required.

The customer must always be involved in this activity because the criteria for a successful project are established here. At a minimum, the customer must provide the high-level success criteria and approve the detailed support requirements.

Test Planning

The software test plan provides a vehicle for the software manager to document plans, procedures, and practices that will be followed in qualifying the software. This early planning is critical to the long-term success of the project, for project effectiveness during this period is a key component of project health and development productivity. Through this planning the manager anticipates predictable crises that will, in all likelihood, occur during the testing. These crises, summarized in Figure 6.2, will occur during the testing period and must be addressed during the planning period when solutions are feasible and may be planned for. If not effectively dealt with, these crises can cause the software project to stop during the most critical period of the development; integration, test, and system qualification.

Because of the pressures on the software manager during the planning period, there is a tendency to defer test planning until "we can get to it." On the surface it appears that there is plenty of time to resolve testing issues as there is no immediate pressing need for answers to the test problem. There is a temptation to look on it as a problem whose "time will come."

Deferring test planning is a key trap a software manager may fall into early in the project. The test problem is the most stringent of all project requirements necessitating the effective implementation, integration, and application of a variety of project disciplines to succeed. These disciplines must be initially defined and implemented in accordance with the overall requirements for testing in order to ensure a smooth project transition for software implementation to test and integrate and adequate project controls over technical products and project resources during this period. The software manager must, from the outset, plan for the worst and assume that from the beginning software testing will not go well and will continue to be difficult until the last customer acceptance test has been run. There is no room for optimism in test planning.

Development and specification of software test requirements is an iterative process paralleling the software design and development. Basic software test planning during the initial segment of the project specifies a test philosophy and structure tailored to project environments. As illustrated in Figure 6.3, the philosophy defined should describe six distinct software test

Problem	Early symptom	Effect if not corrected	Possible planning option
1. Schedule difficulty due to extended development and code time	Software not ready when tests ready for execution	Insufficient time to test software resulting in schedule slip	Phase software testing into build testing software when available
2. Inability to translate requirements and design to test procedures	Nonfunctional software test procedures	Delivery of a system not responsive to user needs	Conduct customer/ user reviews of test data iterating requirements and specifications when needed
3. Inability to develop executable test cases from procedures	Test personnel cannot specify test script from procedures	Test scripts not adequate representation of software execution characteristics	Phase development personnel into test planning activities
4. Nonavailability of hardware or key testing resources	Schedule delays due to hardware slips	Software schedules keyed to hardware availability	Simulate critical hardware interfaces and support
5. Insufficient interface definition and inability to duplicate exact test conditions	Nonpredictability of test results	Software systems with known problems delivered to customer	Hard code test scripts readable through simulator
6. Ambiguous user specifications or system operator instructions	Insufficient data to develop procedures	Procedures that do not match system support requirements	Plan tests early and iterate details as system detail increases
7. Unavoidable schedule delay between system releases whill new software configurations stabilize	Repeated delays in qualifying system release	Significant schedule impacts due to poor initial performance of software	Schedule informal software burn-in period with each release
8. Insufficient labor during testing	Excessive overtime required during test	Employee demotivation and turnover	Provide for labor pool, sharing resources between test, development, and support

(continued)

Problem	Early symptom	Effect if not corrected	Possible planning option
9. Delays associated with correction of problems	Repeated slips due to problem correction delays	Poorly qualified systems	Plan for software configuration management and overlap system releases
10. Insufficient internal data available to diagnose and correct problems	Necessity to retest repeatedly to diagnose problems	Poorly qualified releases	Plan simulation and instrumentation development, installation, use, and removal
11. Baselines lost during development and corrections lost during test	System releases not controlled or of unknown content	Frequent test and development restarts	Plan, implement, and integrate strong, effective software configuration management

Figure 6.2. Testing crises.

stages, each integrating or demonstrating progressively more complete system segments. These stages, although consistent with hierarchical testing methodologies, modify the approach to recognize schedule, cost, implementation, and project realities. The six stages follow:

1. Module Testing (level 1). This stage tests the smallest identifiable segment of the software. The testing is primarily accomplished by programmers' inspection of source code and executing major paths through the module through drivers.

2. Unit Testing (level 2). This stage integrates all modules comprising a unit into an operational configuration. The unit test exercises sequences, data interfaces among modules, and the functionality of the integrated unit. As with module testing, integration of the unit is accomplished through execution of the drivers.

3. Build Integration Testing (level 3). This stage integrates qualified units into a hierarchical software system configuration providing a subset of overall software support requirements. Build integration tests integrate units and data structures into an executable configuration and test the functionality of the integrated software. This testing primarily uses external simulation to stimulate the software tests.

4. Build Functional Testing (level 4). This stage tests the functional integrity of an integrated build, the visibility of intersoftware and intrasoftware interfaces, and data support. As with build integration tests, functional tests are driven through external simulation.

	Test type	Organizational support	Software control characteristics	Documentation	Document formality
1. Module test	Informal	Programmer	Programmer control	Programmer's notebook	Informal
2. Unit test	Informal	Programmer	Development organization control	Unit development control	Informal
3. Build integration test	Informal	Development team	Formal project control	Build test plan	Informal
4. Build functional test	Formal	Independent test organization	Formal project control	Build test plan/ procedures	Formal
5. System integration test	Informal	Independent test organization	Formal project control	Software test plan/ procedures	Informal
6. System functional test	Formal	Independent test organization	Formal project control	Software test plan/ procedures	Formal

Figure 6.3. Test levels.

5. **System Integration (level 5).** This stage integrates qualified software builds into an operational software configuration. The primary emphasis of these tests is to take individual builds from different software subsystem and integrate them across subsystem boundaries. The tests will exercise system internal and external data interfaces, transaction processing, and software functionality.

6. **System Testing (level 6).** This stage demonstrates the functionality and the integrity of the software in a variety of system environmental conditions. The tests are all driven externally and are the final phase of software qualification.

In the software development plan, the manager describes what procedures and actions are to be applied in testing the software and demonstrating adherence to functional requirements. These basic requirements must be translated into a testing structure, which will address all segments of testing software, and procedures, which will result in a fully qualified software product responsive to the needs of the user and the application.

The software manager must define, document, and implement a software test structure and environment that will provide a smooth and controlled flow of data and project responsibility as the software flows through the phases of testing. This structure should encompass specific procedures defined for each of the six stages of the test program, define the role of project organizational elements during the testing stages, describe how the activities of these groups are to be orchestrated, monitored, and controlled by the manager during each testing stage, and specify the responsibilities of each organizational element during testing.

The configuration management tools, techniques, and project methodologies to be applied by the project in support of testing should also be defined. This definition is a statement of configuration management and control requirements as they are applied to each of the six test stages and a definition of how, where, and when these requirements are to be detailed, documented, and incorporated into the project. The test planning specifies only what has to be done in the areas of software configuration management to support test, not how the requirements are to be satisfied. Subsequent planning and project practices document this level of detail.

The specific techniques to be followed for each of the six testing stages must be evaluated and documented early in the project. The relationships and technical flow and overlap between each stage should also be identified.

The manager must define and document a project structure and review procedures which provide accurate and timely visibility into the testing process. These should provide assurance that the software undergoing test is of acceptable quality and is adequately controlled and that the testing material, tools, and data are consistent with project requirements and the needs of the test program. This planning will set the requirements for project and quality monitoring during the test stage of the project. Each of the six software testing stages has differing, although overlapping, requirements that must be addressed and used as the basis for software test planning and implementation.

Module testing is the means by which programmers demonstrate that source statements that execute in accordance with software design requirements defined in the program design language or flowcharts approved at the unit design walkthrough. At this stage of the development, the software configuration is very preliminary and requires significant modification to complete the module testing requirements.

The software testing environment during module testing should be loosely structured to allow the programmer the flexibility to test his or her software whichever way best satisfies the physical, environmental, and support equipments of the module, is consistent with the experience of the programmer, and is appropriate with the project testing environment. The general requirements for a module should be documented in the programmer's notebook and reviewed as part of the design walkthrough. The general attributes of the module test process that should be incorporated into the programmer's test planning follow:

1. A clear demonstration, either through external code review or execution of prespecified test cases, that the code characteristics are consistent with documented project standards and conventions.
2. A demonstration that all major functional and control paths defined by the module design and approved as part of the design walkthrough have been exercised. This is the only time in the entire test progress that the internal flow of a module will be exercised and, as such, this aspect of the testing is an essential component of software integrity.
3. An analysis of all interfaces to related modules to ensure that when they are integrated into a unit configuration, the internal module interfaces will match and support each of the modes of support required of the module.
4. Verification that all error conditions and recovery modes required by the module design and execute properly in response to indications of system malfunctions. As with the module path testing, this is the only opportunity to exercise these aspects of the module in a controlled, standalone configuration.
5. A collection of module performance and sizing characteristics. These statistics will be used in conjunction with data from other modules to define an accurate identification of software size and performance characteristics and to verify that the code has been de-

veloped in accordance to the documented part. The correspondence of code to design will be developed through inspection or execution of test cases. The results should be a fundamental part of the unit test walkthrough.

All software used during module testing should be under informal programmer control; however, the module design specifications that form the basis for the test planning should be approved by completion of the design walkthrough and be controlled by the program support library. All module test results should be informally reviewed by the task leader responsible for the software. Formal approval of the results should be delayed until the unit test walkthrough.

Unit testing is the phase of the test program that integrates individual modules into an executable configuration to support an indentifiable segment of the software configuration. Through these tests, the smallest component of the software configuration is derived from individual modules, and the unit functional requirements specified in the software program specification are demonstrated. The requirements for unit testing are approved at the unit design walkthrough. During unit testing the software is still volatile and undergoes significant and often dramatic changes to facilitate the requirements of the testing. For this reason, the controls over unit testing should be localized within the software development organization and must be flexible and adaptable to changing test and support requirements.

Unlike module test activities, which are conducted by and affect a single programmer, unit testing may involve software that has been developed by several staff members. Software discrepancies found during unit testing may impact other technical organizations and may affect controlled software.

The software manager must define a unit test structure that satisfies the requirements of the unit test environment, is flexible in response to changing test needs, and provides sufficient rigor and control to minimize problems resulting from inadequate configuration control, poor communication among programmers, and changing software requirements, design, technical characteristics, and baselines.

The unit testing structure should be documented generically in the software test plan and be tailored to the characteristics of the particular unit in the unit development folder. Generally, this structure should follow the guidelines listed in the following paragraphs.

1. The unit tests should demonstrate the interface integrity between individual modules that comprise the software unit. These tests should exercise each intermodule paths defined between modules and exercise the data interfaces supported through shared data base elements and components internal to the unit.

2. All major functional and control requirements of the unit allocated through the software program specification should be met. The tests should be defined in the unit development folder and approved at the design walkthrough. The module test results, as well as the results of the unit testing, should be reviewed and approved at the unit test walkthrough when the software is placed under configuration management.

3. The software unit should be exercised in a variety of operational, environmental, and support configurations controlled through the test environment. These tests should stress the software, evaluating the effects of changing data requirements, error conditions, and system resource availability on the integrity of the unit configuration.

4. The software unit design and architecture should be rigorously controlled through project configuration management after completion of the unit design walkthrough. Because of the dynamic nature of the software during this phase of the testing, control over code, test, and data base elements of the test configurations should be rigorous but centered within the team integrating the software. The team leader responsible for the unit development should have control of all test configuration and be responsible for any discrepancy correction or testing conduct.

5. The unit test execution review and monitoring structure must recognize and be responsive to the phased availability of software modules that comprise the unit. Because of the phasing of functional availability through the build testing structure, certain modules that make up the unit may not be available until late in the development cycle. The unit test structure, walkthrough, and scheduling and control requirements must provide for the conduct of the overall unit test requirements at various points keyed to module availability.

6. Error recovery and support characteristics of the unit should be exercised and evaluated in relation to requirements of the performance specification. The error conditions and environments should be defined through the test procedures document and be varied to the actual software execution environment projected for the software unit.

The process of unit testing is an essential part of the software test program. Because it is the final opportunity to test the software in a totally controlled software test environment and configuration, it is the last time that the software configuration is maintained or controlled by the group responsible for developing it. After the unit test requirements defined in the unit development folder have been successfully completed and approved through the structured test walkthrough, the unit will be released to configuration management for integration into a system configuration.

Build integration testing is the process by which qualified units are integrated into an executable software configuration and released for functional qualification. The process of build testing is iterative and begins with the integration of a limited subset of the system configuration and ultimately results in a fully integrated system supporting the full range of system requirements.

Build integration tests qualify the design integrity of individual units and interunit interfaces. The tests are conducted by a team assigned responsibility to integrate the software and are based on the design documented in the software detail design specification and approved at the preliminary design review. The specific criteria for tests are provided in the software test plan, with test specifics being documented in build test plans to be provided for each major version of the system by the build integration team.

The software used during this phase of the testing has started to stabilize and is less apt to require significant and dramatic design modification during this testing phase. There is, however, a significant labor penalty associated with inefficiency, ineffectiveness, and poor control over test resources, software updates, and test materials. During build integration testing, any software modifications improperly made or applied to the system result in testing delays. Any use of software that is of insufficient quality to justify integration impacts not only the team integrating the software version but also the development organizations who are responsible for making software modifications in order to correct problems. *An inability of the software project to deal with these issues effectively during build integration testing can dramatically impact project cost and schedule performance and affect the long-term health and progress of the project.*

The test structure must recognize this potential for impact and provide a structure for build integration testing that is both rigorous and controlled, as follows:

1. The orderly addition of prequalified units into an executable test configuration should carefully match unit development and test schedules, thus ensuring availability of working software for testing. Each build configuration should also represent a logical functional system subset, minimizing the requirements for environmental simulation. Emulation of critical functions needed by a build configuration at this late stage can severely impact system release.

2. The software configuration used for build testing must provide internal instrumentation to monitor internal software data values and changes in data base settings resulting from test execution. Because the instrumentation normally requires a long lead time to develop, the functional requirements, performance criteria, and restrictions on usage during testing must be defined very early in the project, preferably during the initial planning stages.

3. Build integration testing marks the transition from development design testing to integrated functional testing. The software manager must ensure that a structure will facilitate the receipt of software from the development organizations, control the integrity of changes, and monitor testing performance and technical, cost, and schedule integrity.

4. System error recognition and recovery modes inherent in each build configuration should be exercised as part of the integration testing and provide a controlled test bed for causing and monitoring responses to erroneous system conditions.

5. All major interfaces and data paths through units as specified in the unit development folder should be exercised by build integration tests when the unit is integrated into the system test configuration. The procedures and techniques to be followed during build integration testing should be defined in the software test plan, tailored through test procedures and techniques to the specific build configuration described in the software test plan, and detailed in scenarios and data definitions. The test plan should describe how each build is to be qualified. Specific tools, techniques, methodologies, software components, and test criteria must be provided in build plans for each major system release.

6. The test environment should be modifiable in a controlled manner. During the execution of build integration it will be important to evaluate the effect of changing loading parameters and dynamic system conditions on software design integrity. The planning for build testing must consider that a static demonstration of software design may not qualify a build configuration for functional testing.

Build testing is the last point at which the internal execution of the software is evaluated and assessed. Software discrepancies noted after this point are more difficult to correct because of the organizational relationships and potential for conflict during subsequent functional testing. For this reason, the project organization and development structure must provide for a detailed review of integration results at the completion of each major build. This review should serve as the basic checkpoint required to release a build to functional test.

Build functional testing is the first time that the software configuration is driven from external data sources and evaluated against functional requirements specified in the software functional specifications. This phase of testing evaluates system external performance characteristics during test execution rather than monitoring internal software execution parameters. The test environment, structure, organization, and support requirements for this testing are entirely different from those used for the previous design tests and, as such, should be treated separately and distinctly by software test planning. During this test phase, versions of the software system whose design has been qualified through integration testing are qualified. Although the software configuration is stable during this stage of testing, there is a certainty that there will be a substantial impact on the software configuration. This impact results from improperly interpreted requirements or poorly defined technical parameters, improperly implemented internal and external software system interfaces in the software configuration, and inconsistent software performance and response characteristics with system or user requirements. During this phase of testing it is important to ensure that the test bench is documented. Problems noted during testing must be reproducible, and sufficient data based on a known test configuration must be collected, documented, and provided to personnel responsible for correction. Regression tests must be executed on exact configurations to qualify system corrections and new system releases. *As with build integration testing, the labor penalties associated with ineffective build functional testing are significant.*

These penalties range from poor cost, schedule, and project performance to inadequate functional testing, with associated long-term software acceptability and reliability impacts. Functional testing at the build or system level provides a vehicle to assess independently the quality of the software in relation to the functional requirements specified in the software requirements specification. Organizationally, this check is ensured by isolating all functional test planning, test case development and implementation, and test execution and results analysis in an independent organization reporting at the same level as the development activities. All data developed or used by this test organization are released to or acquired through the configuration management organization. Changes to this data require approval by the software configuration review board before use in the test program.

The software test plan provides the general guidelines for conduct of these tests and the relationships between this testing and other segments of the test program. Specific techniques, tools, and functional requirements must be validated, as they will be addressed in build test plans unique to each build and procedure developed for each test case. The preliminary verification and validation plan should, however, describe an environment for build functional testing and be characterized by the following:

1. There should be a smooth and controlled flow of data from the design testing areas through project configuration management and control to the functional test activities. This flow of data must be two-way. It must allow test personnel to report problems encountered during testing and to monitor correction as well as receive and test the latest baselined software phase.

2. There should be an objective analysis of software quality and validity in relation to approved software functional requirements documented in the software requirements and system/subsystem specifications. In the case of these requirements, all test stimuli should be external to the software configuration through external simulation, with performance and internal execution characteristics monitored only where necessary through software instrumentation and performance monitoring.

3. A test architecture should provide sufficient flexibility to exercise all functional software requirements in a controlled and reproducible manner. The specified test should identify facilities to vary the test execution se-

quence dynamically. The test should also modify the ambient test environment, dynamically control the test input, modify or terminate execution of test instrumentation affecting performance of the system, and select and monitor the settings of key system parameters and data values during test execution. This dynamic test environment is an essential component of build functional test success. It must be planned for at the outset of the test planning period because of the extremely long lead times associated with specification, definition, development, and qualification of software tools, data, and system and environment simulations. These functional test components must be tightly coupled to other testing requirements specified in the software test plan and, as such, must be integral parts of the testing process.

4. There should be an exercise of specified software error recovery and degradation modes using external data and, where possible, actual system error conditions. These tests and test monitoring techniques are more stringent than normal functional testing activities, because of the high incidence of system and test failures during this test phase. Associated losses in test data and the frequent nonreproducibility of failures are due to unexpected system responses or error conditions. The software test plan should deal with the essential differences between normal functional testing and those test requirements defined specifically for the demonstration of software error conditions. The plan should specify modification to, or additional categories of, test tools that support this testing. The plan should also provide unique data collection techniques to be applied and differences in data collection and analysis techniques to be used when testing error recovery functionality.

5. It should be specified how system interfaces and external data sources are to be supported in both nominal and heavily loaded system environment: The requirements for interface testing defined in the software test plan should specify the sources of interface data to be used to develop the tests, the availability of data sources to be used as test stimuli, and equipment for data simulations to overcome hardware nonavailability limitations and scheduling incompatibilities.

Build functional testing is the first point at which the software configuration is evaluated functionally. Discrepancies noted during this testing are normally more significant than bugs found during previous design-testing activities. The problems are normally based in software design inconsistencies, improperly specified requirements, or inadequately specified or misinterpreted software interface designations. The reporting of problems by the independent test team during this phase of testing must be rigorous, clear, and effectively controlled if testing success is to be expected. The correction of these problems and installation of modifications to software test configurations must follow positive and complete control procedures over test configurations.

In parallel with build functional testing, the software integration team will take various individual components of qualified software builds and integrate these across subsystem boundaries into an operational software configuration.

This phase of the testing will exercise and qualify internal interfaces between software subsystems as well as the performance and integrity of integrated components when executing in an operation configuration. The purpose of these tests is to qualify the software configuration against design requirements specified in the system/subsystem and software product specifications as well as against the interface requirements defined in subsystem interface specifications. The testing done during this phase will, for the first time, integrate software developed by different organizations using varying standards, project conventions, and development and project control methodologies.

Software configuration management control during this phase of the testing must be implemented in a software system basis transcending individual development organizations and subsystem responsibilities. System integration responsibility and software error correction must be assigned on a system basis not reflecting subsystem or project area biases. In order to avoid organizational conflicts associated with testing, the roles and responsibilities for each organizational element must be defined during test planning stages before the organizations and development staffs become parochial and protective of their particular development areas. This early resolution of testing requirements and system responsibility will greatly help maximize productivity during system integration. The environment specified for system integration should meet the following requirements:

1. The testing structure must provide for the efficient analysis of software discrepancies during testing. It must allow the identification of responsibility for correction and assignment of work, qualification or corrections from different development organizations prior to use of a test configuration, and positive quality monitoring techniques to ensure the adequacy of the update package before placing it under control. The software test plan should specify what project requirements will be levied in satisfaction of these test requirements and how each is to be implemented in the project organization.

2. As with the build integration testing, both nominal and anomalous system conditions specified in the system/subsystem and software product specifications should be testing during this phase. The testing criteria specified in the software test plan for reproducibility, control, and execution integrity should be carried forward and extended to encompass the requirements for software system integration. The modifications to the build integration structure and additional control procedures required to tailor the build environment to system integration requirements should be described in the software test plan. This environment and the associated

tools, techniques, and methodologies associated with the system integration problem will be detailed in the software test plan.

3. As previously described, the key system integration problem to be resolved is to orchestrate and control the technical interactions and software quality of several supporting organizational elements. The software test plan must define, in some detail, (1) how these organizations will interact, (2) how the data products developed by each are to be monitored and controlled, (3) how resources are to be allocated and controlled between project organizations, and (4) how priorities are to be established, modified and enforced and conflicts resolved during the system test period. This plan, again, describes how the system test organization is to be structured.

4. The software test plan should tailor software instrumentation, simulation, and test control requirements specified for build integration and build functional testing to the more demanding rigor imposed by system integration. This tailoring should consider the differences in the two test environments rather than differences associated with the software configurations and technical attributes of the test. The software test plan will detail specifically the requirements imposed on the suite of tools associated with the documented differences.

5. As with the build tests, the system integration requirements should specify requirements for qualifying and controlling interfaces between software system components. The test planning should identify major interfaces to be qualified, general guidelines for generation of test requirements, and how tools, system, and simulation resources are to be applied in exercising the interfaces and monitoring the integrity and performance.

6. System performance and accuracies should be evaluated during this test phase using data collected during testing. The general ground rules for collection of these statistics during this phase of the testing should be provided in the preliminary plan. Analytical techniques and methods to interpret the data identified and procedures for evaluating the results against performance budgets also should be described. The test plan identifies the requirements for performance monitoring and specifies how these requirements are to be satisfied in the actual system integration test environment.

This software system integration testing marks the end of design testing conducted to verify software integrity. When the final build has been qualified through system integration testing, the software configuration is assumed to be complete and, at least from a design standpoint, ready for the final test stage of software system functional testing.

Software system functional testing is the means by which software is finally qualified for operational support. The test cases represent a full demonstration of all functional requirements specified in the software requirements specification. The testing structure during this stage should, to the minimum possible degree, represent the actual operational configuration of the software and system environment. All instrumentation should be removed, and where possible, simulated interfaces should be replaced by actual system hardware and support equipment. This level of testing deals totally with system externals, treating the software configuration as a "black box."

The requirements to be addressed are a blending of the requirements specified for build functional testing and system integration testing. The test environment, test techniques, test execution, test control, and error correction procedures applied to the conduct of software system functional testing are a direct transfer from the integration testing. The general requirements for these tests are extensions of those specified for build functional testing. These extensions are concerned with the differences between qualifying software at the component level versus qualification in a fully integrated environment.

Software test architecture that drives test case execution of the outermost extremity of the software configuration must be specified. During this level of test, the test cases are structured to monitor performance in actual operational configurations, with no attempt to monitor internal execution characteristics or system performance.

Functional problems identified during this phase of testing are always significant, for they invariably involve support from multiple organizations and entail modification to baselined system requirements, functional and interface allocations, and changes to design specifications and software support. As with software system integration testing, absolute control and configuration management must be maintained if the testing is to have any possibility for success. The project control must span organizational boundaries.

Any problems corrected during this testing phase require full regression testing through all the test phases to requalify the new configuration for functional test support. This regression testing is essential to ensure that the final configuration of software qualified through successful test execution was fully validated and will work through all operational environments and system support nodes.

The software test plan will provide general guidelines for planning, implementing, executing, and analyzing system functional tests. The plan identifies the relationships between software system testing and the baselined documentation and requirements. The plan describes how the tests are to be developed, and it defines the specific requirements of each functional test case. These data are to be developed for each software subsystem from which procedures, test scripts, and data are developed. The subsystem's specific test tools, techniques, and methodologies will be defined in the software plan.

Test Documentation

The initial release of the software test plan is the basis for all subsequent test planning, development, execution, definition, and integration and project testing interfaces. The plan must be sufficiently detailed to allow the software manager the option of initiating critical or long-lead-time testing tasks, which if not completed in a timely fashion, could limit or constrain project programs. The software test plan is the basic testing document establishing testing rules, criteria, organizations, and specific test care specifications for the functional test case.

Careful planning early in the project is an essential prerequisite to success. This planning has the following components:

1. **Purpose and Scope.** A clear understanding of the purpose, expectations, scope, and limitations of the software testing program should be made, documented, and agreed to by all parties associated with the test effort. This early agreement is essential, for it provides the basic criteria on which organizational relationships and project responsibilities may be made.

2. **Test Organization.** The organizational roles and project responsibilities should be identified, documented, and approved by each project organizational element. The responsibilities should be consistent with the identified test purpose and scope and reflect the organizational commitments, goals, and objectives of the test program.

3. **Test and Verification Approach.** The test and verification requirements and general approach toward satisfaction of the requirements should be defined, documented, and agreed to through the software test plan. It should address each phase of the testing, individually identify how each segment will be supported through the test program, and specify requirements by phase that must be supported to complete the test effort. In the preliminary test planning phase, the emphasis is on what is to be accomplished by the test and verification approach at each phase of the testing rather than on how the requirements are to be satisfied.

4. **Test Support Requirements.** The planning should identify the test environment required to support each phase of testing, the flow of data between the test phases, and manual and automated tools, techniques, and procedural support requirements that will support the satisfaction of test goals and objectives during each test phase.

5. **Test Management and Control.** The requirements for management of the test program at all levels, as well as definition of requirements for the control and flow of data as the testing proceeds through each test phase, should be identified, documented, and reviewed with each test organization.

6. **Test Specifications.** The specifications of requirements for each test case to be developed for functionally qualifying the software at the build functional and system functional tests should be identified.

7. **Schedule and Expected Test Program Performance.** General task categories for support of each phase of testing should be identified. The schedule requirements and task phasing should be described, documented, and agreed to by the responsible test organizations. The software test plan should be available and coordinated through the various management levels and project organizational areas before any software tasks are initiated on the project.

A single test plan should be developed for each subsystem. Once approved by the customer, the test plan becomes the basis for implementing test activities in the programming process. The test plan may be modified as approved changes are made to the program requirements specification or to reflect changes in the planning process. The latter would generally involve the customer and the programming organization.

Software Test Procedures

The test procedure is the basis for preparing, conducting, and evaluating the functional test cases. The procedure describes the goals of the test, the responsible organizations, the method of reporting the test results, and the sign-off procedures. The procedures contain the following types of information:

1. Identification of the software to be tested.
2. Test objective.
3. Test equipment to be used in test.
4. Step-by-step operational instructions for executing tests on a test-case basis.
5. Criteria for passing or failing the test.
6. Specified tolerances of operation.
7. Initial settings for all controls, equipment, software data values, and changeable test parameters to be set prior to the test.

The test procedures are prepared concurrently with the design and coding phases and should be available in draft form for customer review prior to conducting the specific test. Each test procedure is reviewed by the customer to determine if the test is redundant and if the procedures are adequate for fulfilling the goals of the test. Any changes must be approved by the customer prior to conducting the test.

A test procedure should be developed for each functional test to be executed at the build and system test levels. The procedures define the specific system inputs that will initiate specific test sequences and the expected system responses.

Test Scenarios

The most time-consuming and difficult test-planning activity is the development of test scenarios. They match the requirements of the test case as defined in the test procedures with the software execution characteristics. The procedures define on a step-by-step basis how to initiate a test step and the expected system outputs, but they do not define the intermediate operational, data, and control steps that simulate the operation of the software and establish the environment required to execute the test.

The scenario is a definition of the time-phased sequence of software execution and the simulated or live data messages required to establish the conditions and environments of the test. As illustrated in Figure 6.4, the scenario documents the sequence of data and control required to support execution of the test. The test scenarios are developed for each test case and are sequenced to the start of each test step.

The scenario, when completed, will define exactly what messages must be provided, when, and from where to satisfy the objectives and requirements of the test case. From the scenario, the data required for the test case are developed.

Development of the test procedures requires an understanding of how the system is supposed to operate as documented in the user's manual, requirements specifications, and interface and functional specifications. Test procedures are oriented toward how the system may be controlled operationally through the normal operational modes or system control positions during a test. Scenarios, on the other hand, require an understanding of how the software executes as documented in the functional and design specifications. The development of scenarios is based on the specific execution characteristics of the software.

For the sake of objectivity, both the functional procedures and test scenarios should be developed by an independent organization not reporting to or controlled by the development organizations. Using this technique, the manager gets an independent view of the operational integrity of the software. The specified tests and test detail will not be based on assumed design or implementation characteristics, on operational assumptions, or on implementation characteristics or development trade-offs. They will be based solely on the specified requirements of the system as interpreted by the test team.

Test Data Development

The development of test data is straightforward if scenarios are properly defined. For each of the messages defined in the scenarios, a specific data

Test case	Test stimulus	Test reference (time from test step start)	Data message identification	Control message identification	Data base setting	Test case output	Notes

Figure 6.4. Test scenario form.

record must be developed, time phased to the test requirements and defining a means for recording and identifying the data that result from execution of the test. The scenario also defines and controls messages and protocols required to keep system interfaces and test equipment operational during the test.

All test data, scenarios, procedures, and supporting data should be placed under software configuration control after review and approval at the appropriate review or walkthrough.

Unit Test Plan

The unit development folder (UDF), begun during software systems design breaks the implementation of the design into small, measurable, and meaningful steps and provides a structural mechanism for organizing software development products requirements, design code, test plans, and test data as they become available. It is an important part of the development environment, in which unit-level schedules and responsibilities and their step-by-step accomplishment are made visible to management and the customer.

A unit test plan is developed and maintained as part of the UDF. It establishes the order of testing for each unit, specifies the required inputs and outputs with their sources, and checks the completeness of the unit. The test exercises all branch points and validates the internal computations and functional capabilities of each unit. These include not only nominal data but also singular and extreme values in order to stress the unit. Without such stress testing, anomalies can escape discovery until the program is declared operational. Reprogramming at that point is unacceptably costly and time-consuming, and the operational difficulties caused by such anomalies are often unacceptable as well. The unit test plan is approved at the design walkthrough and baselined through the PSL. The results of the testing are evaluated and approved at the unit test walkthrough.

Build Test Plan

Prior to planning or scheduling the specific builds to be used to integrate and qualify the software, a build test plan should be developed, reviewed, and approved by the software project through a build test review.

The operational requirements for build testing are defined in the software test plan. In the test plan, the rules, guidelines, and techniques for build testing are specified. The build test plan defines specifically how these requirements are to be translated into a test structure compatible with software development schedules, the technical requirements and characteristics of each build, and the functional capabilities to be integrated into each build.

The build test plan should be developed by the independent test team.

The plan identifies specifically the software units that will be integrated into each build, the functional capabilities to be qualified by the qualification segment of the build testing, and the environment, tools, techniques, and acceptance criteria. The specific test cases for each build should be identified in the plan, and the software, data, test configuration, and schedule for the build should be specified. The plan should be produced before any meaningful build test development is started.

The build test planning should be reviewed and approved by the software test manager prior to authorizing the build requirements. The build review should evaluate the schedule, management, control, and technical plans for the build. The review should be chaired by the software test manager, attended by the technical leaders responsible for each unit to be included in the build, members of the test team responsible for integration and qualification of the build, and representatives from PSL.

The build review is informal and conducted in a walkthrough format. The test team leader proceeds through the plan in a step-by-step fashion. The walkthrough will evaluate the plan, and any discrepancies noted should be corrected prior to approval of the build for development. At completion of the build test review, the build test plan will be approved and baselined under configuration management.

The execution of module, unit, and build integration testing is informal, conducted by the development organizations, and consistent and compliant with the documented requirements of the appropriate test plan. The results are documented as software problem reports processed through software configuration management.

The functional testing must be conducted in strict compliance with the approved test procedures. The tests must be performed in the presence of a customer-approved representative. All software problem reports must be handled by the approved configuration control mechanism.

Successful completion of the test and sign-off of the test approval report constitutes acceptance of the software product or versions and authorization for the next phase of testing. If there are any open problem reports, acceptance is contingent on successful requalification tests.

Test Approval Report

An approved report forms a part of each acceptance, requalification, and qualification test procedure. It may become necessary to perform on-the-spot changes to the test procedure. These changes require test witnesses and customer and software authorization with appropriate documentation. When changes become excessive, these test witnesses have the option of scrubbing the test until a reasonable test procedure is provided. These changes must be incorporated into a revision copy of the test procedure by the proper documentation organization and made available to all test participants as soon as possible after the test.

SUMMARY

The process of software testing is the most difficult of all the development tasks. As described, the planning, execution, and conduct of the test requires a close integration of management, technical, and control disciplines. The software manager must plan this process from the very outset of the project, continually refining, reevaluating, and restructuring the plans as the development proceeds. The degree to which the manager solves these problems is the measure of productivity.

7 Interfacing to the Program Environment

If software is being developed as part of a larger system, it is important to understand the special constraints the program environment imposes on the software organization.

As illustrated in Figure 7.1, software development in a program environment is only one of many components of the program that must be coordinated and integrated by the program manager and his staff.

From the view of the program manager, the design, development, integration, and qualification of a system with several hardware and software components is an overwhelmingly complex task requiring superhuman commitment and effort to manage, coordinate, monitor, and control.

The main problem facing the program manager is the complexity of interactions between program elements. The numbers of activities that must be managed within all of the program areas and the conflicting goals, objectives, and motivations of each of the program areas are just a few of the problems to be faced by the manager. The lack of program visibility into the day-to-day activities of functional organizations and an inability to assess and anticipate technical progress and problems are largely responsible for the lack of an immediate solution. Unless the manager is extremely perceptive and effective, he must rely on the functional organizations to report progress, often resulting in a distorted perception by the manager of the health and status of the program.

PROGRAM MANAGEMENT RESPONSIBILITIES

When assigned responsibility for a program by a company, the program manager becomes accountable for the technical, administrative, contractual, and overall performance to the basic requirements and constraints of

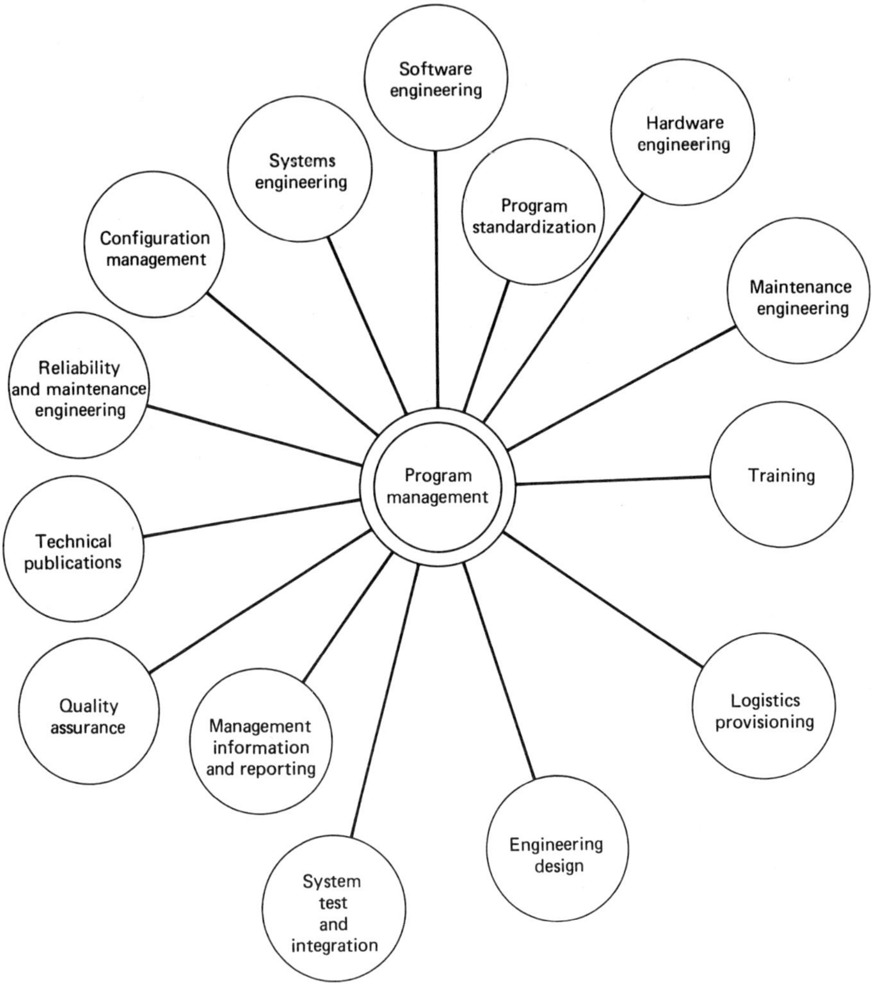

Figure 7.1. Program relationships.

the program. With this accountability comes broad responsibility and freedom of action. Normally the manager may organize and plan the program as he sees fit, allocate and control resources in any manner provided it is within budget and schedule constraints, technically develop the system following any methodology or methodologies desired, and manage and control the program as tightly or loosely as required to meet program milestones with quality data products.

The program manager is accountable for performance in each of the many functional and support areas of the program and is responsible for the technical adequacy, quality, and control of all data developed internally or delivered to the customer.

In order to provide a program structure that will minimize the risks associated with managing the program, the manager organizes the project to maximize visibility while providing tight fiscal and technical control. The nature of the organization implemented depends on the characteristics of the program and may change as the program evolves. The basic program office is staffed with a control organization that includes the personnel required to administer a contract. These administrators are individuals from contracts, marketing, financial control, material, and the functional departments assigned technical responsibility for implementation of the program.

The program organization consists of two basic elements: a program "office," which directs, controls, and monitors the technical and production tasks and conducts essential administrative activities; and a program "team," which performs the technical and production tasks. The organizational philosophy and the program office organization is usually predetermined by the proposal and contract. The program team is organized from within the function organization to meet the needs of the development.

Just as the program manager is responsible for the management activities that will ensure acceptable program performance, the functional organizations are responsible for the technologies and their application to develop a quality system within the technical constraints of the program. The relationship between the program and the functional organization can best be described as a partnership. If one fails to meet its obligation, both fail.

SOFTWARE COST NEGOTIATION

The functional organization components are predetermined by the technical proposal, and the magnitude of their participation is predetermined by the cost proposal. The functional organization was normally party to the technical and cost proposals, participating with the program in its resource planning. The specific personnel who developed the initial cost and schedule projections are often reassigned by the start of the program, and, as a result, a key planning legacy is lost.

With the initiation of the program, the program manager must coordinate with the affected functional organization components any changes in task or budget that resulted from negotiations. If the functional organization had no part in the development of the proposal or if the projected cost commitments have changed, the program manager must then negotiate with the affected functional organization for the support needed.

This negotiation is often difficult because of differing objectives of the two groups. The program wants to get the maximum value for the resources it allocates, whereas the functional organizations want to minimize risk by committing the minimum resources against the maximum schedules, retaining or increasing the budget commitments.

The software manager should recognize the importance of this negotiation to the long-term health of the software project, as well as the problem being faced by the program manager. The program manager has fixed resources to be allocated to each of the functional and support organizations within the program. Each of these organizations is convinced that their budgets are inadequate and that adequate performance with the specified or revised budgets is impossible.

The program manager must assess risks associated with the restructuring of budgets, allocating additional funds to those organizations that, in his opinion, will impact program performance most and taking resources from the functional organizations that will have minimal impact on program integrity or performance. The software manager, however, must also understand that the budgets negotiated during this phase of the project are the criteria by which the success or failure of the software project will be measured. The manager too often feels that because the initial estimate was done before the contract was awarded and because the technical basis of the estimate was, at best, questionable, the negotiation with the program should be based on a new set of parameters. The software manager then proceeds to negotiate a new set of budgets with the program on less than adequate technical or project information. These budgets have no more validity than the previous estimates.

Before pressing forward with cost, schedule, and technical planning, the software manager must be aware that parameters are often poorly defined early in the program, causing project plans to be invalid or inconsistent with program objectives. The software manager must recognize the essential relationship between basic program parameters: the effectiveness of the project structure, the validity of the software project structure, the financial and resource projections, and the development schedules.

The software manager must translate basic program parameters into a project structure tailored to program characteristics while anticipating development requirements and the flow of work as the implementation proceeds. The results of tailoring are described in a series of planning documents and tools that provide the hub of the project and give it form and substance.

From this planning base, the software manager then must implement each of the documented project parameters, organizational and administrative controls and practices, budget, schedules, project monitoring practices and procedures, and the technical, development, and project control methodologies to be used in developing the software. Then the manager is in a position to negotiate valid cost projections, program organization and initial support.

PROGRAM RESOURCE MANAGEMENT

The software implementation is initiated to make a profit for the company or enhance company effectiveness or productivity, not to advance the state of the art or to solve a difficult technical problem. Software managers often lose sight of this pragmatic reality, limiting the success potential of the software project and greatly increasing the development risk. The software manager often forgets the program profit commitment and critical financial and schedule constraints in the pursuit of technical excellence.

Although these program requirements are not readily perceived by the software development staff, they bear a significant relationship to the success of the project and the ability of the software manager to meet project goals, commitments, and objectives. The software manager must come to grips with his own reluctance to deal with what appears to be unnecessary administrative trivia and recognize the importance of program control, performance monitoring, and resource management. The prudent software manager recognizes that control over resources during the development period and early recognition of schedule, cost, and performance problems will have a positive effect on the ability of the manager to redirect resources, reallocate work, or modify project parameters to solve the problem.

Within the program environment the software to be produced is only one of many program elements, any one of which has the potential for delaying or impacting program success. In a typical program, these elements include system engineering, hardware development, integration and test, installation, logistics support, training, and others, which must be effectively managed at the program level. The program manager must orchestrate the activities of each functional area of the program, manage the interactions, interfaces, and overlaps between them, and control the flow of work and allocation of resources between organizational elements of the program. The degree to which the manager is successful in these roles has a direct relation to how successful the program is and, as a result, how successful the software development is in the context of the system objectives.

For the program manager, the overriding concern is to be sure that the activities of these diffuse project elements work together in an effective and controlled manner and that the program is developed within preallocated schedule and budget constraints. To the program, a smooth running project is more important than technical excellence.

As illustrated in Figure 7.2, the program manager has available to him at contract award a series of costing inputs, a proposal describing how the project development was described to the customer, and an organizational structure, in many cases, bearing only a passing relationship to the requirements of the program. Using this information as a base, the program man-

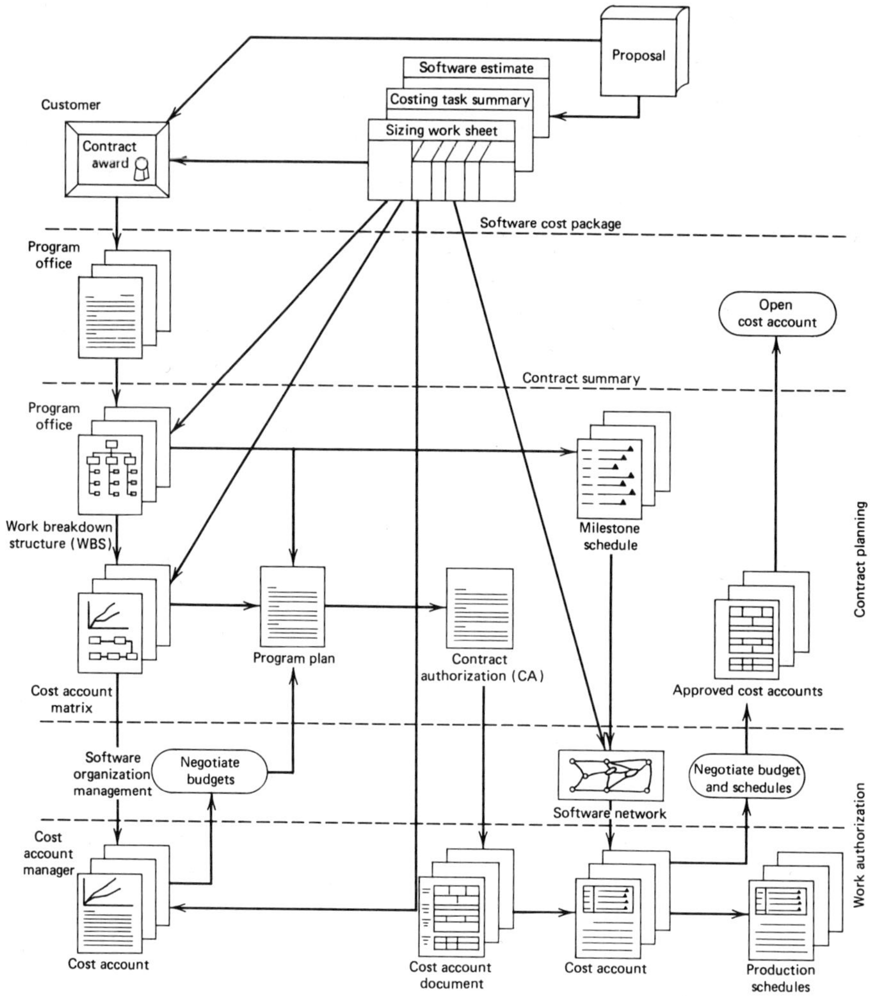

Figure 7.2. Typical program control flow.

ager often develops a contract summary. This summary is primarily a financial document describing costing and profit projections, schedule commitments, and contract risks. This summary is the first communication that a program manager has with management that commits the program to performance constraints. And from this summary, the manager develops the program work breakdown structure (WBS) and program schedules and tasks the software staff to develop cost and schedule projections.

The work breakdown structure is the prime means by which the pro-

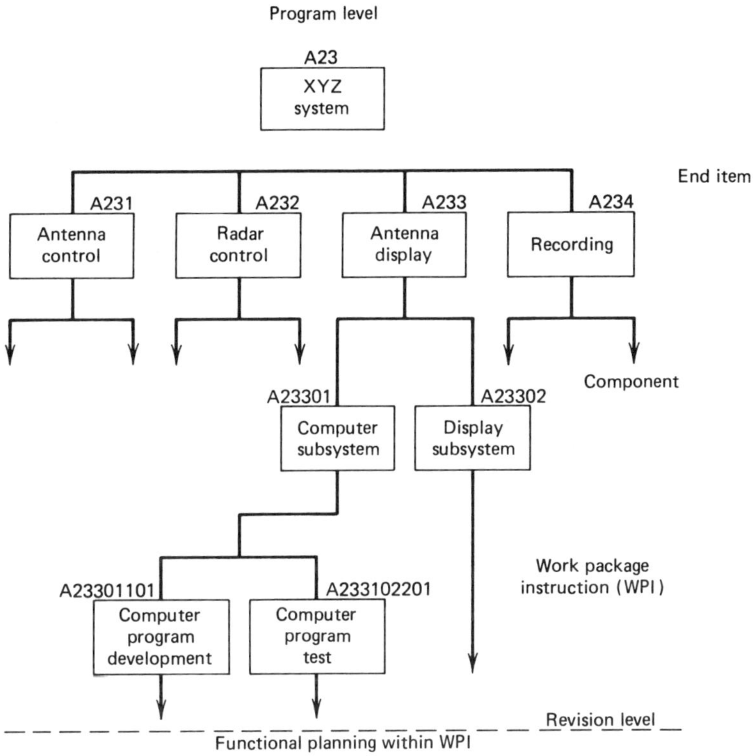

Figure 7.3. Sample work breakdown structure.

gram office organizes and allocates work throughout the organization. As illustrated in Figure 7.3, the WBS is a product-oriented division of hardware, software, services, and other work tasks that organize, define, and graphically display the work to be accomplished in order to develop a specified product.

A WBS is a graphic illustration of the determination of program objectives and the progressive passing down of these objectives from higher to lower levels of management. Its configuration, content, and detail will vary and will depend on:

1. The status of the program.
2. The size and complexity of the program.
3. The organizational structure of participating organizations.
4. The arrangement of responsibility for the work to be performed according to the judgment of management.

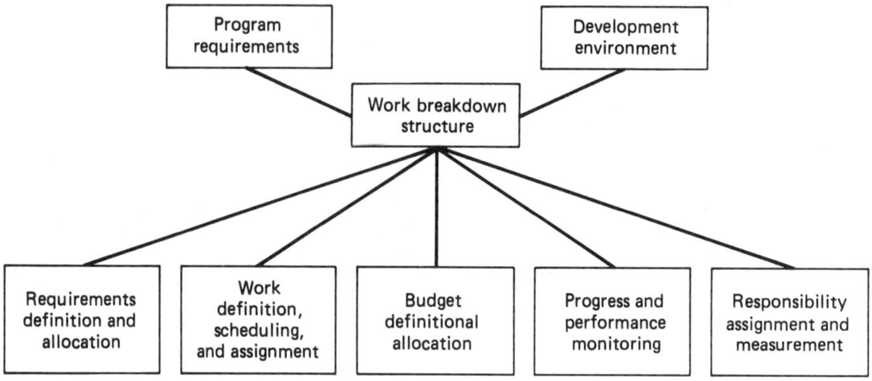

Figure 7.4. The program planning process.

As illustrated in Figure 7.4, the WBS is the root of the program planning process.

The initial and possibly the most important step in the program management process is the determination and definition of program objectives for the proposal, contract, and customer documentation. Objectives must be based first on the total program and then extended downward to the more detailed levels. The objectives used as the basis for the WBS should ensure that the project objectives are fully supported by lower-level objectives, that the project structure is fully integrated, that each part of the project is consistent with and related to the project as a whole, and that useful summaries of project information can be made.

At the top level, the WBS is an identification of the program. From the program the end items that are major segments of the program or system to be developed are defined. These then are allocated into all required components of the product, the specific work package instructions, and finally all revisions to work packages and functional planning. Use of the WBS by a program manager forces the proper allocation of work through the project, from the top down.

The WBS subdivides the work into manageable units through the various levels of hierarchy described and illustrated in Table 7.1.

These basic program objectives form the core of the program planning process and, when properly expressed and translated into a WBS structure, provide focus and organization to the program activities. This is accomplished by:

1. Providing a framework to identify project requirements separately from the performing organizations, cost estimating and accounting systems, funding sources, and so on.
2. Providing insight into project element interrelationships and overlaps.

Table 7.1. WBS hierarchy

WBS Hierarchy	WBS Product or Process
Level 1	System
Level 2	Prime deliverable
Level 3	Software, hardware, and so on
Level 4, software branch	Software Subsystem, Software Subsystem, . . .
Level 5, software branch, subsystem 1	Subsystem requirements, subsystem design, subsystem implementation, subsystem test and integration, and subsystem documentation
Level 6, software branch, subsystem design	Subsystem preliminary design, subsystem preliminary design review, subsystem detailed design, subsystem critical design review

3. Identifying specific work packages for time, cost, labor, and material estimating; pricing; budgeting; work assignment and authorization; accounting; and reporting.
4. Allocating system reliability requirements to subsystems and components.
5. Establishing a specification tree for defining documentation hierarchies and production requirements.

As illustrated in Figure 7.5, the WBS is the basis for planning and defining a structure for the program and allocating work to and tasking individual organizational elements in a coordinated and focused manner.

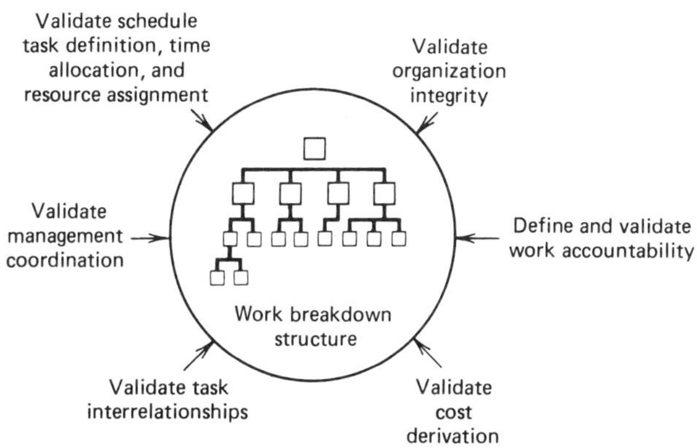

Figure 7.5. Work breakdown structure and program relationship.

WBS Development

The work breakdown structure, developed by the program office, decomposes work throughout the project into successively lower levels, portraying this decomposition process graphically through a hierarchial diagram. The WBS is developed by starting at the top level, which is the program definition, and through an interactive procedure, decomposing work downward until all levels of the WBS have been satisfied. The number of WBS levels required is a function of:

1. Contract size.
2. Cost accounts and work packages dollar size.
3. Personnel requirements for the program and for individual task areas.
4. Task duration and schedule.
5. Number of milestones in each task.
6. Implementation cost.
7. Management confidence.

The lowest level of the WBS is the point at which the program manager delegates direct management control to the functional or development organizations.

The basic data used to define the tasks are the program proposal, contract, schedule cost, and technical data derived as part of WBS planning activities. From these data, a WBS dictionary is developed. This dictionary identifies each task and support tasks that are required specific WBS elements. Each element included as part of the dictionary should be clear and meaningful, including all tasks required to develop or support a WBS element (an element is a definition of a specific system component from which specific tasks may be described and assigned to the functional organization). All program WBS components that have significant dollar or personnel commitments should be described as individual WBS elements.

As illustrated in Figure 7.6, the dictionary describes those tasks required to support each element of the WBS. For the software elements of the WBS, the task descriptions are extracted from the software costing task summaries used as the basis for software cost and schedule derivation. For use in the definition of the WBS dictionary, these task descriptions must be specific, directed toward specific organizational components, and described so that they are unambiguous and usable in the definition of software work authorization documentation. The task statements included as part of the dictionary are developed by the manager responsible for each program development area based on data describing program commitments, constraints, and planning parameters. The dictionary is used with

Level

3 4 5 6

2.3 Antenna display — Dictionary definition

This WBS component provides all system components required to display and retrieve operator data describing the status of all antenna systems. The component is in two parts: the display subsystem described in WBS element 2.3.2 and the computer subsystem described under 2.3.1. Under this component all tasks required to design, implement, integrate, demonstrate, and document antenna display components are included. — Summary paragraph

2.3.1 Computer subsystem — Dictionary definition

This WBS element provides the computer support required to support the antenna display requirements. Integration and demonstration requirements are included under WBS element 2.9.6.1. The tasks described in appendix B are integral parts of this WBS element. In addition, the system engineering and design tasks required to define the POLYP interface are included in WBS element 2.6.3.2. If the software integration task requires simulation, these are included as part of this WBS element. — Summary paragraph

Figure 7.6. Sample WBS dictionary and summary paragraphs.

the WBS to amplify the program development and organizational requirements indicated in the WBS.

The WBS may be used to define a cost account matrix. The matrix provides a check of the WBS, for tasks defined in the wrong level of detail for assignability and manageability to a given organization are obvious. Each matrix entry correlates on a one-for-one basis with activities on the Program Evaluation and Review Technique (PERT) network. The matrix is formed by placing the WBS on the vertical axis and the complete organization structure on the horizontal axis (or vice versa). The organization structure should display all program organization components and segments, other organizational segments supporting the program, and major subcontractors. When completed, the matrix provides a single framework for further planning and control by identifying and assigning individual tasks to be used as the basis for development of the program cost structure. In the planning process, each organization assigned task responsibility provides schedule, labor, cost, and technical information, including the contributions required from support organizations. The application of task and organization code numbers based on the WBS allows unique identification of each matrix entry. The framework of the matrix and associated technical information, schedules, and cost projections provide the basis for work authorization and measurement criteria for control purposes.

Cost Accounts

Cost accounts represent the effort to be performed by a major organization in support of a single WBS element. They are used to accumulate summarized project performance data and represent the lowest level in the work breakdown structure at which actual costs are required to be recorded. The planned value of work performed is summarized in such accounts for comparison with actual costs directly into the work breakdown structure without requiring splitting costs between two WBS elements.

Cost accounts should be a natural contact point for cost schedule-planning control and represent a point at which the organization structure and the contract work breakdown structure are linked. Planning an appropriate account code structure based on the WBS dictionary, facilities, the summarization of data through the cost accounts and WBS is essential. For large projects, work authorization to various functions such as engineering, software, or purchasing may be at a higher level than the cost account. They may consist of other authorized cost accounts and planning packages.

Work Packages

From the cost accounts, the next logical subdivision for planning and control is a breakdown of each end item subdivision into specific work packages. As illustrated, the work package describes the specific requirements, by task, to be used in controlling development.

Work packages are detailed descriptions of work to be accomplished or required to complete the contract. A work package:

1. Describes manageable units of work.
2. Is unique and clearly distinguished from all other work packages.
3. Is scheduled with a start and completion date, has defined, documented scope, and is controlled by budgets (expressed in labor hours, dollars, or other measurable units).
4. Assigns responsibility for performing the work to a single organizational element with any suballocation of work done by the assigned organization.
5. Is integrated with detailed engineering, manufacturing, and other schedules as applicable.

A work package is job-specific, resulting in a specific set of products or services, such as a report, a piece of hardware, or a service, that is in the responsibility of one operating unit with an organization. Work packages plan what must be accomplished, by whom, and under whose responsibility and estimate the resources required.

Work packages should be small in order to facilitate easy management while affording flexibility in the development effort, minimizing the need either to reorganize or to rewrite them as the job proceeds and basic project criteria change.

Work packages defined in great detail often are without the flexibility to anticipate problems that, when encountered, require reallocation or redefinition of the work package and a major replanning or rescheduling or the total program. The relationship of the technical accomplishment to schedule and budget is a key problem facing program management. Large work packages covering a major portion of the work make monitoring of technical progress in relation to budget and schedule projections difficult to determine.

Failure to accomplish assigned tasks on schedule does not become evident until a major milestone is missed, which, in turn, necessitates the readjustment of, and reorganization of, schedule and resource allocations throughout the balance of the program. The size of work packages depends on the degree of management visibility desired and the extent of control to be exercised on the project.

Work Breakdown Structure Organization Matrixes

The management tool for relating work defined by the WBS to organizational units, subcontractors, and individuals is the WBS-organizational matrix. As work and organizational responsibilities become clearly defined on the program, a responsibility assignment matrix is developed. The personnel responsible for accomplishing specific WBS tasks within defined budgets and schedules are identified, and the organizational relationships and structure are defined.

The matrix includes major subcontractor assignments and relates statement-of-work paragraphs to WBS elements and organizational elements to cost accumulation codes.

The matrix must not only list contractor and subcontractor personnel but also identify customer counterparts responsible for tasks within specified WBS elements.

PROGRAM PLANNING

In planning the program, generic program objectives are converted to detailed planning requirements and assigned to organization managers for implementation. The managers develop these plans down through the cost account level.

Cost accounts may be summarized to represent the effort to be performed by a major program organization in support of a single WBS element. These are selected at varying levels of the WBS based on size and criticality of the task and provide a definition of work requirements, total dollar value by cost element, a listing of major milestones, and technical performance parameters if applicable. The program manager ensures that these account summaries are approved by the performing organization before their release for use in the program. The work authorization ensures and documents that the program manager and supporting organizations have a thorough understanding of the requirements and that the assigned work has been accepted and understood by the performing group.

After the program manager and performing organizations agree to the budgets for the cost accounts within each area, these are issued as an integral part of the work authorization process and become the basis for cost performance measurement. Resources that have been negotiated but have not been authorized to the performing organizations are maintained as planning packages within each organization. The planning process constantly reassesses the work definition against progress and the remaining schedule and resource constraints—which is the process of phased program planning. Replanning exercises continually result in new or revised work authorizations that modify, delete, or add to tasks, schedules, technical requirements, or resource commitments.

Task Descriptions

The task description is an expansion of the contract statement of work and is developed concurrently with the WBS dictionary and organizational structure. The initial descriptions are assembled from task statements prepared by the performing organization under applicable WBS element codes. The summary paragraph for each WBS element is prepared by program management based on the WBS dictionary.

Schedule Planning

Schedule planning is the preparation of project schedules and includes the development of project master schedules and subordinate schedules, based on the WBS. Schedule planning ensures that all elements of the program are delivered on time and that the activities of program organizations are integrated and focused to specific milestones. Work authorizations clearly identify work statements, schedule requirements, and cost elements to the lowest level of planning and control.

Schedules summarize numerous organizational activities into time-phased milestone plans and provide the project manager an overview of integrated plans for hardware, software, and documentation development and delivery.

Types of Schedules

There are several different levels of schedules by which a program manager controls, orchestrates, and monitors performance. The top level, the master program schedule, identifies the overall goals and objectives for the program. These top level schedules are the schedules that control development of the second-level WBS tasks.

The master program schedule has two major objectives:

1. To provide a technical planning base.
2. To smooth the allocation and application of resources.

The master project schedule is based on the customer's planning schedules, and its development starts in the concept phase. The schedule is progressively refined through the customer's request for proposal (RFP), proposal, and negotiation phases and is finalized after contract award.

Through the master schedule, specific project requirements, objectives, and ground rules are established, project deliverables and interim products are defined, and a project logic network is established. This network establishes the task sequences and interdependencies required to satisfy the contract as well as describe baseline documents, requirements, design, development, facilities, associate contractor, subcontractor, material requirements, fabrication, assembly and checkout, software, and all supporting activities. A scheduling team composed of functional personnel estimates the time required for each task and relates the time estimates to the requirements and the events on the logic network to develop a preliminary master project schedule and subordinate schedules for WBS elements.

From the master schedule, the performing organizations develop more detailed subordinate element schedules, which are integrated into the higher level schedule plans. Informal working-level schedules are developed down to the individual working level and are continuously reviewed and analyzed to ensure that they are compatible with program activities and experience. Schedules are integrated with the WBS and the cost-schedule-planning control system.

Scheduling is an interactive and dynamic process that, like all planning, starts with a broad plan that is then successively decomposed to lower levels an then adjusted as more information and facts become available and as changes, modifications, and revisions occur as a result of both in-house and customer action.

There are two basic scheduling techniques most often used to interface and control software development and provide current data to the program concerning project progress:

1. Gantt charts.
2. PERT.

Gantt Charts

A Gantt chart is basically a bar chart showing planned and actual performance for those resources that the manager wishes to control. Many factors that create variances—money, overproduction, underproduction, and so on—can be coded and depicted on the chart. The Gantt chart was designed for and is most successfully applied to highly repetitive production, although it also can be used for development operations. The key deficiency of a Gantt chart is that it does not express development logic and constraints well.

Performance Evaluation and Review Techniques (PERT)

A PERT network is a graphic illustration of events connected in logical sequence showing all activities necessary to complete a project or program. The network shows interrelationships and dependencies between events in the project as well as identifies constraints and limitations.

Networks are built from events, activities, and activity time estimates that represent definable points in time by which an activity starts or completes. Once the program and supporting objectives have been diagrammed, the network may be expanded to include all the work packages necessary for the accomplishment of each objective. The network should be comprehensive, including all significant interdependencies and interactions required to perform program work packages.

A PERT activity is a procedure occurring between a beginning (predecessor) and an ending event (successor). Activities may be the work related to such various functions as design, procurement, production, or even the time required for the administrative decision-making process and represents the elapsed project time required to accomplish a program event. This time is indicated on the network. These time estimates are a projection of how long it will take to accomplish an activity or event. PERT can be successfully used as a tool for the programming of a single component or subsystem as well as of a complete system.

Scheduling Detail

After the scope of application has been determined, the optimal level of detail to be included on the networks must be defined. Level of detail refers to the relative number of project events and activities shown on the network and primarily depends on the degree of project information predetermined to be necessary for adequate programming and control purposes.

As a general rule, the level of detail should be determined beginning with top management information needs and working systematically down through the various organizational levels. This top-down approach reduces the risk of accidental omission of important events that must be monitored. The level of detail may be increased as tighter control is determined to be needed for more extensive planning and control of critical path activities. The relationship of PERT, WBS, and work packages is direct and is maintained through the charge numbers and program summary number defined through the WBS dictionary.

Scheduling

Scheduling is the bridge between the planning and implementation phase of the program. At this stage, the PERT schedule is time phased by adding elapsed time projections for the accomplishment of each activity as indicated on the network. These time estimates are projections based on knowledge and are furnished by the person or persons with understanding or experience relating to the predicted accomplishment of the activity. With these established time estimates, latest allowable dates for the accomplishment of every event and activity can be developed. Then, expected completion dates for the same events and activities are developed. Slack time is the difference between the latest allowable dates and the expected dates; it shows how much time the program is expected to be behind or ahead at each point in a network. These calculated dates can then be correlated with other formal program schedule dates to determine if current planning is realistic in terms of the time allotted for the accomplishment of project events.

The PERT network shows the sequence of activity events expected to impact planned schedule performance. The sequence of activities projected to take the longest time is the critical path. There may be more than one critical path shown for a project, and all must be identified and controlled. Managers must focus their efforts on the critical paths identified through the PERT source, for any slip in these areas delays the program schedule and impacts delivery. Slack reports identify surplus resources that possibly could be reallocated to critical path activities. The scheduling function must provide clear data identifying the competition for available resources both within the project and between projects within the organization, and it is this slack time that permits work packages to be scheduled so as to make maximum use of the available resources.

Network timing, and the resultant identification of the critical path and program slack, also serves to validate work packages and total program elapsed-time estimates against calendar due dates and indicates where revisions must be made in the program plan for timely completion.

Milestones

Milestones are identified on the network to measure progress against the program plan. Milestones represent the completion of a total work package or some component part thereof that is significant to some other phase of the program. There should be periodic progress reporting against milestone performance by the personnel responsible for the various work packages, and the manager should use these reports to make the necessary management decisions and actions. In order to provide this data it is desirable on the PERT schedule to have at least one milestone per work package per reporting period, even if it is not significant in any other way.

TECHNICAL PROGRAM MANAGEMENT

Besides fiscal and schedule responsibility, the program manager is responsible for the accomplishment of all tasks necessary to meet program requirements and achieve the objectives of the program. This responsibility not only is for the technical tasks required by the contract but also, as many program managers painfully find out, encompasses the administrative and support requirements essential for program implementation.

The management, planning integration, monitoring, and effective coordination of these technical and support tasks in the program environment is the primary responsibility of the program manager and is the single most critical factor leading to program success.

The basic engineering tasks and systems engineering design, development, and test are the basis of the technical structure of the project. The program manager, through the program office, will normally define a central point in the project technically responsible for the system design and development. This system engineering position within the project is responsible for:

1. **System Analysis.** This system analysis step includes any one of a number of tasks in order to obtain an understanding of the actual system requirements. In addition, the analysis functions may include studies which define the system's technical and operational characteristics. Technical analyses may also be conducted to address alternative means for satisfying the system needs.

2. **System Concept Formulation.** This step will develop the system concept for the hardware or software system. It is typically a top-down design approach defining basic functions into successively lower levels of abstraction. As each step, a particular function and/or element in the system is described in greater detail. This approach enables the design decision to be indentified so that the basis for selecting alternatives is apparent. Through this process, alternative concepts are identified and a decision analysis methodology is employed in which the selection criteria and alternatives are explicitly identified.

3. **System Requirements Definition.** The system definition step identifies the equipment and software that must be bought, developed, and obtained to implement the system architecture and satisfy the user's operational and performance requirements. System performance specifications

are delineated in terms of the architecture. Key subsystem characteristics are identified, and hardware specifications and software requirements are developed.

4. System Hardware and Software Design. Once the system characteristics have been defined, design efforts for the hardware and software to be developed can be undertaken. Hardware design engineers address the tasks of hardware design, fabrication, and unit testing. Software engineers develop the overall software design and estimate software size, requirements, and cost. Documentation, data, quality assurance, and logistics support efforts are also analyzed and estimated during this period. The major system engineering tasks are to interface with the hardware and software design engineers, specify design interfaces, perform program configuration management, identify areas appropriate for further analysis, and perform trade-off analyses.

5. System Integration, Test, and Acceptance. As the subsystems and software modules are completed, the systems engineer must integrate them into a complete system. The systems engineering staff prepares detailed integration plans and designs partial and overall system tests. The systems engineer or an independent testing staff then conducts and coordinates the actual integration of the system. When system testing is complete, the systems engineer recommends to the technical manager that formal acceptance tests be scheduled with the customer. The systems engineer, supported by design task managers, design engineers, and quality assurance personnel, is responsible for conducting and coordinating the acceptance tests.

6. System Development Support. Once a system has been accepted by the customer and installed, normal contractual requirements have been satisfied. Because of the operational nature of many systems, however, the customer and contracts usually have a continuing interest in system support. This support may require an understanding of the overall system concept and how the system was designed to meet the requirements. If the operational environment changes significantly from that for which the system was designed, the systems engineer will be able to recommend engineering changes to the customer. The basic objective of system engineering in a program organization is to specify the hardware, computer programs, facilities, personnel, training, and procedural data needed to meet the requirements of the system as defined in the contract and succeeding specifications. The fundamental purpose of the system engineering organization is to provide a single analysis, definition, trade-off, and synthesis of requirements and design solution within the program for the whole system. Design trade-offs must be made in terms of performance, cost, and time, with these factors being weighted, as appropriate, for the item being developed.

The system engineering process is used to evaluate logically each of the many technical and economic variables involved in total system design. System engineering is fundamentally concerned with deriving a system design to achieve stated requirements. Those responsible for system engineering must recognize that engineering specialists play a predominant and highly complementary role in satisfying total system design requirements, and this relationship must be understood by the performing functional organizations.

The program or project manager must integrate the business and technical management systems into an integrated performing program structure. The better trained the project manager and his team are in system engineering and system analysis, the better the system will be. Through systems engineering, the program manager plans and controls the engineering effort. Specifically included are:

1. Identification of the elements of the contract work breakdown structure.
2. Development of the design and related test requirements to subordinate product elements of the contract work breakdown structure.
3. Identification of critical areas and definition of the requirements to be met in the technical program tasks of design, development, test, and evaluation.
4. Monitoring the conduct of the technical program and providing design and associated technical program alternatives for the resolution of problems affecting the software project. These may be identified through cost, schedule, or technical performance measurement.

In a typical project the output of the systems engineering effort is a technical management structure under which the software project along with the other engineering segments of the project will be developed.

As illustrated in Figure 7.7, the technical structure is documented in the systems engineering management plan (SEMP), which has three major

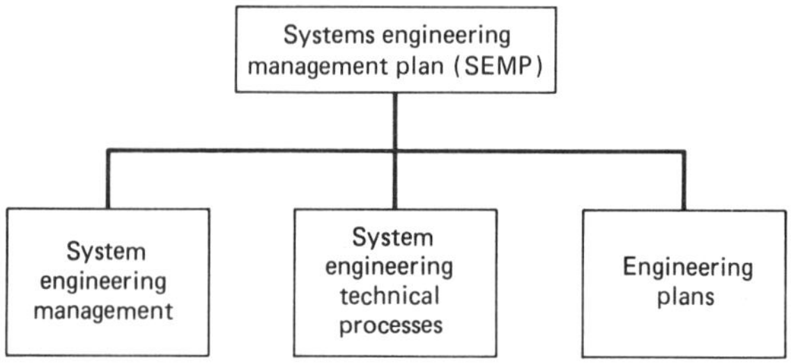

Figure 7.7. Systems engineering management planning.

parts: systems engineering management; a description of the process of systems engineering in the program environment; and the engineering specialty plans describing how the specific development resources programs are to be developed.

Systems Engineering Management

The systems engineering management component of the SEMP documents how the system engineering is to be managed, organized within the program, and controlled. It also identifies the requirements and program constraints that limit the technical and engineering prerogatives of the staff and the specific system requirements to be satisfied by the program implementation. Normally the systems engineering management structure, as it affects the software project, has the following parts:

1. *User requirements and constraints* interpret, clarify and validate basic requirements inputs to the system engineering process.
2. *Responsibility and authority* identifies organization(s) and key personnel for managing the system engineering effort and defines responsibilities, lines of communication, and fuctions of personnel associated with system engineering policy.
3. *Resource allocation* allocates resources of budget, schedule, and expertise necessary to achieve effective system engineering and systems engineering management.
4. *Procedures* are established for formal progress for implementing system engineering and systems engineering management through all phases of the program.
5. *Documentation and format* establishes procedures for the generation and management of all system engineering documentation and specifies formats of documentation.
6. *Design reviews* establish schedules and procedures for the comprehensive examination and review of all aspects of the design.
7. *Interdisciplinary integration* establishes procedures to ensure design compatibility from the standpoint of all pertinent engineering and scientific disciplines.
8. *The Engineering decision* process establishes formal internal procedures utilizing system effectiveness models, trade-off studies, risk analysis, and so on.
9. *Program assurance* identifies technical measures that can reduce the risks and unknowns associated with critical areas of the program and selects measures to be implemented.
10. *Change control* establishes formal internal procedures necessary to control all technical data that have an impact on configuration, per-

formance requirements, design constraints, or functional-physical interfaces.

11. *Work breakdown structure* identifies the structure of products and services comprising the entire work effort.
12. *Training* identifies and establishes methods and procedures that will be used to train selected personnel in the system engineering process and systems engineering management methodology and rationale.
13. *Technical performance measurement* identifies items that have a significant impact on system effectiveness; identifies and quantifies parameters that have a significant impact on system effectiveness; establishes analytical or test criteria for the estimation or measurement of technical performance; and evaluates and forecasts all significant technical performance characteristics of the system through the design activity.
14. *Tailoring* deletes, alters, or adds requirements in order to adapt this manual to the peculiarities of specific systems or subsystems.
15. *Milestones and schedules* identify and establish cost, time, and performance accomplishments that are essential at a specified point in time to meet the objectives of the system engineering effort.

When implemented, these systems engineering management specifications define the program environment under which the software project must be developed. The software manager must be cognizant of all systems engineering management requirements defined in the SEMP. The software manager must ensure that any organization supporting system engineering effectively interface with the system engineering, and technical, and control organizations.

The software management must establish a software project structure that has a point-to-point relationship to the systems engineering staff. Data and control must flow smoothly through both organizations, and there must be a clear relationship among the various components of both organizations.

Systems Engineering Process

Besides defining how the engineering organizations interface with and take direction from the systems engineering organizations, planning the systems engineering activities should also define the technical theologies to be followed in defining, designing, and implementing the system. These methodologies are the technical basis for the project, and all technical development by any engineering organization supporting the program must be consistent with them. The systems engineering process should identify technically how the program will define and conduct the following steps:

1. *Function analysis* defines functions and function performance requirements that must be met in order to accomplish the operations, maintenance, test, production, and development requirements of the system.
2. *Synthesis of conceptual systems* depicts a complete response to functional needs, provides alternatives for trade studies, depicts compatibility between system elements and interfacing systems, and provides traceability between system elements and their functional origin in the operational stage.
3. *Evaluation and decision* selects the best combination of system elements to meet the mission objectives and support requirements as a balance of cost, performance, and schedule.
4. *Description of system elements* produces engineering data that identify, describe and specify the configuration, arrangement, and usage of all system elements and their effectiveness in achieving functional performance. It controls the design, development, test, production, and deployment of equipment and facilities, the selection and training of personnel, and the development of procedural data and computer programs. It provides a basis for change control.

This definition of systems engineering functions at the program level technically constrains the software manager. Whatever methodologies are employed to define software requirements, to decompose functional requirements, to synthesize design, or to conduct control coding, test, integration, and documentation of the software must be consistent with the requirements of the program systems engineering methodologies.

The data and technical requirements must be consistent, and the technical products must be compatible. Above all, the systems and software engineering efforts must operate smoothly in the program, resulting in a quality system responsive to the needs of the user and the contract.

Specialty Plans

The system engineering organization develops a series of plans that detail how certain critical functions of the system development are to be integrated into the product. These plans address specific areas of the project of concern to the program systems engineering customer or technical staff. Those plans that affect software frequently include the following questions:

1. Reliability. How do all segments of the program plan to meet the reliability commitments and obligations of the program?
2. Maintainability. How are system maintenance requirements integrated into the system, and how are they measured and evaluated?

3. Human engineering and human factors. How are human engineering requirements defined and integrated into the system, and how are they evaluated?
4. Personnel requirements. How are the types, requirements, and sources of personnel used throughout the program?
5. Standardization. How are engineering and project standards used throughout the program?
6. System cost-effectiveness. How are measures applied to the program. How do engineering efforts ensure and measure the cost-effectiveness of the end product?
7. Quality assurance. How are quality assurance techniques used to monitor system quality and adherence to program standards?

THE SOFTWARE PROJECT PERSPECTIVE

The role of the software manager in a program environment is difficult not only because of the technical difficulty inherent in the development of a system but also because of the conflicting goals, objectives, and perspectives of the different organizations.

The program is most concerned with meeting the fiscal and schedule commitments of the program with minimal technical risk and exposure. *The software organization, on the other hand, is concerned with meeting the technical requirements of the software project, not with understanding how the initial cost and schedules were derived and how the technical requirements of the program can be satisfied adequately within these artificial constraints.* It seems that there is never enough money, time, or resources adequately to satisfy the program and at the same time implement the software in accordance with the requirements of the contract.

The software manager, when looking up through the various organizational levels of the program, is often appalled at what appears to be total lack of organization and progress. The program seems to be insensitive to the real problems of the program, all of which are focused on the problems being experienced by the software project. *The software manager must recognize that although the control and limitations that the program exerts on the software project are restrictive and burdensome, they are absolutely essential if the program objectives are to succeed.* In the program environment what is important is not what the individual projects that support it do, but rather that they interface and support the program objectives.

The critical understanding that a manager must have if he is to succeed is that the manager is in the middle of two responsibilities. Above are the program responsibilities and requirements that cannot be controlled but must be supported. Below are responsibilities he has to orchestrate, coordinate, and manage the many facets of the software project.

8 Estimating Software Costs and Schedules

The value of initial software cost and schedule estimations is totally determined by the amount of planning on which they are based and the level of commitment that is thereafter applied to meeting them.

The software development industry, unlike older, more established industries, has not yet developed standard tools and techniques for estimating the cost and length of time a particular job will take. One of the main reasons for this situation is that there is no standard method employed for producing software, and thus there is no basis on which to develop standardized estimation techniques.

Software projects typically overrun schedules and budgets—often by as much as 100%—sometimes resulting in financial disaster for the software contractor, and sometimes resulting in large losses by customers who have spent all the money they can afford to allocate to a system and have a half-finished, and thus worthless, product to show for it.

Research in the area of software cost and schedule estimation has generally taken a backseat, in terms of time and dollars spent, to the development of new methodologies for the technical tasks of design, coding, and test. As a result, the research that has been done in this area yields data concerning the cost and number of labor hours that have been expended to develop particular kinds of software systems under the specific project structures employed. Efforts are being made to isolate and quantify the factors that influence the cost of a software project, but much more analysis needs to be done in order to produce a generalized method by which a particular software development job can be estimated with reasonable accuracy.

This chapter will explore the problems involved in estimating the software project, present guidelines for producing the best possible estimate within the framework of the current research, and try to place this process in perspective, given the dearth of tools with which the software industry has to work.

SOFTWARE COST, SCHEDULE, AND LABOR ESTIMATION: AN IMPOSSIBLE PROBLEM?

How much time, how many people, and how much money will be required to develop a particular software system?

In industries where the work is mechanical, the time and costs involved can be estimated fairly easily and accurately. Workers themselves know how long it will take them to complete a job based on previous measures of the same task.

Software development, however, is not a purely mechanical job. The work in producing lines of code is mainly a cerebral activity, like solving a puzzle. The heart of the entire activity is the devising of a series of logic paths that will cause certain physical processes to take place according to the general desires of the user. Almost nothing is a "given," for the inputs and outputs to computer programs can be designed in a multitude of ways to produce the same end result. The best input for one part of a software system may make the coding of another unnecessarily complicated. Fixing all the parameters associated with the logic paths is the main thrust of the software problem, and each designer goes through the process of trying and changing combinations of these parameters until a set that works is found. At any point in time, software developers fix as many parameters as they can and proceed to work through them until they find they must change one of them. It is imperative that the process is documented, especially if more than one person is involved. Someone must control this seemingly uncontrollable process and provide schedule and cost estimates for it, if for no other reason than that a customer is paying for the product and deserves to know how long it will take and how much it will cost.

THE BASIC INDUSTRY METHOD

In many other industries, the price of a product can be determined on the basis of a quantifiable measure that has a clear impact on the work to be performed. The price of a house is directly related to the number of square feet constructed. The cost of moving across the United States is calculated on the basis of a price per pound of material to be moved and a rate per mile traveled. For these kinds of work, the customer knows or can specify a ceiling for the quantities involved, for the quantities are clearly related to what he wants to purchase.

Determining the Base Measurement for Software

The software industry has searched for a way to quantify the work to be done. The industry has most often used the lines of software code produced as a basis for estimating software costs, because this is really the only quantifiable measure of the size of the end product. This measurement is not a good one and is similar to predicting how long it will take to produce a painting by estimating the number of brushstrokes that will have been applied when the painting is complete.

First of all, there is no obvious relationship between the lines of code produced and what the user really wants to buy. Although it means something to a customer buying a house to say that he wants approximately 2000 square feet, it means nothing to a customer buying a software system to say that he wants 100,000 lines of code.

Secondly, most programmers do not know how to estimate lines of code and wonder what significance it has, anyway. Most programmers have not done the same work over and over again and do not have a reference point from which to measure. Programmers do not want to code the same application over and over again, and before they get to the point at which they could tell how many lines of code a particular application will take, they have requested to change areas or have even moved to another company, looking for a different software challenge.

Finally, there are many ways a set of specifications can be coded to achieve the same basic result, even when the input and output formats are fixed. Ask any teacher of computer science to quote the range in lines of code produced by 20 students responding to the same homework assignment. The highest number of lines of code may be five times as great as the lowest, and the difference in the amount of time spent by the students on this problem was probably minimal.

Even if lines of code could be estimated with any accuracy, this quantity would be clearly useful only when the functions to be coded are defined with regard to input, processing, and output. As defined in Chapter 2, three entire stages of the software development process are spent fixing these parameters. Specifying the job itself is a major part of the work to be done.

The customer cannot be expected to provide detailed software specifications—this is the specialist's job. The software organization cannot wait until the specifications are complete to establish schedule and budget parameters. Therefore, like it or not, software developers must estimate not only how long it will take to build the product but also how long it will take to determine exactly what the job is until a cost relationship between user requirements and the work that must be done to meet these requirements is discovered. Research efforts in the area of software estimation should be directed at defining a relationship between user requirements and the cost of the resulting product, for "plain English" user requirements are all that will ever be available at the beginning of a software project.

Determining Productivity

The next step in the classic industry estimation procedure is to produce a figure that will predict how long it will take to produce a certain number of lines of code. This is usually done by dividing total lines of code produced on a previous project by the total number of labor hours spent on the work, yielding a number of lines of code produced per person per period of time, such as a month.

The figures, called "productivity" figures, produced from these studies vary so much from project to project that it is difficult to determine how the information can be used. The literature sees variation in lines of code produced per man-month from 60 to 1000 or more lines of object code. It is seldom specified whether technical effort alone was considered, or whether all who worked on the project were included. If so, how many were technical, how many support? How were the people organized? Who documented the final system? What documentation was produced, when, and how were changes to documentation and source code handled?

In trying to account for the great differences in productivity figures across projects, the industry has begun to identify the factors that influence productivity. Walston and Felix (1977) listed 13 environmental factors, such as complexity of the customer interface, overall personnel experience and qualifications, and turnover rates, and studied the effect of each on productivity. Scott and Simmons (1973) list 35 such factors. There are probably hundreds more that could be identified and studied. Is new hardware being developed at the same time? How hard is it to find programming talent in your area of the country? How difficult is it to procure equipment or personnel through your company?

As illustrated in figure 8.1, the harsh reality is that software development is extremely sensitive to the total environment in which it is developed. Each software development project has a character all its own, which is shaped daily by the complex interactions among the people involved, the organization of the project itself, the organization of the company, the customer relationship, and the technical demands of the system. Attempting to determine what the productivity of a given set of software developers will be within a predicted environment is tantamount to attempting to predict a particular human being's behavior by factoring in all his personality traits, previous experiences, and the current environmental conditions in which he lives.

As if this is not enough to show that a sound basis for generalized software estimation procedures is a long way from becoming a reality, the studies have also shown that the productivity rate varies significantly from

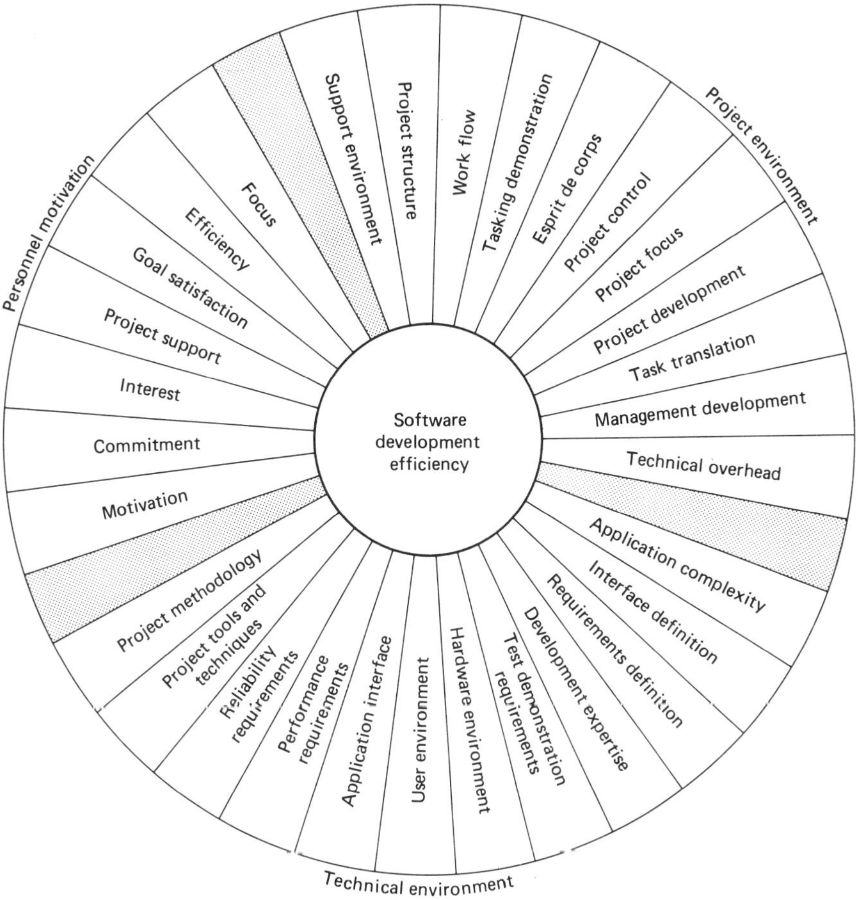

Figure 8.1. Software productivity factors.

software component to software component, depending on the complexity of the particular code required. The factors that have most often been reported to affect the productivity for a particular software function are the type of language used (high level versus assembly or machine level), the type of function to be coded (for example, algorithm versus data base management versus time critical process), the subjective determination of whether the function is "easy," "average," or "hard" to implement, and the familiarity of the staff with the hardware, operating system, language, and the application itself.

Brooks (1975) mentions several studies that show up to a five-to-one productivity increase (based on the number of words produced) with the use of high-level versus machine-level code. Wolverton (1972), Donelson (1976), and the RCA parametric software costing model PRICE-S use clas-

Wolverton (1972)	Donelson (1976)		PRICE-S cost model
Control routine: controls execution flow and is not time critical	Data definition books: file record and transaction layouts that are stored in a library and copied into programs as required	Edit modules: programs that ensure the logical integrity of data entered into the system and that provide error listings or alerts (one module per transaction type or family of transactions is assumed.)	Operating systems: task management; memory management; heavy hardware interface; many interactions; high reliability; and strict timing requirements
Input/output routine: transfers data into or out of the computer	One-time utilities: programs to create files, generate test data, simulate processing, and test called subroutines	Update utilities: programs that update the data base	Interactive operations: real-time man-machine interfaces; human engineering considerations and error protection very important
Prealgorithm or postalgorithm processor: manipulates data for subsequent processing or output	Conversion utilities: programs to convert or reformat data files and transactions from existing systems to the new system format	Processing modules: programs that do extensive calculations, analysis, and manipulation of data, resulting in possible additional file maintenance	Real-time command and control: machine-to-machine communications under tight timing constraints; queuing not practicable; heavy hardware interface; strict protocol requirements
Algorithm: performs logical or mathematical operations	General purpose utilities: modules to perform repeated functions that are used by different control modules (data conversions, table lookups, calculations, etc.)	Major data base extracts: programs that select data from the data base for subsequent (or simultaneous) analysis and reporting	On-line communications: machine-to-machine communications with queuing
Data management routine: manages data transfer within the computer	Data base interface utility: a	Minor data base extracts: same as above, but less complex	
Time-critical processor: a highly optimized machine-dependent code			

"bridge" between application programs and most data base management systems that relates functional entry points (open, close, read, write, explode, implode, etc.) for application modules to technique-oriented entry points and commands supplied by data base management packages (MRAN, CDIR, ADD-M, DELVD, GET UNIQUE, etc.)	Major reports: programs that report the results of major extracts and processing and that are complex in nature (multiple levels of control breaks and totals, suphisticated row and column formatting, and possibly further access to the data base)	allowed; timing restrictions not as restrictive as with real-time command and control
	Minor reports: same as above, but simple in structure	Data storage and retrieval: operation of data storage devices; data base management; secondary storage handling; data blocking and deblocking; hashing techniques; hardware oriented
		String manipulation: routine applications with no overriding constraints; not oriented toward mathematics; typified by language compilers; sorting; formatting; buffer manipulation; and so on
		Mathematical operations: routine mathematical applications with no overriding constraints

Figure 8.2 Comparative software categorizations.

sifications into type of software required to derive module-specific costs. These classifications are shown in Figure 8.2. Wolverton (1972) and Griffin (1980), each apply a subjective complexity rating ranging from easy to difficult to each piece of software. The PRICE-S model accounts for several complexity factors, such as staff experience and the familiarity of the application itself. Is the technology required "old hat," or does it involve state-of-the-art or breakthrough technology?

The problem with using any of these data on a particular project is that, again, they do not portray the "whole story" with regard to the context in which the reported factors were quantified. What base productivity rate was used? Was the lines-of-code estimate based on machine-level executable instructions, or was it based on lines of source code, no matter what language was used? It is a mistake to apply a weight for each factor that has been identified, because their effects on one another undoubtedly overlap. For example, in categorizing software functions into basic types, have they automatically been rated as difficult, medium, or easy to implement? A look at the categorizations that have been made in the studies seems to support this theory. Most software managers will choose a high-level language for development if possible. Does the fact that an assembly-level language has been chosen imply that the function is "difficult"? It seems valid to assume so.

What the studies have shown is that a given company can improve its estimates by collecting and analyzing productivity figures from previous similar projects. This is because the complex environmental factors, both known and unknown, that are contributed by virtue of the basic project organization, type of software development, and company environment have remained relatively constant from project to project and have thus been automatically factored in.

A software manager should thus be able to improve sharply his estimates by analyzing his own past projects. Given the time, the manager could set up the procedures by which labor hours are recorded so that they correspond to the project structure used, then at project end, he could determine what percentage of the project was spent on each stage and on each type of activity. He could categorize software components according to basic type for his sphere of business and analyze the differing productivity rates that occurred during design and implementation. This information could then be used to estimate the next project with more accuracy. Unfortunately, software managers are not usually given the time between projects to analyze historical data.

Software development companies would be wise to invest time and money analyzing past projects in an attempt better to estimate future jobs. Many have done so, and have enjoyed success within the company. The industry can be helped from these studies in direct proportion to the detail with which the project structure of the past projects is described.

Determining Labor Allocation

Once the lines of code and productivity estimates are made, what is the next step? If the project is estimated to take 10 man-years, can we assign 10 people to the project and complete it in 1 year? Of course not. As Brooks (1975) has pointed out, software tasks are not equally partitionable, because time must be added for the required management of the interactions among people.

This principle is not unique to the production of software. If a tailor shop has two identical jackets to sew, it can assign a jacket to each of two people and have a chance of producing two jackets in half the time it would take one person. What if the two jackets were assigned to four or more people to produce? The individual tasks needed to complete a jacket must be understood, as does the order in which these tasks must be completed. The seemingly simple problem of producing two jackets now involves a great deal of planning, coordination, supervision, and knowledge of what the exact process of making a jacket entails on the part of someone who is responsible for the project. The time involved in this coordination must be added to the total project time. If constant attention is not placed on this aspect of the project, the jackets will never be finished. Depending on the partitioning, we may not even produce one jacket by the deadline, but instead on the delivery date will find pieces of jackets lying about all over the shop. There is a point at which the number of people assigned to the two jackets will increase rather than decrease the amount of time it would take to complete the project had it been left to two people (at a clean partitioning) in the first place. Can this point be determined mathematically in the case of the jackets? Perhaps. We are certainly a long way from determining such a figure for the software industry.

Thus, software developers must learn to find the "clean breaks" when partitioning software into separate work packages, and must assign development tasks so that the impact of human interfaces among individuals and across functional groups is minimized.

In order to allocate labor to the entire project, the manager needs to know how much of the total project time is expended on each task. Industry studies have supplied what is known as the "40–20–40" rule, which allocates 40% of the total effort to design, 20% to coding, and 40% to test. This rule, although valid for the division of percentages across project stages, does not assist us in determining how much labor is required for support areas such as configuration management, independent test, project management, secretarial, and clerical. Are the total labor hours calculated for the project to be spent only on the technical effort, or are they inclusive of support areas and products also?

The percentages we need must be derived according to the specific project structure and life cycle employed. As there is no standardized software development life cycle or project structure, these figures are not available from industry studies, and estimate them as well.

Basic Industry Method: Conclusions

Given the problems described above, how can a software manager produce a reasonably sound estimate? Several conclusions can be drawn, as a result either of examining industry studies or of using common sense:

1. The length of time it takes to produce a software system varies grossly with the number of lines of code generated.
2. Overall productivity becomes lower as projects become larger and more and more people are involved.
3. Productivity varies from technical task to technical task within a project, depending on the complexity and characteristics of the particular task.
4. A software project cannot be scheduled and costed on the basis of any universal method, but each project must be analyzed with regard to the particular tasks involved in the context of the environmental constraints that are placed on it, applying commonsense principles and a knowledge of the software development process.
5. Software estimates are probably going to have to be based on lines of code and productivity figures from past projects, because these are the only figures available at this point.
6. A great deal of the factors that the authors feel affect productivity are under the direct control of the software manager, such as devoting attention to planning, intelligently assigning tasks, controlling the communication of information across interfaces, applying corrective action to problems as they arise, and anticipating when resources will be needed and acquiring them by that time.

The next section of this chapter provides the reader with some approaches to estimating software size and projecting development costs based on project experience. The approaches presented are meant to serve as guidelines for software managers and other personnel who must deal with the issues and problems associated with estimation.

SOFTWARE ESTIMATION: GUIDELINES

The software manager has the primary responsibility for directing the estimation and scheduling process, defining the methodology to be followed in projecting software costs and schedules, and ensuring that the proper resources and data are available, when needed, to support these activities. In this role, the manager orchestrates the diverse activities of several disciplines, often under unrealistic schedule constraints.

Unfortunately, the software manager is faced with an unresolvable dilemma. On one hand, the software estimates must be accurate, because they are used to define budget and schedule requirements, but on the other hand, there is invariably insufficient time or information available to define a detailed software structure, convert this structure into size projections, and translate the size estimates into valid projections of the required development resources.

The prudent software manager recognizes the importance of these initial estimates as well as the inherent inaccuracy in the procedure. The estimates derived during this phase of the project, despite absolute commitments from marketing, higher management, and customer representatives that they will be considered preliminary and not binding, are, in fact, used throughout the project to measure management effectiveness and project success.

The manager must ensure that the procedures used to project software size and complexity are based on engineering rather than on marketing or nontechnical considerations. This means not that the software manager should not consider external requirements and realities, but rather that the estimate should be based on engineering principles and follow a rigorous discipline during development.

As illustrated in Figure 8.3, the discipline of software estimation we shall describe consists of several distinct steps:

1. *Software requirements definition* is the generation of software requirements that serve as a basis for the sizing and estimation process.
2. *Software architecture definition* is the derivation of a preliminary partitioning of system functions into a set of software components that will support the requirements as defined.
3. *Software sizing* is the estimation of the number of lines of code to be produced.
4. *Productivity estimation* is of the amount of work that can be done within a unit of labor hours.
5. *Complexity weighting* is adjustment to the software estimate to reflect the complexity of the individual components.
6. *Schedule development and labor allocation* is an identification of the number and types of labor required to implement the software through preliminary scheduling.
7. *Other direct costs estimation* is the determination of all nonlabor costs to be incurred during development.

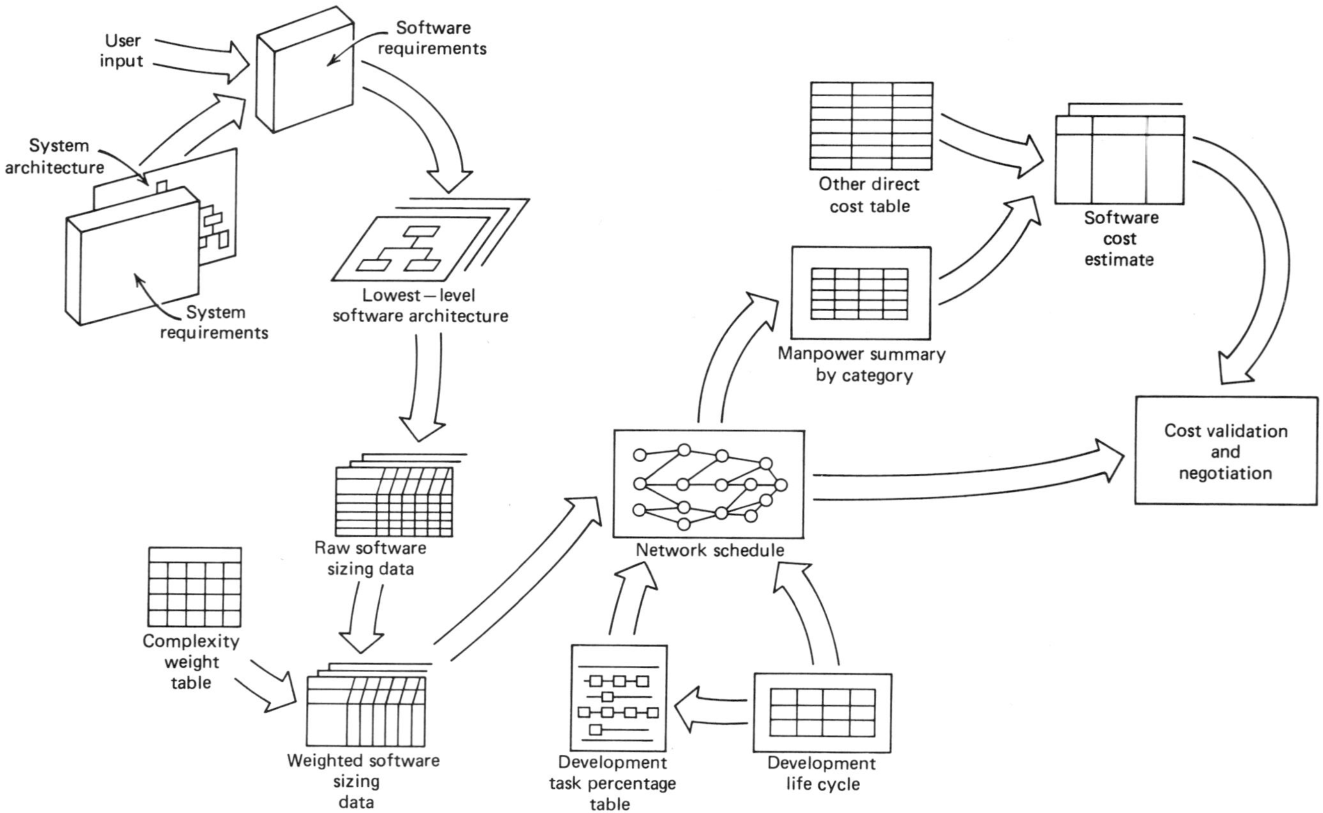

Figure 8.3. The software estimation process.

Software Requirements Definition: Defining the Job

Before specifying a projection of development costs, the software manager should have a clear, negotiated set of requirements on which the software architecture may be designed.

The customer should provide the contractor with a requirements document describing, from his point of view, what is desired from the system. If the customer is unwilling or unable to produce such a document, the contractor must work with the customer to produce the initial requirements. Under no circumstances should a schedule or cost estimate be made without having this document.

The software manager and a small technical staff may now begin the task of refining and expanding the basic requirements. If at all possible, the technical people who are involved at this stage of the project should be the future key people in project design and implementation. Much time is lost in software development projects when personnel are constantly reassigned from one project to another.

This task should be allotted enough time to do a thorough job without waiting for the "perfect" set of specifications. This document, as all others that will be produced, is subject to change and is needed as a basis from which to start planning the project. During its production, this task should be the only one with which the manager and staff are concerned.

The effort must be well coordinated and supervised in order to be a success. There must be an outline of the document being produced that is followed by all who are working on it. The work must be split, then brought back together. The document should contain a section introducing the nature of the project and telling in general terms what it is that is to be produced. The document will be used to acquaint new project members with what the project is all about. This written introduction to the project is missing in so many projects, and its absence accounts for the long period of assimilation on the part of new personnel. A new employee first wants to know, What is this system I'm working on supposed to do? Often, a long period of time is spent rambling in the gory details of the system, gleaned from scattered documents and sources, and often the minds of old project members, until one day the employee suddenly realizes the purpose of the entire system. He will always feel better when this day comes and will not be entirely productive or enthusiastic until it does. No matter how large and complex a system is, its main purpose and reason for existence can be explained in one or two paragraphs of plain English.

The basic requirements for the system should then be presented, delineating any imposed methods of input or output, timing requirements, and the order in which events must occur. What computer system will be used to execute the software? Will the same computer system be used to develop the software? These decisions must be made within this time frame and incorporated into this document. The staff must determine whether other factors as yet undecided will have an important bearing on the scope of the problem and have them resolved and documented at this time.

The software manager should submit the document to the customer as the basis on which schedules and budgets will be created, and the provisions therein must be negotiated until the customer agrees to the resulting specifications. It should be made clear that changes in these requirements may have an impact on the project schedules and budgets and that any changes the contractor wishes to incorporate must be approved by the customer before they are made. If the software manager gets this far, he is well on the way to making a reasonable estimate and meeting it.

Software Architecture Definition: Breaking the Job into Manageable Pieces

The only way to develop a preliminary software estimate that has a chance of accuracy is to spend time defining the required system in as much detail as possible. This process is a microcosm of the first three stages of the project, and the end product is a proposed software architecture that identifies the software components that must be coded and the major files and external interfaces with which they will interact. Each software component may then be estimated as to lines of source instructions required as the basis for the system cost estimate and the preliminary project schedule.

Figure 8.4 illustrates the steps involved in producing the preliminary software architecture to be used for sizing purposes. First, the user interface must by thought through in some detail in order to determine how the requirements of the system will be allocated to software components. The major points at which the system interacts with the outside world should be identified, as well as the kind of information that will enter and leave the system. This method will shape the determination of the major pieces of software to be developed and the major files required.

A high-level tour through the system from the user's point of view should then be designed and documented. It may exist in pictorial or narrative form, but it should be shown to the customer and discussed with him as the estimation process proceeds and questions inevitably arise that will greatly impact the scope of the project.

From this high-level specification of the user interface, the major functions of the system and the interfaces among them can be identified. Each major function will be allocated to a software component. At this level, the software components may be called "subsystems," and each should be given a unique name by which it and its subcomponents can be identified.

At this point, each major software component can be analyzed and broken down into its required subfunctions. These functions can be summarized and grouped together so that the best allocation to software components is made. This process consists of performing a hierarchical decomposition of the software system into smaller and smaller pieces that, when coded separately and integrated together, will satisfy the require-

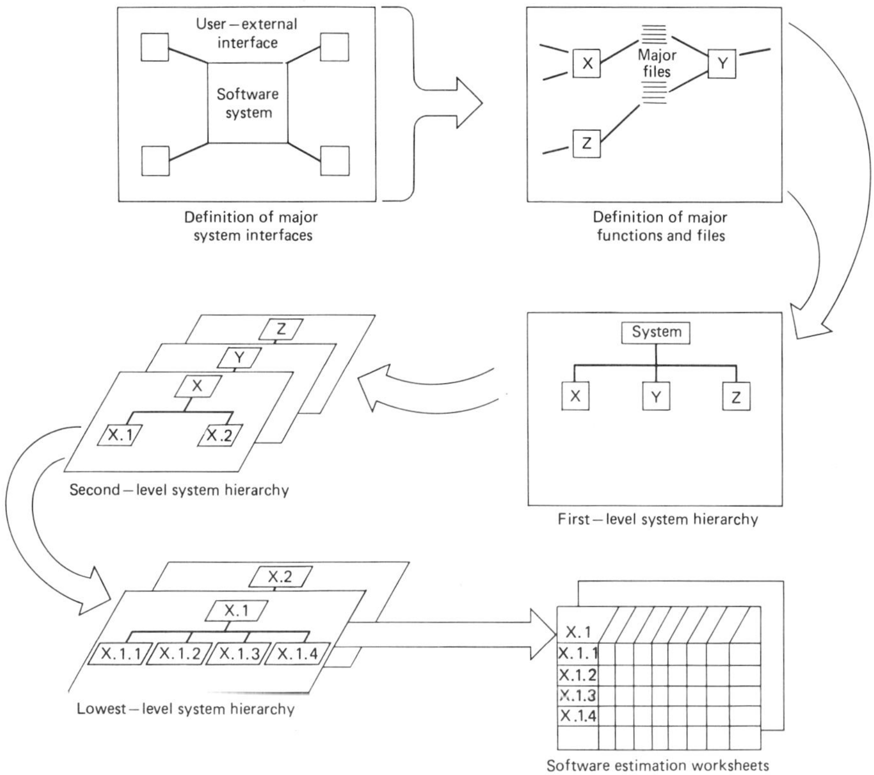

Figure 8.4. Producing the preliminary software architecture.

ments for the system. The principles behind this process have been described in detail in the literature under various terms: *Functional decomposition, top-down design, structured design,* and *stepwise refinement,* to name a few. The main idea behind the approach is to determine the major functions of the software system and allocate these functions to software components, each of which can be further broken down into a series of subfunctions.

The analysis proceeds in a stepwise fashion until the components can be separately coded, documented, and maintained. Generally, this process means that the component is compiled or assembled separately. We have called these pieces of software code "modules." Within this definition, modules that are extremely large can be designed. The aim in this approach is to partition the software in such a way that modules are as small as is reasonable for the system being developed. The literature on the decomposition process details various methods by which this goal can be achieved.

The result of this analysis is a proposed software system architecture that can be represented in a tree diagram showing the software components at each level of decomposition. It is important to stop after each level of the tree is generated and examine the decomposition to ensure that:

1. The interfaces between components are specified and are kept to a minimum.
2. The inputs, processes, and outputs to each proposed component are specified in enough detail to allow the further decomposition of that component.
3. The requirements from which the analysis began are being satisfied thus far.
4. Any like functions are identified and redesigned so as to meet the requirements of all the higher-level functions identifying them.

At any level, the decomposition of a node in the tree may be assigned to an individual designer to complete, but the preceding checks must be made jointly among designers to ensure that a system perspective is maintained at all times.

One side benefit of this approach is that the system is being partitioned with an eye to minimizing interfaces from the beginning of the project. Minimization of interfaces is the key factor in maximizing the total schedule time to be gained by partitioning the work.

The architecture resulting from this analysis is used both as a basis for estimating the size of the total job by estimating pieces of a manageable size and also as the basis for allocating labor to the design and implementation phases.

Software Sizing: Estimating the Scope of Each Task

The next step in the estimation process is to predict the number of source instructions that will be required to code each module. There are two primary techniques that may be employed in the generation of sizing estimates. The first of these techniques, engineering judgment, relies on an experienced software engineer to predict how many lines of code a particular subfunction will require. This method provides an educated analysis of system size based on the broad level of experience possessed by the estimator. The use of a seasoned professional software engineer to predict software size ensures that those technical parameters that might be ignored by the novice will be considered.

Another technique often used to size a software subfunction is to base the estimate on the known size of an existing, similar piece of software. It is important in using this technique to take into account the differences between the existing software and the software to be developed.

The method used to estimate the lines of code for most software components will be a combination of these two approaches, as the estimator usually consults listings of previously coded modules to extract instruction counts for similar subroutines and uses his or her judgment based on these previous counts.

The software estimation work sheet illustrated in Figure 8.5 provides the

Software Estimation Worksheet	Raw Size Estimate				Complexity Weight	Productivity Estimate	Total Effort	Comments, Risk Factors
Project ______ Subsystem ______ Function ______ Estimate preparer ______ Project base productivity estimate ______ Module Identification	New or Modified Code N = new, M – modified	Sizing Basis J = Engineering Judgment, P = Previous System (If Previous, Identify)	Source Language	Number of Statements	Complexity Weight	Productivity Figure Applied (Lines/Man-week)	Total Effort Required in Manweeks	General Specific
Totals			Statements			Manweeks		

Figure 8.5. Software Estimation Worksheet.

estimator with a convenient means for collecting descriptive costing information about a software element and, at the end of the estimation exercises for all such software elements, provides the manager records for assembling the total system estimate and performing initial project scheduling.

One such sheet should be prepared for each collection of related functions that can be implemented relatively independently. The first step in completing this form is to identify the functional group that comprises the modules to be estimated, along with all higher-level identification at each node of the tree. For each module, the estimator identifies whether it involves the development of new code or whether an existing piece of code can be modified to meet the requirements.

The basis for the estimate is then identified. If the estimate is based on a specific existing piece of software, that software is identified by name.

Next, the language in which the module is to be written is identified. The number of statements will be the estimate of the total number of source statements to be coded if the code is new. If an existing module is to be modified, the estimate is the number of statements to be added or changed.

The source statement is chosen because it is easier to estimate, for it is what will be coded, and it is easier to check after the module is coded. Also, it is highly likely that the increased productivity for high-level languages is somewhat accounted for by the fact that one statement of a high-level language usually translates to multiple machine-level instructions.

The next sections of the form will be filled out as the estimation process continues.

Productivity Estimation: Projecting How Much Work Can Be Done Per Period of Time

The next step in the estimation process is to define a base productivity projection. This projection is a figure representing how many lines of code can be generated for a given number of labor hours expressed in man-weeks, man-months, or man-hours.

As discussed previously, there is no scientifically sound method for projecting productivity. The best projection, however, will be derived from historical data for projects developed within the same basic environment and within the same arena of technical requirements. It should be ascertained that the total lines of code for the selected historical project is divided by all the labor hours, including management and support, that were charged to the project.

If no such historical data are available, the software manager should research the literature and use an average productivity figure reported for the same basic type of software (business applications versus real-time versus compiler development, for example) with the same size. There is no need for a first-time software manager to assume the worst for his project.

Neither should the manager be willing to assume that he will do much better than any of the findings reported by industry peers. The resulting productivity estimate is the most reasonable one a software manager can make. It will be used as the base productivity measure from which the total labor hours required to complete the job will be derived.

Complexity Weighting: Taking the Characteristics of the Individual Pieces into Account

As discussed previously, productivity rates vary from function to function, depending on the complexity of the function. These differences should not greatly influence the total cost estimate, because a base productivity rate derived from a project of the same basic type of application will, it is hoped, average out the factors affecting individual modules. When the scheduling begins, however, it will be necessary to know how long a particular module should take to design and implement, and it will not be reasonable to expect that a simple Fortran application will take as long per statement as a machine-language telecommunications interface.

The problems associated with defining a set of complexity factors based on previous studies have been discussed. The ideal way to make a scientifically sound complexity adjustment is to identify a set of characteristics affecting productivity rates from one software component to another and to derive statistics from a previous project quantifying the effect of each characteristic. Although there is little chance that a software manager will have the time or resources necessary to conduct such an analysis during the estimation process, he should define a basis for the estimation of the current project that will provide a starting point for analysis and refinement once the project is complete. No matter what methodology is chosen, it should be documented and used by every estimator assigned to the system for the sake of consistency and traceability.

In order to define a methodology for adjusting base estimates for complexity, it is necessary to analyze the processes the typical software estimator routinely uses. In reality, most complexity judgments are made according to the estimator's instinct that a particular application will require more or less effort than the "average." It is worth investing the time to identify the reasons that cause an estimator to feel that an adjustment is necessary for a particular estimate.

Select a set of software components from the job to be estimated, and identify the "most complex" and the "least complex." On what basis did you choose these two components? Write your reasons down on paper, no matter how illogical they may seem. Next, rank the remaining components in order of complexity, and write down the reasons. Involve other estimators within your shop if time permits. A pattern should begin to emerge. An exercise such as this will most often reveal:

1. A classification into types of functions that have been required repeatedly for the projects with which the estimator has been associated.
2. A determination of relative complexity among the types of functions identified.
3. An automatic ranking of "complex" for functions that are unfamiliar or that have not been implemented previously by the staff.
4. A consideration of the staff familiarity with the hardware, operating system, compilers, and other development tools under which the software will be developed and executed.
5. A consideration of the stability of the hardware, operating system, compilers, and other development tools under which the software will be developed and executed.

The classification into type of processing required is a good basic discriminatory factor, as it will automatically include and combine many of the complexity factors that could otherwise be identified separately. For example, the "type" of code requiring much direct interface with hardware will have to be written in a machine-level language. The more we attempt to quantify separate complexity factors, the more we complicate an inherently inaccurate process.

The results of your particular analysis should be recorded in a table, such as the one shown in Figure 8.6. The table defines, as a reference point, the characteristics of the "easiest" and "most difficult" functions imaginable. The actual definition and ranking of the types of software should be performed according to the typical applications with which the specific software shop normally deals. Notice the vast difference between the software categorizations produced by Wolverton and those produced by Donelson in Figure 8.1. In Wolverton's environment, real-time command and control systems are being developed. Donelson defines his sphere of influence as that of commercial applications, in a batch, COBOL, IBM 360 environment. There are no doubt many different classifications that could result from analyses of the business base for software shops within each of these two basic application areas.

Because the staff to be assigned to each function is often unknown at the beginning of the project, familiarity with the application, the hardware, and the development environment should be judged by the likelihood that a software engineer of average experience and skills will be acquainted with these particular conditions. As the staff is selected and assigned, these factors can be corrected to tailor the project characteristics to staff experience. These parameters will identify those areas for which there is little likelihood or no possibility of staff familiarity. This evaluation, therefore, is helpful if for no other reason than to alert the software manager that for-

Rating Weight Criteria	Very simple .5	Simple .7	Average 1	Difficult 1.3	Very difficult 1.5
Software classification	Module performs routine calculations on validated data and returns unformatted results				Module receives data directly from peripheral devices
	Module selects records with specified values from a previously created file				Module schedules others in time-critical environment
Staff familiarity	Familiar application				Unfamiliar application
	Familiar operating system, compiler, assembler, development tools				Unfamiliar operating system, compiler, assembler, development tools
	Familiar hardware				Unfamiliar hardware
Risk factors	Stable operating system, compiler, assembler, development tools				Operating system, compiler, assembler not field tested
	Does not interface directly with hardware				Interfaces directly with hardware currently under development

Figure 8.6. Sample software component complexity weight table.

mal training is necessary and must be planned and scheduled, and the costs added to the software cost estimate.

If the hardware with which a software module must interface is being developed at the same time, the software manager should be alerted to the importance of the human interface between the hardware and software organizations. The software manager must identify what information is needed from the hardware group by what times, include these external constraints on the software schedule, and establish communication and cooperation between the two groups.

The weights to be applied are, for the first project, a "best guess" as to total range of effect of the factors. They serve as a starting point for further analysis.

In constructing the complexity table, do not include factors that do not apply to your area of business. For example, in Donelson's environment, the direct interface with hardware currently being developed would not likely be a factor. Also, identify any factors that will, in reality, apply across the board, and adjust the base productivity for these instead of adjusting each estimate.

The advantages of constructing and using a complexity weight table such as the one we have described are:

1. The criteria for complexity weighting within the familiar business base have been identified and documented.
2. The weighting is applied consistently throughout the system.
3. The results for this project can be anaylzed and the table refined for use in the next project.

The complexity weight thus determined for each component will be identified on the software estimation work sheet.

Complexity weighting may be done by altering the lines of code estimate or by adjusting the base productivity projection. Because a total labor hours projection from the division of the lines of code by the productivity rate will be derived, adjusting the lines of code has the advantage of simplicity of calculation. The lines of code may simply be totaled, then divided by the base productivity projection to yield total labor hours for the system.

Adjusting the productivity rate has the advantage that the basic estimation parameter—lines of code—remains unchanged, and thus the accuracy of at least this estimation can easily be determined at project's end. If estimators can become better at estimating lines of code, they gain a strength in the estimation process and can analyze the complexity factors separately. When the lines of code are adjusted for complexity, it is easy to lose track of what the original estimate was, and thus, it cannot be determined how close the estimate came.

At this point, the projected number of labor hours required for the completion of each software function may be derived by dividing the size estimate by the productivity estimate. This figure should be recorded on the software sizing work sheet for each software module being estimated.

In order to keep a perspective on this inherently inaccurate process, it is desirable to have the estimators cross-check one another's work. If time permits, a good approach is to provide several estimators or teams with the same basic data from which to derive an estimate. The individuals or teams work in parallel and independently, then collaborate on the separate results to produce a single estimate.

To derive a total labor hours estimate for the system, simply sum the hours for each component estimated. During the last steps the estimators have been concerned with small pieces of the system, therefore now is a good time to check the total labor hours estimate for reasonableness. This estimate is checked by comparing the system estimate with actual labor hour expenditures for previous similar projects. Any great variance should be examined in light of the differences between the two systems, and areas that seem suspect should be reevaluated.

Schedule Development and Labor Allocation: Dividing the Work among People

Now that a total labor hours projection for the development of the system is available, a delivery date as well as dates by which major project milestones can be met must be projected. In order to project these dates, it must be determined how long each major technical task will take and how many people can be applied to the task such that the total hours for the task realistically can be divided by that number of people. It must be determined what tasks and activities can be performed in parallel and, for each task, which tasks must be completed before that particular task can be begun.

It is necessary to plan a product-oriented life cycle, such as the one presented in Chapter 2, in order to determine the tasks and activities that must take place. This life cycle must be based on the products and activities required by the contract, higher management, and the company, as well as the internal products and activities the software manager determines are essential to support the development. The logical relationships among the tasks and activities thus defined must then be determined. The use of a PERT or similar schedule network is the only way to define with accuracy the logic to be followed in peforming the tasks and to determine quickly the effects of changing labor levels in individual tasks. As shown in figure 8-7, this type of scheduling technique graphically portrays the events that must take place, which events are dependent on others, and which tasks can be conducted in parallel.

Time spans must now be assigned to each task. The software sizing work

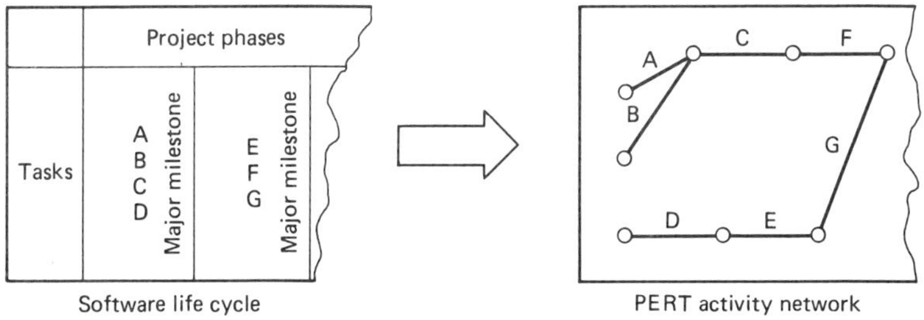

Figure 8.7. Derivation of activity network from the software life cycle.

sheets provide the raw labor hours estimate for each software component. These labor hour estimates include all project activities that must be carried out in support of the component's development. In order to determine the lengths of time and numbers of people that must be applied to the schedule, it is necessary to estimate what percentage of the job time is spent on each major task and activity category. The percentages must be based on the actual work flow and project structure to be used. For example, if the data entry task for all documentation is to be performed by staff within the software organization, it must be determined what percentage of the total labor hours will be spent on this activity. If the data entry services are purchased on an as-needed basis from an outside organization, the cost can be calculated from estimates of page numbers to be produced and added into the total cost estimate in the category of "other direct costs."

As mentioned previously, this percentage breakdown must be estimated for the particular life cycle identified. Figure 8.8 shows a sample percentage breakdown of the activities and tasks defined in our basic life cycle as a basis from which to schedule the work. It is important to remember that characteristics of the particular project must be taken into account and the figures adjusted accordingly.

In contrast to the 40–20–40 rule, some of the time that is classically allocated to the technical code and test phases is allocated to configuration management and independent test activities at the beginning of the project, because the careful control of interfaces and the detail with which the design is specified in our life cycle reduces the time required at the end of the project. The remaining time is taken from the technical tasks and distributed to mangement, clerical, and ongoing configuration management and test team tasks.

The ideal situation would be one in which the software manager could plan to collect costs by activity category and product for the life cycle he derives, so that at the end of the project the manager could analyze the results and better the estimations for the next project. If the customer or higher mangement legislate the way project costs will be collected, the software manager can ask the staff to keep track of key categories separately. The software manager who pays attention to such details is already planning for the next project. If he does not get a chance to evaluate his estimates and learn from them, he has no way of improving his future estimates.

The total hours delegated to the detailed design and implementation phases be scheduled first, with an eye toward assigning modules and units so as to minimize interfaces. The development of the system must now be looked at with regard to the most efficient way the software can be developed and integrated at test time. For example, if a software component adds records to a major file that is accessed by many of the other components, it should be developed and tested first, so that it can be used to integrate the remaining modules. This process will save time by removing

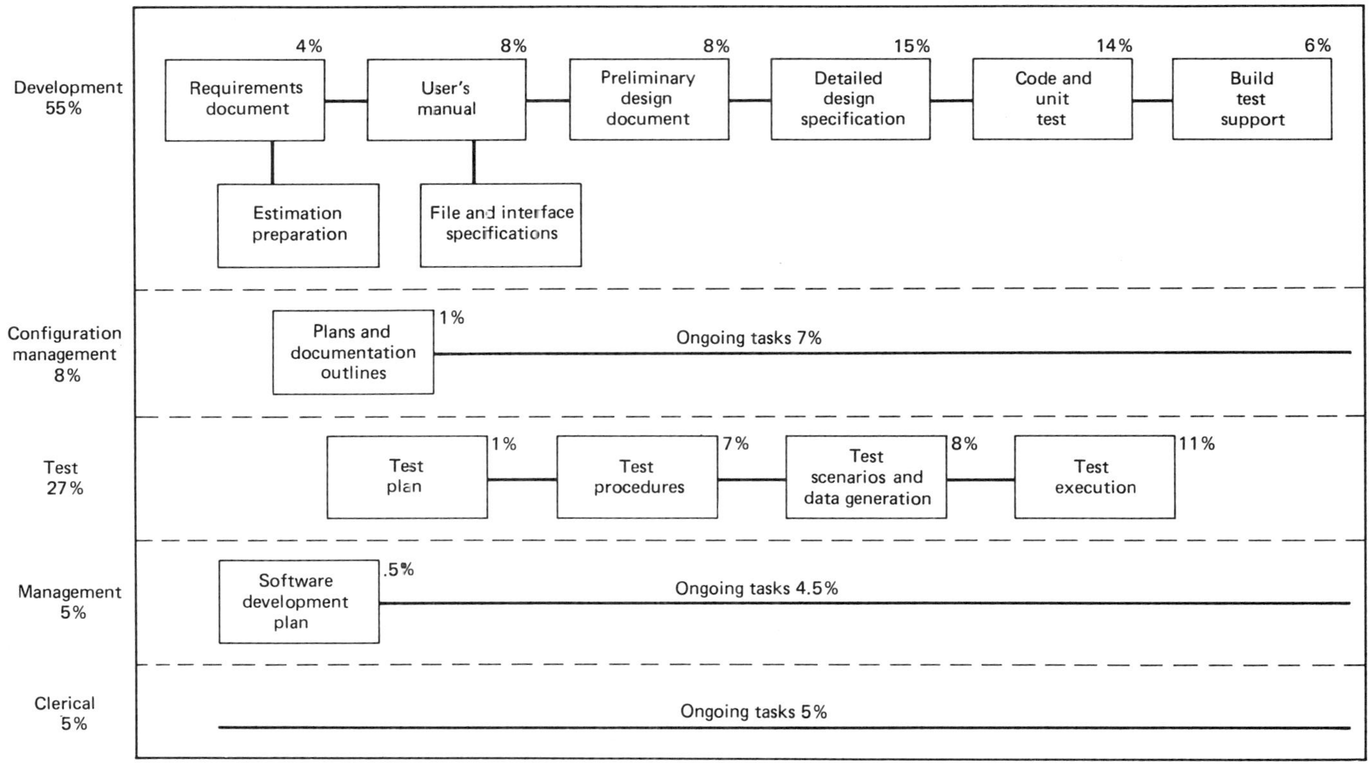

Figure 8.8. Sample development task percentage table.

the requirement to create simulated records for the testing of the other modules.

The resulting schedule and allocation of design and implementation tasks gives a feel for the length of time the design and implementation stages will take. The support tasks can then be allocated labor by dividing the total project time by the hours estimated for a specific category to see how many people can be supported.

As a guide to loading manpower to the project, for the development group, the specification of the basic requirements, the user's manual, and the file and interface layouts should be assigned to a small number of senior engineers in order to reduce the number of interfaces and conflicting approaches to the design at this level. At this point, the integrity of the system as a whole is the emphasis. Later, in the production of the preliminary design document, a few more people may be added to break the subsystems into units and modules and specify design requirements for each. At the detailed design stage, more junior-to-entry-level staff can be added to design and code modules from specific input and output requirements. Staff should be added in advance of the time they are to be considered productive so as to account for learning curves. People will begin to phase off the project as their units complete build testing successfully.

On completion of the scheduling and labor allocation exercise, another reasonableness check can be made against the length of time and number of people applied to a previous similar project.

Assembling the Total Direct Labor Cost Projection

The cost estimation for the direct labor charges to be applied to the project may now be derived by determining the labor category required for each position identified during the labor allocation exercise. The specific labor categories are almost always defined by company standards and policies. In general, however, they fall into four categories:

1. **Entry Level.** This level includes individuals with basic software or support skills but no project experience. These individuals require training and day-to-day supervision and direction. They are capable of simple programming and support tasks.

2. **Junior Level.** This level includes individuals with software or support skills and some project experience at the entry level. These individuals require frequent direction and review and are capable of performing development or support tasks under the direct supervision of senior personnel.

3. **Senior Level.** This level includes individuals with software project experience and a proven ability to work with little direction. These individuals are capable of high-level system design, direction of a technical sup-

port area, and/or supervising and planning the work of less experienced personnel.

4. Management and Staff. These are senior project personnel who have a proven ability to plan, manage, and direct the activities of others. These individuals require no direction and are capable of planning, coordinating, and directing the technical activities of senior personnel.

If there is any doubt of the labor category required to fill a specified position, it is wise to estimate the highest level reasonable to accomplish the task.

On compilation of a total number of labor hours required for each job category, the software manager may deliver these figures to pricing personnel, who will generate the direct labor costs by multiplying labor hours by the hourly average direct labor rate for that job category and applying the company's overhead and general and administrative rate. The costs will then be summed across all job categories, yielding the final direct labor costs.

Other Direct Costs Estimation: Determining Nonlabor Costs

The final category of costs to be developed is those additional costs required to support the development of the software application. The following categories must be considered:

1. *Computer time* includes costs associated with the acquisition, installation, administration, operation, and maintenance of all computer resources.
2. *Publication charges* (usually quoted from external publication facilities as a fixed price per published page) includes costs associated with production and editing of project documentation.
3. *Supplies* includes costs associated with project, office, and computer supplies.
4. *Training* includes costs associated with the training required to enhance the technical skills of the staff.
5. *Travel* includes costs associated with travel to or from external facilities, including transportation, food, and lodging expenses.
6. *Photocopying and reproduction* includes costs associated with the day-to-day copying and reproduction of project material for dissemination to the staff and external organizations.
7. *Special software* includes costs of software tools or utilities that may be purchased to support the activities identified on the schedule, such as automated configuration management or test tools.
8. *Books and manuals* includes the cost of any books or manuals that must be purchased.

9. *Subcontractor services* includes the cost of any subcontractor required to develop, document, or support development of the software.
10. *Miscellaneous* includes those nonlabor costs, such as consultation, that are not included in the direct labor estimates but that are required to develop the software system.

These costs are combined with the direct labor estimates, and the profit is computed from this base. The resultant estimate is the total cost estimate for the software project.

Cost and Schedule Verification and Negotiation

As the area of software estimation is notoriously inaccurate, the costs and schedules produced are bound to be suspect, especially in the eyes of higher management and the customer. Verification techniques may be employed by the software manager or required by company or customer policy to evaluate the validity of the estimate.

Cost Verification Techniques

Several techniques are available to evaluate software estimates developed for a particular application:

1. *The Delphi* technique is a forecasting technique by which the opinions of several experts can be merged to produce a single solution to a problem.
2. *Parametric cost models* are computer-based software costing models that have been developed to predict software costs based on industry experience.
3. *Independent audit* is an audit by an objective, experienced third party of the estimation procedures used and the estimation results.

The Delphi technique is a technological forecasting procedure that is characterized by the independent parallel assessment of a problem by several experts, none of whom ever consult with one another on the problem, but all of whom receive the anonymous opinions of the others as a basis for revising their own opinions. This procedure is iterated until each expert stands firm on his opinions. It was developed in order to eliminate the effects of persuasion and peer pressure, which are great during the normal "group discussion" methods of obtaining consensus.

This technique can be applied to the evaluation of the procedures used in producing the software estimates by selecting several individuals from a base of experienced software managers. These individuals will be chartered with independently evaluating the validity of the basic estimation process and parametric data used to support it. These data are provided to each of the individuals as an ordered list summarizing the tasks performed to derive the estimate and the parameters used in the estimation.

Each individual is then asked to rate the effectiveness or validity of each list item from minus seven to plus seven, with zero being neutral. The results of this rating are collected and distributed to the individuals, who can then use the opinions of the other evaluators to influence their ratings for the second iteration. The process is ended when none of the evaluators wants to change his or her ratings. The final results are then examined by the original estimation team, and areas in which there is much disagreement or in which the evaluation is negative are investigated.

A second technique for evaluating software estimates is to use a computer-based parametric model. These models are designed to assess project cost parameters in relation to a standard development structure. The model provides a means for conducting a comparative evaluation of pricing against an analogous historical data base. This process reduces the use of empirical data except for cases of significant technological or economic differences between system characteristics and the pricing model.

Using the model, the estimator may input project descriptors and customized parametric values along with technological and economic factors to produce a cost and schedule projection. The model should provide for impact assessments and project development sensitivity based on historical project experience.

The model also provides a facility by which a software estimator may evaluate a cost projection against a predefined historical data base and project experience. Execution of the model results in a cost projection that may be validated against the project estimate. If the estimates differ significantly, further analysis must be conducted to isolate the areas of contention and adjust the estimate if required.

The final validation technique is to assign an objective auditor to evaluate the estimation process for adequacy and accuracy. The auditor reviews how the estimate was derived, including the software architecture on which the estimate was based, the projected sizes for the components, the productivity projections, the complexity definition, and the labor mix projected for the implementation of the software. Any areas he finds questionable are flagged for further analysis by the estimators.

NEGOTIATIONS

The cost estimate and schedule produced will undoubtedly undergo a series of negotiations with higher management and/or the customer. If the software manager has directed and documented the procedures used in order to derive the estimates, he may enter the negotiations with a degree of confidence that otherwise would be lacking.

It is at this point that the true constraints for development are revealed. It is rarely possible to reduce schedule and cost at the same time, so a choice ultimately will have to be made. As Putnam and Fitzsimmons (1979) have pointed out, money can be saved if the schedule is relaxed. Why is this true? One reason is that in order to reduce schedule, the options are expensive. First, the most experienced staff available may be hired. Second, overtime may be required. Both are costly. Finally, more people may be hired and the work partitioned further than what was thought reasonable during scheduling. As mentioned previously, this latter action is likely to cause problems in managing the interfaces and is inherently expensive, because a one-day slip now costs a multiple of what it would cost if less people were on the job. A combination of these three actions dramatically increases the cost and may even yield no gain in schedule.

One realistic option open to the software manager is to negotiate a reduction in the scope of the work. This solution means identifying those requirements that can be easily removed without disturbing the rest of the system and quantifying the savings that will be realized.

If the software manager has confidence in the methods by which the estimate was produced, he should clearly refuse to commit himself to a gross reduction in budget or schedule. If the manager must agree to unreasonable constraints, he should, at the very least, identify, quantify, and document the risks involved.

PERSPECTIVE ON THE SOFTWARE ESTIMATION PROCESS

As shown, the estimation process is based on:

1. A necessarily "quick and dirty" design, which will certainly change as the actual project work is done.
2. Two estimated quantities—lines of code and productivity—neither of which can be assumed to have an accuracy within a known range of error.

The software manager must recognize that this phase is not the end of the scheduling and estimating, for as more data become available, the schedules and estimates should be reworked to reflect the added knowledge.

The true value of the estimation process lies in the planning that has been required of the manager. At the end of the estimation process, the software manager will possess a negotiated set of requirements, and so a preliminary design, and should be aware of the technical task required. He will possess a schedule showing exactly how the job will be broken into tasks and how many people will be required at any point in the project in order to perform them. In order to produce this schedule, the manager will have had to make a decision as to the organization of the project. In order to complete the costing for the project, he will have made decisions concerning the computer system and software development tools to be used and the facilities required for development and test. In order to project costs for training, he must have made decisions regarding the use of any new methodologies and evaluated the probable expertise of the projected staff with regard to the skills required for all aspects of the job, including support areas.

If the software manager has looked on the estimation process from this point of view, the cost estimate and schedule will now provide the basis for running the job, and the milestones and budgets will be considered goals that the manager and the present and future staff strive to meet.

If, instead, the manager has haphazardly produced figures and schedules that are not backed by in-depth planning, using the inherent inaccuracy of the process as an excuse, the estimates have little chance of being met, for the software manager is not prepared to proceed with the job in the controlled, orderly manner required for success.

As figure 8-1 shows, the three general categories of project characteristics that interact to affect the development productivity of the project are:

1. *Project environment.* Those factors that determine how effective the project staff will be in working as a unit to produce the software products.
2. *Technical environment.* Those technical project attributes that impact the effectiveness of the project staff or affect the resources required to support development.
3. *Personnel motivation.* Those individual factors that account for the influences in individual productivity.

Many of these factors are under the influence, if not the direct control, of the software manager. The final cost and length of time required for the project, then, should not be regarded as predetermined quantities that will remain a mystery until the project is complete. Rather, the manager should recognize that his job is to influence the outcome of the projections by constant attention and intervention into the project's daily affairs.

A manager who channels his energies into the following tasks can, barring catastrophes from external sources, influence the productivity projection to fit the estimate by:

1. Assigning tasks immediately and making sure the requirements for each task are understood.
2. Keeping abreast of the status of all tasks and reviewing the products for quality as they are produced.
3. Giving the staff positive feedback and constructive criticism on their work.
4. Readjusting personnel, tasks, or schedules to solve problems that arise and to keep the project going.

5. Keeping track of what resources must be available to the staff and acquiring them by the time needed.
6. Making sure the lines of communication among staff members, with higher management, and with the customer are always open.
7. Promoting enthusiasm for the project.

Hence, these areas are where the manager's attention should be placed for the rest of the project.

9 Planning the Project

Even, or especially, in a project with an extremely tight implementation schedule, the planning process cannot be ignored.

As illustrated in Figure 9.1, the establishment of an effective software development environment is a layered definition of data, with each individual set of parameters providing the basis for the next planning level. At the lowest level, there are a set of fundamental project parameters that drive the planning, organization, administration, and execution of the software development project. These are:

1. The technical requirements as expressed by the user and defined in approved system technical and operational specifications.
2. The availability of resources that will be available to the project throughout the development period.
3. The cost estimates that establish the commitment for allocation of project resources and serve as the basis for project budgets.
4. The schedule derivation that translates customer, manager, technical, and project parameters into a work plan for development of the software.
5. The personnel requirements and availability of specific personnel categories and experience to the project.
6. The review and documentation requirements that determine the specific software development products and requirements for review and audits that evaluate and approve them.
7. The customer and contract environment that determines and constrains the project environment.
8. Program and customer interfaces, both technical and contractual, that limit, structure, and define the project environment.

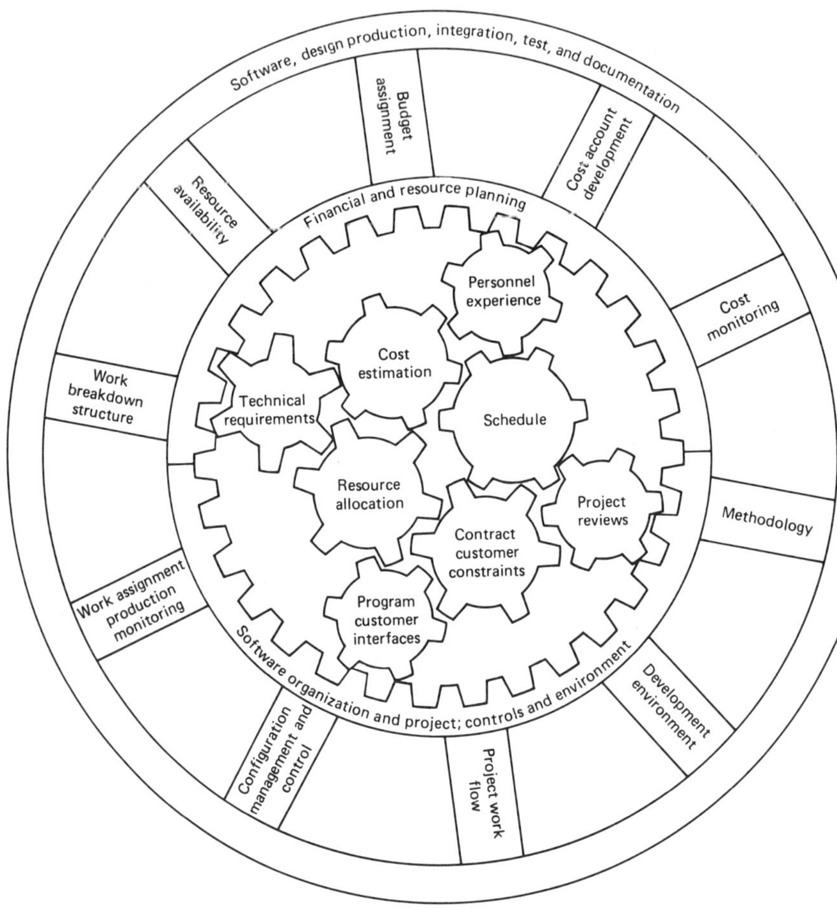

Figure 9.1. Software planning parameters.

The degree to which the software development satisfies these requirements is the ultimate yardstick by which software development success is measured.

Resource and schedule projections committed to by a software manager provide the basic constraints within which the project must be developed. The definition of a software development environment that will support and facilitate software production within these resource constraints and the successful implementation and integration of the software production environment is the cornerstone of a successful project.

As we have seen in Chapter 8, much planning was required in order to produce the cost estimation and schedules for the software effort. Now the software manager must expand on the decisions he made concerning how the project will be staffed, scheduled, and controlled and document these plans in detail.

Unfortunately, during the project definition period there are many conflicting priorities that compete for the software manager's time. These include:

1. Essential customer interface requirements, which engender long-term project good will, technical concurrence, and project awareness of customer expectations and administrative interface requirements.
2. Short-term development and contract milestones, which require a major commitment on the part of the manager and his staff, represent the first customer deliverable, and must be developed using minimal project and technical data as a basis.
3. Recruiting and staffing requirements, which are essential to support project schedules, provide management with essential backup in key areas, and allow the staff to get on with the technical aspects of the project.
4. In a program environment, program interface support is required to plan the program, define the role of the software development organization, and participate in the design of the system.
5. Essential administrative tasks required to define and implement cost accounts, authorize acquisition of project support facilities, and perform those administrative tasks required by the company to monitor and control the project.

Each of these project requirements is important to the early success of the project and, as such, must be fully supported by the software staff.

The conflict facing the software manager is that if short-term program requirements are to be supported adequately, there is not sufficient time to plan and implement the project environment and staff and control those initial project tasks essential for long-term project success. The common, and disastrous, resolution to this conflict is to establish a set of management priorities that deal with short-term project issues first, deferring long-term planning issues to "when I have time." By "tackling the biggest bear in the woods," the software manager establishes a style of crises or reactive management that will, in the long term, significantly impede development effectiveness and increase the risks associated with project development cost, schedule performance, and ultimate acceptability of the software.

A key to the resolution of this dilemma lies in the perspective of the software manager, his commitment to planning, and his ability to convince the customer, higher management, and staff personnel that planning, structuring, and implementing a smooth, effective software development environment supersedes any requirement for short-term project progress.

All the issues described must be dealt with, but only when the manager can address them in the context of a consistent software development plan dealing with long-term project issues. This plan should address project goals and objectives, management techniques, organizational and technical environments to be implemented, the development methodologies and project controls to be followed, project resources and work flow, and the checks and balances that ensure the quality of the software product, integrity of the implemented system in relation to customer and designer requirements, and acceptability in light of contract standards.

These basic parameters must be defined if the project is to begin productively and not bog down or stop during the development. The planning is what gives form and structure to the project, anticipates predictable crises that occur as the software is implemented, and provides the smooth flow of work, data, and responsibility characteristic of successful projects and evident through the various stages of the development. Unless planning parameters are effectively defined, tailored to the characteristics of the specific project, vigorously implemented and enforced, understood and supported by project personnel, and reviewed and modified as project experience dictates, the software development has a marginal prognosis for success.

The software manager and his staff must define and order their work during this period to ensure sufficient time allocations to the planning effort and maintain clear focus toward long-term planning. The priorities are:

1. Development of a software development plan, which is the basic documentation of the software organization and provides a comprehensive definition of basic criteria to be followed in the implementation of the project, defining what is to be done by the software development organization. Subsequent plans, procedures, specifications, and manuals define how these criteria are to be met by the project organization.
2. Refinements to software schedules, budgets, and cost accounts that become apparent during the software planning process.
3. Implementation of those segments of the software plan that must be in place effectively to start the project or that require long schedule lead time to complete.
4. Definition of customer requirements essential to support short-term contract commitments.
5. Identification of administrative obligations required to satisfy company requirements.
6. Initiation of technical tasks relating to software development.

The software manager must then convert these priorities into a short-term plan for completing essential software planning functions. The planning activities must be managed and controlled if success is to be expected. The manager should identify all tasks that must be completed as part of the planning segment of the project and the milestone products resulting from the tasks. A short-term network schedule of planning tasks should be developed detailing the plan for completing these tasks, the logic to be followed in completing the planning, and the schedule commitments for each task. This schedule should include all the planning tasks and documentation, and progress should be measured with formal status-monitoring procedures. The planning requirements should be identified on the software schedule.

As may be readily apparent, these priorities, although essential for software success, are somewhat inconsistent with goals and objectives of external organizations, which, in some cases, pay the bill for software development. This priority conflict is the first instance when the software manager must exercise two key components of software management success—backbone and persuasion. By having clear priorities, the software manager knows what must be done to ensure project success. The manager knows the long-term implications of an evolutionary rather than a planned development and is cognizant that the commitment to meet cost and schedule milestones is his and, as such, must be supported with a project structure that will maximize potential for meeting these milestones while minimizing project risks. The manager must be willing to stand up to external pressures to compromise the priority structure "for the good of the project" until the software development plan is in place. This resistance is often difficult to maintain, but the manager must do so if the software development is to succeed.

The software manager must also be willing and able to convince higher management, customer, and project personnel of the critical need for planning the project, even at the expense of technical progress and customer goodwill. The effective software manager may be accused of being a "snake oil salesman," not sensitive to the difficult technical aspects of the job or to the feelings and experience of the technical staff. This ability to persuade, based on firm priorities, plans, and technical judgment, coupled with enthusiasm and a commitment to proceed in the manner perceived as most effective given the project situation is one of the traits that distinguishes an effective software manager from a marginal performer.

THE SOFTWARE DEVELOPMENT PLAN

The purpose of the production of a software development plan is to create and document a project structure that will support the predictable, orderly

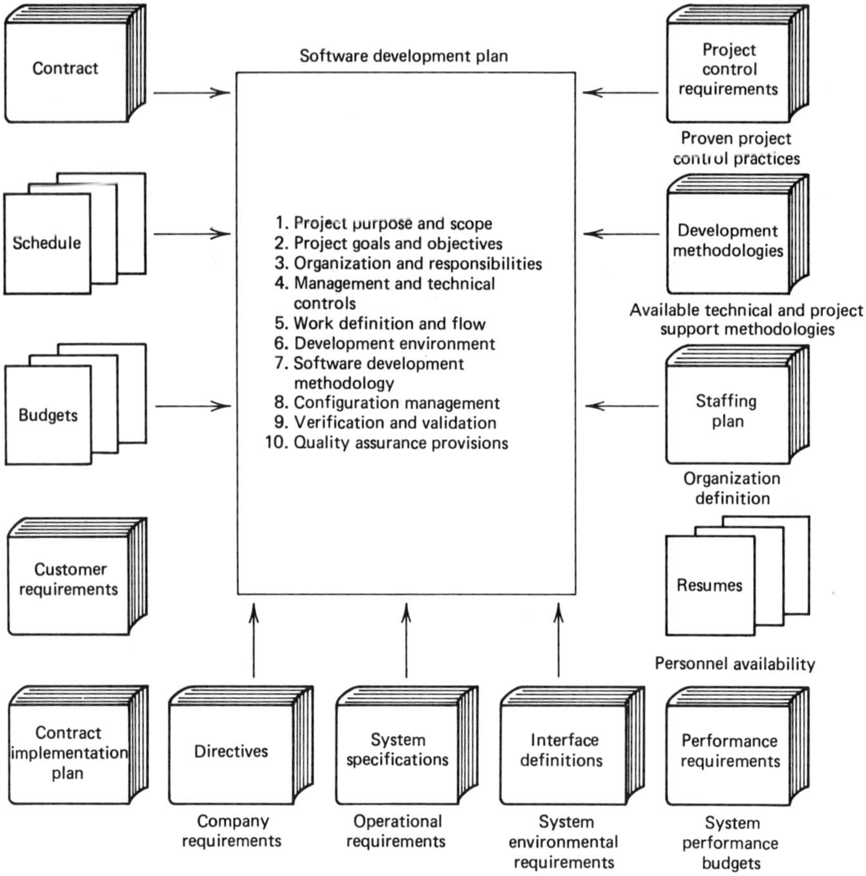

Figure 9.2. Software development plan.

development of the software within cost and schedule constraints. As illustrated in Figure 9.2, the project structure must be tailored to the customer, company, technical, and contract characteristics and requirements. The tailoring process is the means by which the software manager ensures that the selection and implementation of the development, support, and control methodologies are consistent with the needs and characteristics of the particular software application.

The software development plan serves as a guide to the development process for the software manager, software staff, and all external groups throughout the life of the project. The plan should describe the basic project delivery and development requirements, the plans for allocating, controlling, and assigning resources, and the procedures for controlling the development of the software throughout the software implementation period. The software plan should cover the 10 separate areas shown in Figure 9.2.

As the primary software management document, the software development plan should be maintained throughout the development period by the software manager. The manager should provide all updates to higher management, customer agencies, and technical project staff.

The software development plan should address what is to be done in the areas of staffing software development, configuration management, test

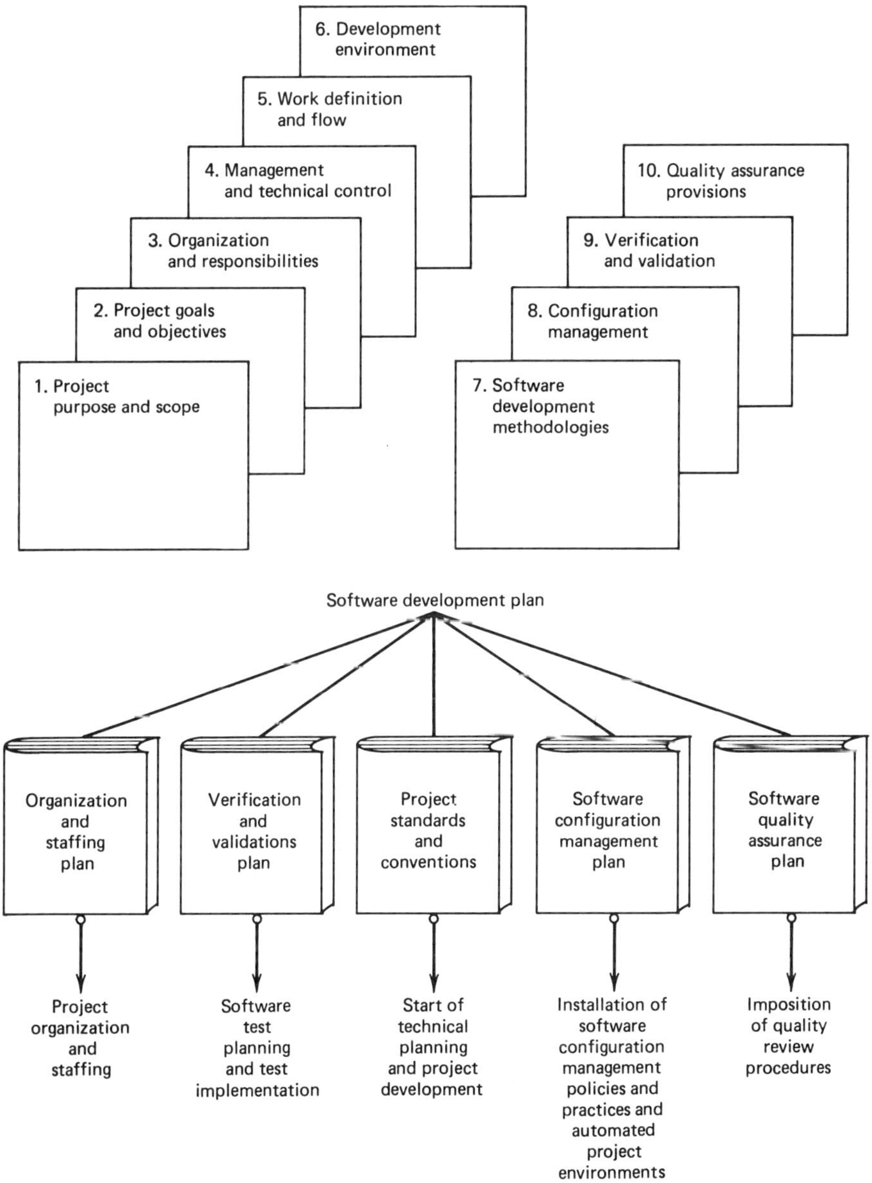

Figure 9.3. Second-level planning documents.

and validation, and quality assurance. Some of these areas will require that a separate document be generated containing detailed procedures for that area, delineating exactly how it will be implemented. This step will result in a number of second-level plans, as shown in Figure 9.3.

There is a temptation on the part of the software manager to unload much of this initial planning responsibility to alleviate front and schedule pressures and conflicts affecting his time and effectiveness. Delegation of this responsibility is a critical error that has a long-term impact on the health and stability of the project. The software development plan must be an expression of the manager's approach at implementation and must represent a commitment on the part of the manager to follow a course of action in developing and implementing the software system. Unless the manager plays a key role in the planning efforts, the plan becomes a document that, no matter how impressive or complete, serves no useful function in the overall project context.

TASKS INVOLVED IN PRODUCING THE SOFTWARE DEVELOPMENT PLAN

As Figure 9.4 shows, there is a logical relationship among the tasks that must be undertaken when developing the software development plan.

Requirements Assessment

Before any definition of individual project components or specific organizational, support, or project control requirements, the software manager must have a clear understanding of obligations levied on the project by the contract, customer, and company. The contractual data requirements used in the costing and scheduling phase must now be examined in even further detail.

The manager, or an individual directly assigned by the manager, should review the contract, any documentation of contract negotiations, and software budgets and schedule information, extracting stated requirements, deliverables, data products, project limitations, constraints, or implied development requirements that will impact the software development. Definition of these requirements should be summarized and listed, with each project requirement identified in the form of a milestone date. The manager must then sort the requirements into five categories that define their effect on the project planning:

1. Formal contract deliverable items that are measured by milestone accomplishment on the schedule.
2. Supporting data products that appear on the software network and that may or may not be contractual but that are required by project or company standards.

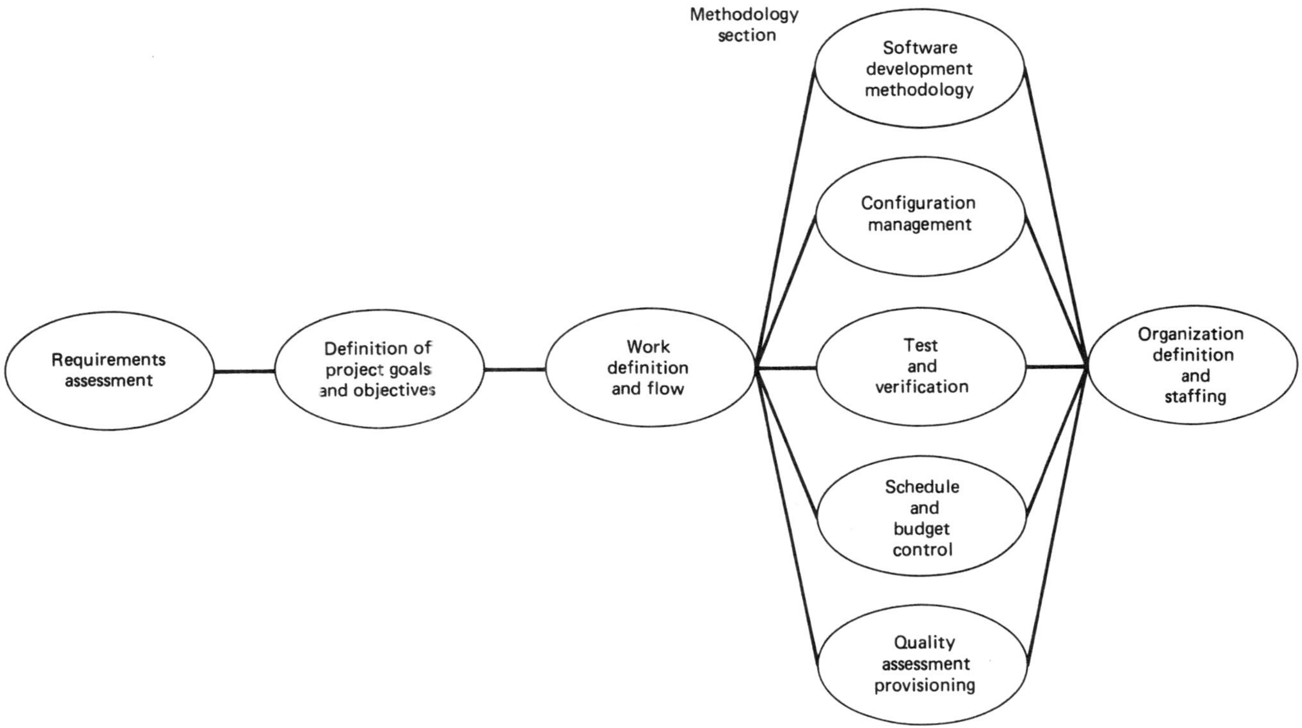

Figure 9.4. Tasks involved in providing the software development plan.

3. Project development methodological and administrative interfaces and contractual or program tools, techniques, or support requirements specified as essential, requiring software project adherence.
4. Technical environmental parameters that define essential elements of the user application and that form the basis for the project technical structure.
5. Software schedule or budget constraints that must be incorporated into any planning effort.

After sorting the project requirements into basic categories, the manager must analyze the list, combining duplicated or redundant requirements, identifying nonachievable, unclear, or conflicting requirements, and flagging project requirements that are inconsistent with good software practice, as determined by the manager. This list is then presented to higher management for their concurrence and modified as required. It should be reviewed with the customer as an interpretation of contract development obligations of the software project.

A parallel task is to define clearly and control a traceable, testable set of technical requirements that will serve as the basis for selecting the development methodologies to be followed and defining the project controls to be applied.

These technical requirements were developed and verified during the costing and scheduling phase. Now they must be formally controlled. Despite assurances that the technical baselines are not critical at this stage of the contract and a strong reluctance on the part of technical personnel to formalize baseline-change control procedure over technical data, the software manager must monitor and control the integrity of technical requirements, identifying and assessing impacts on the costs, schedules, technical assumptions, and project milestones before the agreed-to contract, operational, or user requirements are modified. Acquiescence to requests from external organizations and internal software project members simply to make this small change will lead to invalid software costs and schedule, iterative software design definitions, and a general inability to specify a responsive software architecture.

In order to avoid this problem, the software manager must institute software project control over those parameters defined in the technical requirements definitions; agreed-to and approved technical interfaces; system, software, and operational design requirements; and contract schedule, budget, and project performance requirements as defined in the contract requirement list. A lack of software project control over changes to these basic development requirements, and a corresponding lack of awareness of the technical, cost, and schedule implication and project impact of decisions affecting them, is a root cause of software project performance difficulty and associated development productivity problems. The software manager is placed in the unfortunate position where the customer and technical pesonnel are making agreements and decisions concerning substantive modifications to the technical, administrative, and contractual fiber of the software project structure without an understanding of the impact of these decisions on segments of the software not represented in the decision-making process. Contractual scope, schedule, and funding analyses are not made prior to agreeing to a course of action if the change control process is not formalized, and the software manager finds eventually that there is no clear understanding on anyone's part of what has to be delivered, what agreements have been made, by whom, and why, and what methodologies or resources are to be applied to the project and when. Basically, without formal control of changes to the project, the manager is left with the project responsibility but without the authority or cognizance of basic project requirements essential for success.

Definition of Project Goals and Objectives

After definition and approval of contract and technical requirements and institution of a project organizational structure to document, assess, and control changes to the requirements, the software manager must translate these decisions into a clear set of project goals and objectives. These will be used to guide and focus the project activities as well as to provide a clear, concise statement of where project priorities lie and how these priorities will be translated into project action by the manager.

Once defined, these goals and objectives are the basic management expression of what fundamental issues drive the project and how decisions concerning project priorities, application of project emphasis, and commitments of management support will be made. For each of these goals and objectives, a price is paid by the software project in the form of development effectiveness and productivity and the basic ability to satisfy project and personnel requirements and obligations. The matrix in Figure 9.5 provides a representative indication of project areas that will be impacted if certain project goals and objectives are applied to the project. The check indicates the development impact area that will most likely be affected if the project rigorously and consistently uses a specific goal or objective to guide the project. Although not complete, this matrix indicates that decisions made at this level of what basic criteria are to be followed and applied to the project are key to success of the project and must be clearly defined and documented, and the effect on the project must be clearly understood and integrated into the project structure. The software manager may best disseminate these goals and objectives through a memorandum sent to all project and higher management personnel, with copies sent to the customer. This memorandum should clearly state software project goals and objectives and the priorities to be used by the software manager when considering how to develop the project. The manager should gain project-wide concurrence on these goals to avoid conflicts later in the project.

	Cost	Schedule	Technical personnel satisfaction	Productivity	Development effectiveness	Product acceptability	Staffing potential	Customer and program acceptance
1 Technical excellence and application of innovative software development techniques	X	X		X	X		X	
2 Software operational integrity and effectiveness coupled with end user satisfaction	X	X	X	X	X		X	
3 Documentation clarity, support effectiveness, and maintainability	X	X	X	X	X			
4 Software reliability and performance within stringent performance budgets	X	X	X	X	X			X
5 Development of software products within cost and schedule constraints exclusive of technical or operational acceptability			X			X		X
6 Development of acceptable software applying only a given set of personnel and support resources available to the project	X	X	X	X		X		X
7 Use of a given set of project methodologies and development techniques	X	X	X	X	X		X	X
8 Strict adherence to customer, contract, and program requirements, with associated stringent test and demonstration issues	X	X	X	X	X			
9 Effective software support of hardware interfaces and system environments	X	X	X	X	X		X	

Figure 9.5 Goal-impact matrix.

Task Planning and Work Flow

Once the basic development objectives are defined, the software manager must define the technical, administrative, support, and control tasks required to implement the project.

The basic software development tasks were defined, and the order in which the tasks must take place, along with the relationships among the tasks, was determined and documented in the software schedule produced during the estimation process. For the purpose of producing the software development plan, the work flow must be analyzed with regard to the overall project structure, and the following must be determined:

1. What are the major phases of the development project?
2. How does the work in each phase lead to products on which the next phase can be based?
3. For each phase, what are the intermediate tasks and products that lead to completion of the phase?
4. On what criteria shall it be determined that a phase is complete and work can start on the next phase?
5. What staff is involved in each phase, and what are the major duties of the staff for the phase?

Methodology Selection

The software manager must sort through a myriad of inconsistent and conflicting development standards and implementation instructions that are defined as industry solutions to the "software problem." Understanding the requirements imposed by these standards, being able to tailor software development activities to project requirements, and having the experience necessary to define, document, and implement a specific software project methodology and development structure consistent with documented customer and program requirements are absolute prerequisites to successfully performing software development.

Defining a software development structure that satisfies the customer and higher management but still facilitates development productivity and the engineering process is a complex and difficult management planning problem. Successful definition requires management understanding of the implications and intent of software development standards as well as the management experience and ability to tailor these to the project.

Definition of a software project structure and development methodologies to support software implementation is a four-part process:

1. Analysis of the development requirements of the customer profile. This profile defines what documentation, formal reviews, and re-

porting requirements are obligatory and what expectations the customer has in terms of software management technique, project structure, and access to contractor records, internal reports, and personnel.
2. Summarization of the project development standards as modified to reflect the unique requirements of the contract or customer's development environment.
3. Analysis of implications of the software application, including project size, schedule, technical complexity, project personnel, security classification, support facilities, and available development environment. This analysis serves as the basis for defining project structures and a development methodology responsive to actual development requirements of the project.
4. Analysis of parameters resulting from the company's previous development experience in order to derive a project methodology. This methodology will cover all aspects of software development, including scheduling and project budgeting, requirements analysis, design, code production, configuration management and control, documentation, independent test and integration, and software quality assurance.

As shown in Figure 9.4, the methodology selection task involves deciding exactly how each of the following questions will be answered:

1. How will software be designed and coded?
2. How will the large volume of constantly changing project information be kept current and communicated to staff members?
3. How will the software be tested?
4. How will schedule and budget be statused and controlled?
5. How will the quality of the software products be assessed throughout the project?

Guidelines for Methodology Selection

The major guideline for the selection of methodologies to be applied in each of the areas listed earlier is to consider the requirements of the particular technical application involved as well as the project environment dictated by customer, higher management, company, and staffing factors.

Selection of Software Development Methodology

A major software development methodology decision has already been made by virtue of the phasing of work that has been defined and the requirement inherent in this phasing that the job will be defined and documented in terms of what is to be done before design begins and in terms of detailed design, including interfaces, before coding begins.

The most disastrous of the familiar software problems is the inability to make the system work when the separate pieces are integrated. This problem is caused by allowing separate pieces of software to be developed under conflicting assumptions of what the system is to accomplish and how the pieces interface with one another. The problem is disastrous in that it is usually not detected until test time, at which point much work and rework must be done to reconcile the system.

This problem is averted to a large degree by the imposition of the project and product phasing, defined before cost estimation and scheduling or configuration management methodology were performed. As we shall see in the following section, this phasing is only a first step in the alleviation of this problem.

The methodology for the actual design process may now be selected. There are many design methodologies in the literature that are intended to aid a smooth transition from the requirements specification to the partitioning of the system into software components and detailed design. We recommend the adoption of a top-down design methodology that emphasizes the clean partitioning of the software by minimizing of interfaces between the pieces. There also exist automated design tools that aid in the design process.

Before any methodology is selected, the senior technical members of the staff should be involved in the analysis of the existing alternatives. The ease of use, track record of the methodology, and staff familiarity must be taken into consideration.

Launching the use of a new design methodology not previously used by the staff can cause serious problems if the methodology is difficult to implement or not adequately documented. The software manager should consider use of a totally new design methodology as a risk factor and should employ it only if cost and schedule expenditures for training and learning curves on the part of the staff permit, or if the customer insists on the use of a particular methodology.

The main principle to be applied in making the decision regarding the software design methodology, then, is to choose a methodology with which the staff is comfortable and that is thoroughly documented. This decision may result in a methodology based on a particular text tailored to the capabilities and desires of the technical staff.

Selection of Configuration Management Methodology

The configuration mangement methodology selected is the means by which all the products of software development are to be identified, stored, and controlled with regard to changes. Configuration management is the heart of the project, for no matter how rigorously the requirement for documentation of plans and specifications is enforced, if these products are not made available to the staff, if the list of existing products is not known, and if changes to these products are not controlled and communicated to the staff, the interface problems discussed earlier will exist.

The methodology selected for configuration management should espouse the following principles:

1. Configuration identification. All products, both documentation and software itself, must be uniquely identified and an inventory must be maintained so that at all times the products that exist are known
2. Configuration description and location. The form in which each product exists must be known, along with where it is physically located
3. Configuration product approval. Each software product should go through official approval channels before acceptance into the system configuration
4. Configuration change control. A method must be devised by which the changes to the official system configuration are documented, reviewed, and formally approved before application, and a method for keeping track of the different versions of changed products must be addressed.

Selection of Test and Verification Methodology

The methodology selected for the test and verification of the software is vitally important to the success of the project, for test is the major arena for deciding the quality of the system to be delivered and, indeed, whether the system meets the customer requirements.

The overall testing structure, including the test phases to be implemented and the test requirements for each phase, should be selected. The methodology should be selected so that the following are emphasized:

1. The smooth, controlled flow of data and responsibility as the project moves through the test phases.
2. The orderly buildup of system capability and the software configuration. The software manager should define an integrated environment that will provide an assembly line for the integration of the software components into an operational configuration.
3. The use of known, documented system configurations executing in predefined, controlled, reproducible test environments that are traceable to specific baselined project requirements.
4. The use of known, documented test procedures for each system configuration, including a step-by-step description of how each test case

will be conducted, what data will be inputed to the system, and what results are expected.

Informal Software Verification and Build Test. This testing is conducted by the software development organization and qualifies the software into an operational configuration for use in qualification testing. The following should be determined for informal testing:

1. Overall roles and responsibilities of personnel during test.
2. Control procedures to be applied during test.
3. Requirements for module and unit testing.
4. Requirements for build integration testing.
5. Test reviews and walkthroughs and their relationship to testing.
6. Software controls during rest.

Functional Testing. This test phase takes software that has undergone informal integration and functionally qualifies the integrated software against the functional requirements of the project. The following should be determined with regard to the functional test phase:

1. Functional test planning requirements are the formal requirements for test planning and the review and approval requirements for the test plan and the relationship of this plan to other product data items.
2. Build definition is the method by which it is determined what functional capabilities will be added to the system for each major build.
3. Execution control is concerned with how tests are to be conducted, what organizational entities support testing, what technical controls are to be applied to test, and what reviews are required to monitor or quality and completion.
4. Customer interface concerns the test requirements that are contractually binding.
5. Test environment has requirements and limitations that must be determined.
6. Test procedure requirements are the formal requirements for the development of the test procedures and the review and approval requirements for the procedures document and the relationship of this document to other product data requirements.
7. Test data requirements determine how test data are to be created, approved, and controlled.
8. Relationship to program-wide tests concerns how software functional tests relate to hardware and systems tests.

Methodology Selection for Budget and Schedule Controls

The effective development and application of budget and schedule control procedures will have the most dramatic and visible effect on software productivity of all the software planning and production techniques. It is only through a methodology allowing the timely, accurate identification of the project status with regard to schedule and budget that the manager can assess and correct the daily problems of software development and react in time to reverse or diminish their effects.

The software manager normally has the following reporting responsibilities to higher management and/or the customer:

1. Cost reporting through weekly updates to the software cost accounts.
2. Schedule updates as applicable.
3. Progress reporting on a regular basis, including the cumulative percentage of project work completed, the cumulative percentage of total projected labor hours that have been expended, status with regard to the schedule, and a definition of any changes required in the technical approach and plans.
4. Schedule status on request.

Budget Control. Budgets and schedules are interdependent in that the cost expected to have been expended at any point can be determined only by a summing of the labor hours and other direct costs that are to have been required to date. The cost data produced during the estimation phase can be summed by month to provide an expected total expenditure projection, with which to compare each month's actual charges to the project.

The methodology for controlling budgets in most cases will be dictated by the customer and/or company. This situation should certainly be analyzed before any independent methodology is derived. The basic guideline for developing a cost control methodology is to track labor and other direct costs by development area, so that any overruns can be isolated to the activity in which they occur, and corrective action can be taken. If possible, the cost collection and budget monitoring should track with the manner in which the separate budgets were allocated, so that the actual costs for development activity can be analyzed at project end and used as a basis for future estimations.

Schedule Control. The software development network constructed during the cost estimation process provides the basic project schedule and delineates the major tasks and milestones to be met throughout the project. Identification of the project status against this high-level schedule, however, will not be sufficient to detect and correct problems in a timely manner. A detailed production-level schedule that can be monitored on a day-to-day basis must be created in order to control effectively the software development process.

The methodology selected for controlling the software schedules must be based on further decomposition of each task to be performed in order to meet the major milestones. This process must be iterated until clear milestones that take two weeks or less to complete may be identified.

In order to portray the relationships among the tasks necessary to implement project milestones, a logical scheduling network, such as PERT, is the only effective means for representing software production schedules. Because of the detail inherent in this kind of schedule, it is impossible to project accurately schedule and resource requirements more than six to eight weeks in advance. Thus, the production schedules are valid tools only if they are limited to this time period. Any production schedule that spans a longer period of time is at best inaccurate and at worst extremely misleading.

Derivation of the software production schedules is the most difficult of all the software planning activities. Figure 9.6 illustrates the relationship between the software development network and the production-level schedules. First, the manager extracts from the software development network each individual milestone that is scheduled to be complete within the next eight-week period. Working backward, the manager determines exactly what individual tasks must be accomplished to satisfy the milestone.

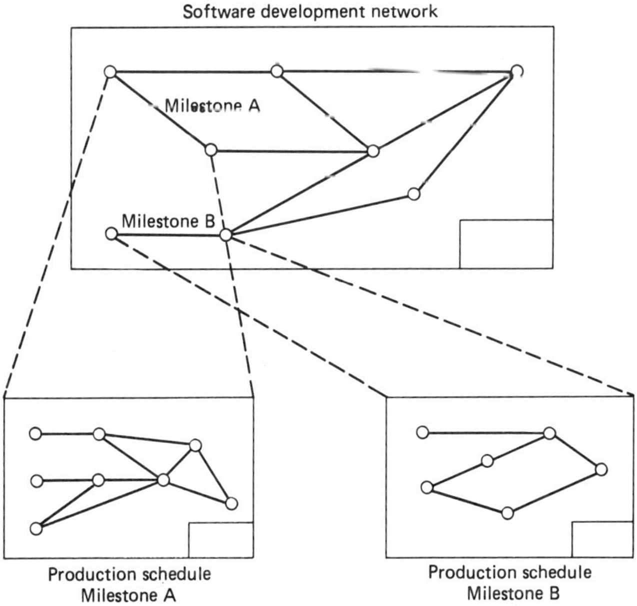

Figure 9.6. Software development network and production schedule relationship.

The manager lists these tasks and then breaks each of these tasks into its component tasks. The process continues until all the work necessary to meet the milestone has been described and listed. Care should be taken to define tasks for which completion can clearly be verified. For example, a milestone of the form "section x of the user's manual written" may be reported complete long before the section is ready to be incorporated into the first draft of the document. This milestone must be broken into the measurable milestones that reflect all the work that has to be done in order to consider the section ready for internal review as part of the draft user's manual. Milestones such as "deliver section x of the user's manual to document coordinator," "section x text submitted for data entry," "section x graphics submitted for drawing," and so on, will make it possible for the status of the task to be pinpointed. This precision will avoid the confusion produced by a schedule that states that section x has been written for weeks when no one can produce a copy of the section that is ready to be incorporated into the draft document.

The logical constraints and relationships among all the tasks identified on the list are then determined and used to develop a PERT network. Using the task list compiled for development of the milestone, the manager reviews this PERT for logic and task completeness. Through this review, inconsistencies in the logic will be uncovered, and essential activities not included in the task list will become apparent. With this updated data, the logic of the milestone production schedule will be updated as required.

The next stage of production schedule development is to assign time spans for each of the individual subtasks identified on the PERT. In order to define these spans, each individual assigned responsibility for a task on the schedule is asked by the manager to assign a time span to the task. It must be clear that this definition represents a commitment and that the individual providing the commitment will be measured for performance against the production schedule.

When spans have been assigned to each task on the PERT, the milestone completion date is computed. This date is matched against the date on the software schedule, and the degree of variance is determined. The manager then determines which task schedules are the most likely to be shortened if additional resources are assigned or if the scope of the task is reduced. When a course of action is determined, the responsible individual meets with the manager, and the new schedule is negotiated. This process continues until the production schedule complies with the software network.

In order to be effective, the time spans assigned to each task on the production schedule should not exceed two weeks, with the ideal span being two to three days. The reason for the short schedule spans is that development personnel are significantly more productive if the milestones are near at hand rather than far in the future. These short milestones also provide the manager positive and early warning of development problems in sufficient time to correct or minimize the problem and to avoid significant unanticipated schedule slippage.

The derivation of such a low-level schedule is rigorous and forces the manager to think through, at a very detailed level, how each individual milestone will be developed. It provides the software staff with granular milestones with very short spans that may be used to guide development activities and monitor progress.

The production schedules are the means by which the software manager plans the development of specific project milestones and communicates this plan to the personnel assigned to the project. In order to ensure that project progress matches the requirements of the plan, a schedule-status-monitoring procedure must be implemented by the manager.

The status-monitoring procedure should serve as a basis for the software manager to determine quickly the status of the software development, completion date projections for each milestone, and a cost-to-complete projection. It should provide for weekly status reporting by all who are in charge of a particular task, identifying:

1. Milestones completed during the week.
2. Milestones that were due to be completed during the week but were not.
3. For each milestone missed, a projection of when the milestone will be complete.
4. Any problem that may impact a future milestone.
5. Any future milestone that is projected to be missed.

In order to determine the percentage of milestones complete, the percentages that were projected for the major tasks during the creation of the software development network in the cost estimation phase can be used as a basis for assigning percentages to each granular task on the production schedule. When identifying status no percentage should be claimed for a task unless it is verified as complete. The validity of the "percentage complete" estimate clearly depends on the degree of granularity achieved in creating the production schedule and the true measurability of the lowest level milestones defined.

As with all project activities, status monitoring must be documented and tracked. A sample schedule status form that can be used during the code and test phase is shown in Figure 9.7.

Methodology Selection for Quality Assurance Provisions

The major guideline for the selection of the methodology to be employed in the area of quality assurance is to plan for checks to be made at major points during the development process, including at a minimum a check on each software product before it is baselined. The checks should be clearly defined in the schedule, and what criteria will be used to evaluate the product should be documented so that the staff can anticipate the checks and work toward specified acceptance standards from the beginning.

Schedule Status Form

CPCI/CPC: ABC/AW Func Area: e3 Task Leader: Smith

Module Name	Strt Design	Rdy Prel SW	Cmplt Prel SW	Start Code	Rdy Peer Rev	Cmplt Peer Rev	Rdy Final SW	Cmplt Final SW	Stp 1 Lev 0 Test	Cmplt Unit Test	Cmplt Sec Test	Cmplt Code Rel
ekebuf	10/20/78	11/20/78	12/11/78	11/20/78	11/27/78	12/08/78	08/11/79		02/20/79	02/21/79	03/11/79	
ekgtrw	10/20/78	11/20/78	12/11/78	11/20/78	11/27/78	12/11/78	08/11/79		02/23/79	02/27/79	03/11/79	
ekmems	10/20/78	11/20/78	12/11/78	11/20/78	11/28/78	12/08/78	08/11/79		01/05/79	02/20/79	03/11/79	
ekreib	10/20/78	11/20/78	12/11/78	12/01/78	12/07/78	12/08/78	08/11/79		02/27/79	02/28/79	03/11/79	
eketab	10/20/78	11/20/78	12/11/78	12/01/78	12/07/78	12/08/78	08/11/79		02/28/79	03/01/79	03/11/79	
			Design Compl			Code Compl				Unit Compl		Test Compl
Sched Date			12/20/78			1/19/79				2/16/79		3/02/79
Proj Date			12/20/78			1/19/79				2/16/79		3/02/79
Actual Date			12/11/78			12/01/78				3/01/79		3/11/79

Figure 9.7. Sample schedule status form.

The checks should be performed by individuals who are knowledgable in the areas being reviewed but should always include reviewers other than those who produced the work being reviewed. The institution of such checks may be resented by the staff unless the following methods are implemented by the methodology:

1. No staff member should be excused from undergoing peer review of his work.
2. No staff member should be excluded from participation in the peer review process.
3. The reason for the checks should be clearly defined by the software manager from the start of the project, and he should allow for reviews of his or her work.

4. The software manager should emphasize from the beginning the common staff goal of producing a superior project and promote the project-oriented attitude to the staff continuously.

Organization Definition and Staffing

The final task in the planning of the project is to synthesize the data resulting from all previous scheduling, budgeting, and work definition and to project how many and what levels of personnel will be needed to execute the tasks and control methodologies selected, how project personnel should be organized, at what times will each position need to be filled, and how will the identified positions be filled.

The organizational approach selected and defined for the project must be tailored to the characteristics and specific needs of the application. As illustrated in Figure 9.8, there is a relationship among the tasks required to implement a software product that a manager must recognize as basic to the structure of the organization if it is to be adequate in supporting software development. At the center of the structure are those tasks relating to software management. These tasks plan and establish the software project environment and schedule, control and monitor the development process. The management tasks orchestrate tasks within and between functional elements of the organization and monitor project performance, taking corrective actions where required to ensure production development. The management tasks are the core of the project, providing a centralized source of responsibility, authority, direction, and control. The next level of functional authority rests with the software systems engineering staff, which provides technical guidance to the project and defines, translates, and interprets the project technical and interface requirements. This segment of the project structure has the responsibility for identifying and documenting all requirements on which the software is based and providing these specifications to the configuration management area of the project for formal control.

Software design authority is centralized in a technical group reporting through the systems engineering function to the software manager. The members of this group are the "architects" of the system, who synthesize a software design from a statement of user and project requirements. The software designers are initially chartered with defining a set of functional requirements and software structures that when implemented satisfy the needs of the application as stated by system engineering. These functional requirements are controlled by the configuration management function. When the design has been fully defined, the team is reassigned to act as either task leaders or system architects, controlling the development of segments of the system architecture. A subset of the team is retained in the design role to act as the group vested with a project-level design authority.

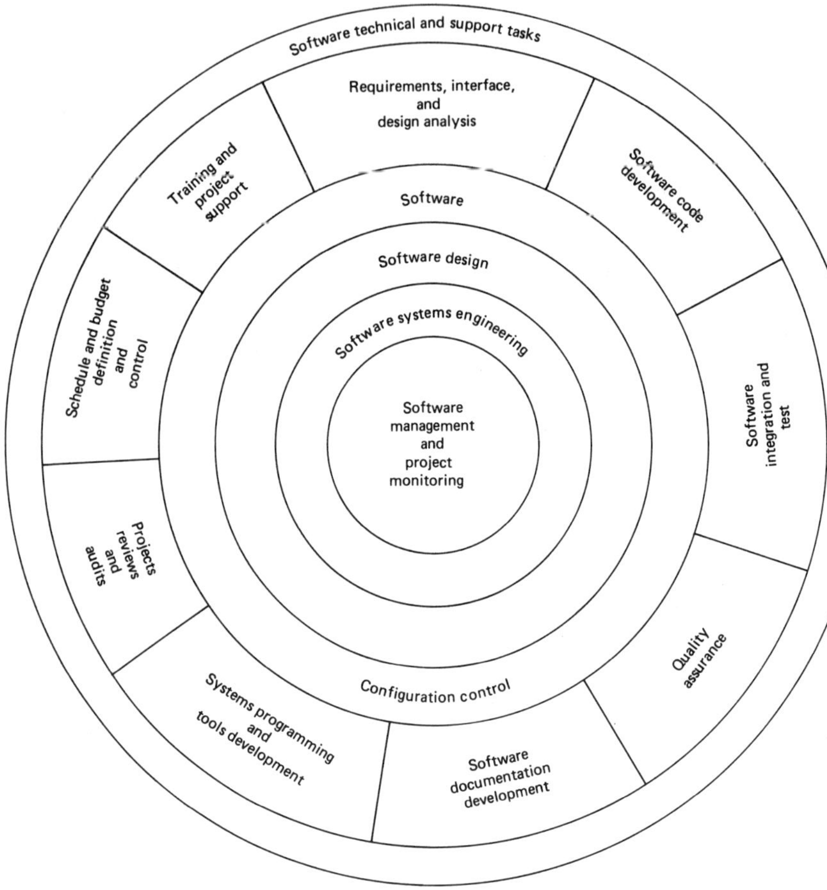

Figure 9.8. Software project organizational structure.

All data developed within the project that have undergone some degree of formal project review or approval will be formally and rigorously controlled by the configuration management and control segment of the project. This element of the project acts as a central point for directing, controlling, administering, and supporting the flow and dissemination of all project data that have been internally reviewed and approved. The configuration management function also has centralized responsibility for the development, implementation, and administration of the tools and techniques required to implement the project methodologies supporting the development and scheduling and acquisition and application of support resources essential for development.

Those specific development areas that result in the production or support of the software product are the final level of tasks the organization must support. The manager may distribute the tasks required to support the process into any structure satisfying the needs of the project and maximizing the productivity associated with all segments of the development process. Two fundamental attributes should be built into the organization structure:

1. There should be a basic set of project checks and balances built into the organization, providing continual accurate assessments of the progress and quality of the development and a redundant level of labor in key project areas so that the loss of a staff member will not cripple the project.
2. The flow and control of data within the project and the transition of responsibility should be clearly defined, so that an effective transition between development phases and organizational entities can be achieved.

The software project organization and its effectiveness in the project environment has a material effect on how productive the development of the software will be and how well the spirit is engendered in the project staff.

The number of people needed at any point in the project and the skill level required for each position was identified during the labor allocation phase of the estimation stage. The software manager must now provide a plan for staffing these positions, identifying a stratgey for obtaining personnel, and the schedule for obtaining them.

STRUCTURE OF THE SOFTWARE DEVELOPMENT PLAN

The software development plan can now be written to document the decisions that have been made as a result of the completed planning tasks. The plan, if structured in the fashion shown earlier, rigorously followed, and kept up to date, will serve as the guiding document throughout the development process. Its various sections are described in the following paragraphs:

1. **Project Scope and Purpose.** This section should identify the project with regard to its official name, the customer for whom it is being developed, and the basic reason for its development. It should provide a clear, concise introduction to the project, including any history that makes the reason for the work and the main functions of the system to be developed more easily understood. This section should also identify the computer systems on which the final product is to operate and any noteworthy requirements or constraint on development.

2. **Project Goals and Objectives.** The goals and objectives that were documented, and agreed on during the second step of the planning tasks

are incorporated here, making them the official guidelines for project development.

3. Organization and Responsibilities. The following five areas should be addressed with regard to project organization.

(a) *Project organizational overview and structure* provides a block diagram of the organization and a description of each major element.
(b) *Roles and responsibilities* describes what functions each of the elements of the organization will perform and the extent and limitations of responsibilities assigned to each.
(c) *Organizational support and work assignment* describes what specific support will be provided by each organizational entity and the work to be accomplished by each.
(d) *Organizational controls and reporting requirements* describes what controls will be placed on each of the areas of the project and how progress, status, and problems are to be reported.
(e) *Staffing requirements and plan* describes the specific labor mix required to support each segment of the project, where the personnel are to come from to staff each position, and when they will be needed.

If the manager determines that a thorough description of these areas will be better addressed in a separate document, he can use the preceding areas as an outline for the separate organization staffing plan. Within the software development plan itself in this case, the manager should introduce the basic organization, briefly describe the major roles and responsibilities of each organizational component, and summarize the organizational controls and reporting requirements. He should then refer the reader to the organizational staffing plan for further details.

4. Management and Technical Controls. This section should provide an overview of the controls that will be applied to the software development process to ensure that the project is on schedule, within budget, and technically successful. It is in this section that the managing philosophy of running a software project is documented. The methodology chosen for controlling and monitoring schedules and budgets should be described in detail in this section. The discussion of methodologies chosen for use in software design and implementation, configuration management, verification and validation (test), and quality assurance should be introductory in nature, and the reader should be referred to expansions on these subjects in later sections of the document. For example, the existence of formal reviews and audits occurring at specific points of development can be mentioned and the reason for their existence explained. Such reviews and audits can be further discussed in the section on quality assurance provisions.

5. Work Definition and Flow. In this section, the software development process is described in terms of the major work phases. A diagram showing the major phases and the major products for each phase should be included to introduce overall work flow. In this diagram, project baselines should be identified. For each phase, a narrative should be included to describe the products generated to mark the end of the phase and the flow of work within each phase.

6. Development Environment Definition. In this section the environment in which the software will be developed is defined for the computer system on which the software is to be developed, its detailed configuration specifications, its location, method of program access, the test configuration (if different from the development configuration), and security access requirements.

7. Software Development Methodology. The methodology selected for software design and implementation should be identified and briefly described in this section. If any special software tools are to be employed as part of the methodology, such as design languages, they should be identified and described. If the methodology is described in the literature, reference should be made to the specific authors and titles. For example, it is not enough to state that a "top-down" methodology will be used; a specific, documented methodology also must be identified. The particular methodologies, standards for development, and detailed procedures for their use should be described in a separate document, which should be referenced in this section of the plan.

8. Configuration Management. This section should describe the general method by which the software products detailed in the work definition and flow section will be controlled throughout the project. It should state in what form the official version of the products will be stored, how access to these products is achieved by the staff, what approval is necessary for accepting a product as "official" and what control and general tracking procedures will be applied to changes in official products. The reader should be referred to the configuration management plan for detailed procedures by which these controls will be implemented.

9. Software Test and Verification. This segment of the plan should introduce the overall testing structure, identify the test phases, and list and describe the testing requirements by phase. It should describe the philosophy of building and testing the system in phases and refer to the documents that will be produced by the test organization. The reader should be referred to the separate verification and validation plan for a detailed description of the test program.

10. Quality Assurance Provisions. This section should enumerate and describe checkpoints at which the quality of the development process will be assessed. It should include a description of all customer-scheduled reviews as well as such internal reviews as design and code walkthroughs and documentation reviews. For each review, the method for reporting the findings and correcting any problem areas found should be detailed. If necessary because of length or customer requirements, a separate quality assurance plan may be generated to describe all the methods by which the software manager will ensure the soundness of the software products being developed.

10 Managing the Process

Technical personnel will not resent management controls and project structure if it reduces the work, focuses their activities, and is enthusiastically supported by management.

Contrary to popular belief, the most critical phase of the project is that period of time at the very beginning when budgets, schedules, and planning occupy most of the manager's time. Any staff members that are assigned to the project at this early stage must be quickly assimilated into the work flow and must be made to feel that the manager is totally committed to project performance and success. They must be given meaningful tasks that contribute to the main products of this period of time, and the manager must communicate his commitment to maintaining a structured project environment in his everyday interactions with the staff. Communication with the staff and direct involvement with the products of their work must be of top priority to the manager, no matter what demands are being placed on his personal time from external sources.

A common management mistake at the beginning of the project is to yield to external requirements to attend meeting after meeting, conduct interview after interview, and leave the staff with nothing to do or to assign meaningless tasks and never review the status or products of the tasks assigned. The manager sometimes feels that he can officially "start" the project at a later date, when he gets organized.

The prudent manager realizes that the project has started, with or without him, and will not wait for him to catch up. The manager recognizes the natural desires of the staff to push the project forward and capitalizes on this tendency. The staff will want to be kept abreast of project events and will want to know what their next assignment is and how it contributes to the project. One day of the software manager being tied up in meetings or locked behind closed doors preparing schedules and budgets can stop project momentum.

It is easy for a manager to allow himself to be guided by external demands. It is much simpler to be told what to do than to get priorities for a project and work through others to get the job done—which is why managers are paid more than their staffs are. If a manager chooses to be guided by external forces, he is not doing the job for which he is paid.

It is difficult to change the tone of project development. A manager who has created an impression of unavailability, unconcern for the project, and disorganization and then emerges one day with a handful of project plans and says, "This project is going to be structured from now on!" cannot expect ready acceptance of the plans or his statement by the staff.

In order to lay the groundwork for a successful project, a manager must possess:

1. A clear understanding of what is involved in establishing a structured software development environment—what tasks, procedures, and controls are necessary in order to direct the effort toward the ultimate goal.
2. A commitment to project success and a firm belief in his or her role in directing the project toward success.
3. A motivation to direct all plans, decisions, and actions to the timely production of a quality product.

Unless the manager truly understands the project structure that must be applied, is committed to project success, and believes that the structure is necessary for the sake of the development of the software and the morale of the staff, he will have no chance of weathering the daily storms associated with implementing a successful project environment. If the manager does understand, is committed to, and is motivated to establish and maintain a structured environment, he will have no choice but to direct all efforts to doing so, because the success of the project is more important than anything else, including pleasing everyone within and outside the immediate software staff. The manager who has confidence in the principles behind the plans he has made will be able to explain the reasons for each component and will be able to stand his ground when faced with the reluctance of customer, higher management, or staff to believe those principles necessary. The manager will also be able to relax or redesign the controls if project conditions dictate, for he knows just how much compromise the structure can bear and still support the orderly production of a quality product.

In the early days of the project, the staff is small, it is fairly easy to establish and promote project communication, and the amount of data to be documented and tracked are manageable. The controls that will be applied are simple, and thus the procedures involved lend themselves to informality. During the planning process, the manager must design an organization and procedures that will support the vast weight of the data that will be generated and the numbers of people that will be involved as the project progresses. These plans will likely describe a level of control that is unfamiliar to many of the current and future staff. A potential problem exists in making the transition from the comfortable informality to the rigid structure described in the planning documents. This transition is extremely important, and many software managers have trouble effecting it. It is important that the software manager understand the problems involved in implementing and maintaining project structure so that he can attack them efficiently.

Software personnel sometimes balk at the structure that is proposed by the manager, stating that such controls are unnecessary deterrents to the creative process of software development. A software engineer may resent the imposition of baselining design specifications before coding begins, knowing that they will be constantly out of date anyway. He may feel it will be a waste of time as well as an embarrassment to undergo formalized procedures in order to correct a coding error the engineer found himself. The engineer may resent having outside testers, who know nothing about the problems he had in creating the code, find that he made an error, feeling that this procedure is an unjust indictment of his work.

This sort of software engineer has evidently not viewed past projects as whole products that the entire staff takes pride in seeing integrated and delivered to a customer. He has no doubt been involved on projects for which his or her contribution is considered as a whole unto itself, for which he was not able to see the entire system and thus was not able to care about the other portions of it. Any changes that were dictated by incompatibility with other portions of the system angered the engineer, because he did not understand why the system could not have been designed that way initially.

Once the engineer finished his contribution, he probably left the project, and problems that arose thereafter were worked out by the newest staff members, who deciphered them by looking at uncommented, undocumented listings as part of their "training."

A software engineer whose career has been launched and nurtured in such an environment has been conditioned to be concerned about his own individual piece of code or the output of his immediate group. He has probably been totally cut off from other development teams within the project and has been acquainted with their work only when a change is required in order to iron out the interface problems. Thus, the other teams have been merely another source of frustration. The only way to survive in such an environment is to have everyone else leave you alone so you can design, code, and test until you are satisfied with your work, then hope to be reassigned to another project as quickly as possible so you will not have to document the code or correct problems that clearly are not your fault.

No doubt this software engineer has felt that things should not be this way. When in training, he thought it was terrible that there was no good documentation and that the code was so hard to follow and was not commented. The engineer probably wished that he knew what the purpose of the entire system was and how his work fitted into the whole. The engineer was probably disgusted when trying to correct a reported error, only to find that the system against which he was testing has been changed several times since the problem was reported. He most likely has been infuriated to receive problem reports of the extremely informative form "Your module blew up!" accompanied by the dictum "The problem must be corrected tonight!"

Unfortunately, however, these irritations have been accepted as a way of life by a software engineer who has never seen any other environment. With no hope that anything will ever be better, the old "initiation rite" attitude familiar in fraternities and military schools prevails. Having suffered through debugging other people's undocumented, unreadable code, the engineer has paid his dues and feels he is now entitled to the luxury of forgoing documentation duties and careful commenting.

A software engineer who has become a technical task leader in such an environment is used to having absolute power over a segment of the system, because the project management has not "had time" to direct his efforts or coordinate them with the other areas of the system. The engineer has been forced to get the technical task done in any way he has seen fit, not regarding any other project area or the requirements of the company or the customer. It is extremely hard for this person to adjust to having a real manager, who actually does direct him. The engineer has tasted independence and is used to it. The management skills he has developed are valuable, yet he has not had to deal with project-wide issues and most probably does not understand them.

It is this former technical task leader who is the most difficult to assimilate into the project-oriented structured environment. His technical knowledge and experience is valuable, if not critical, to the development of the software, but the sustenance of the parochial attitude can destroy project morale, reduce productivity, and lengthen schedules. It is important to recognize the potential adjustment problem this employee may have and to resolve the underlying issues before they cause the software manager to alienate that engineer completely or to compromise the structure the manager has planned. Elicit the engineer's cooperation before the plans are released. Describe the role you expect him to play, and stress the project's need for his expertise and qualifications. Discuss the project plans with the engineer, and describe the reasons you feel the controls are essential. Define what each segment of the structure will do to make his work easier and more satisfying. If resistance is detected, discuss the employee's concerns openly and honestly. Use the old advertising ploy, "Try it, you'll like it." The purpose of this communication with key personnel is to describe your management philosophies informally, and to establish that this is the way things will be done. It should also be made clear that the cooperation of the employee is important, and he should make a commitment to at least try the methods. If this commitment is not forthcoming, it should be made clear that he has the choice of being reassigned immediately, for noncooperation in the project-oriented environment will not be tolerated. As the manager successfully implements the project plans, he or she will find that noncooperation will not be tolerated by the staff, either. There will be too much work to do and too much interdependence among groups to allow this kind of behavior to get in the way of a motivated staff.

This initial communication with key technical personnel will identify early, before much damage is done, those who will never be able or willing to adjust to the structure. It will also establish the manager as the leader of the project. It will establish him as one who is concerned for the attitudes of the employees and who meets problems instead of avoiding them.

Often, managers publish the plans and are taken aback by the criticism and negative reactions that may result. Because they did not recognize the possibility of such a reaction, they are caught off guard and enter a discussion with the critics in which they feel forced to defend the plans or, worse, agree to compromise them without realizing that many of the staff may have accepted and even welcomed the proposed structure. People who are used to a structured environment would not have it any other way. They see the problems that result from disorganization as unnecessary and preventable, and the adjustment from a structured environment to a chaotic one is much more difficult than the reverse adjustment. These people cannot tolerate disorganization and, realizing that they can do nothing about it, finally become apathetic or leave the project. These are the very people who will be the most valuable in the structured environment, and the manager must make as vigorous an attempt to identify them as he does to identify those who may not readily accept the plans.

When faced with any kind of confrontation, the manager must decide what is more important—temporary popularity or getting the job done. Temporary popularity is won at the cost of long-term respect. If a person cannot stand firm for the good of the project under pressure from the staff, he is not going to be a successful manager.

How does a manager create and maintain a project-oriented software development environment? The guidelines discussed in the following sections should assist the manager in this difficult job.

Establish That the Project Has a Leader and That You Are That Leader

It is vitally important that the software manager establish himself as the single point of authority within the project, the one person who is turned to by all components of the software organization for direction, focus, technical and administrative legislation, and task assignments. Although the manager has been given the leadership role in name, he must earn it.

The manager can establish his leadership only through direct communication with the staff—the assignment of duties, reviewing the quality and status of the work, and encouragement of problem discussion. As has been stated earlier, it must be done from the manager's first day on the project. If the manager neglects the duties of directing the staff or if he fails to act on problems when they are brought to his attention, the staff will quickly recognize that the manager is not a true leader.

When the manager must be away from the staff for out-of-town travel or lengthy in-house meetings, he must so inform the staff, appoint someone to take over the leadership role, and make certain that the staff knows this person is in charge during his or her absence. The staff should never feel that there is no leader of the project.

Stress the Importance of the Total Project

The software manager must make it clear that the number one goal of the work that is performed is to produce an excellent system and that everyone on the project is working toward the same goal.

The staff's attention should be focused on the total project as a priority over their own individual piece of work. This can be accomplished only if the goals, objectives, and technical aspects of the entire system are made public to all, preferably within a few paragraphs or pages of the requirements document. The staff must be kept abreast of project-wide issues, and the importance of the project to the company and the customer should be identified and stressed. Project-wide meetings should be held from time to time to impart such information and to allow the staff to interact with one another. Most importantly, the manager should make it clear in everyday decisions and actions that he is considering the total project as his first priority.

Dispel the Counterproductive Myths of Software Development

Many of the attitudes that hamper software productivity and foster separatism within technical groups or among individuals arise from the misconceptions that "good" design should never have to be changed, that "good" coding should produce no errors, and that "good" work will never result in missed deadlines.

Perhaps former management has reinforced these beliefs by giving negative feedback when design changes become necessary, when debugging takes more time than was scheduled for it, and when deadlines are missed. As a result, software engineers are afraid to make public their design and coding efforts, for they feel their work will be judged by the number of errors made. They will always say they are on schedule, until it becomes apparent that a deadline has been missed, in order to avoid being thought lazy or unproductive. This kind of atmosphere is oppressive. No one can produce good software under the pressure created by these erroneous and ridiculous assumptions. If software engineers are allowed to admit what they know to be true—that design changes are a part of the job, that every software engineer without exception makes coding errors, that deadlines may be missed even when an excellent job is being done and extra effort is being expended—they will not feel the need to hide their work from others or be afraid to admit that there will be problems meeting a deadline. Deadlines should not be taken lightly; however, if people are encouraged and feel free to discuss schedule problems as soon as they arise, the manager can take the appropriate action to correct them before it is too late. If the manager reacts to schedule problems by helping the staff and working out alternative ways to increase their productivity, they will more readily report the true status. As a result, the project will be ahead by the amount of time that is routinely wasted between when a problem occurs and when the deadline is missed.

In order to dispel the myth that good programmers do not need to redesign and do not make coding errors, the manager may use a sense of humor, coupled with examples from his own experience or that of respected technical personnel. Errors are not funny, but they are certainly inevitable, especially in the process of writing software code, so it is only reasonable to make it clear that they are not fatal to a career. Most importantly, the manager may foster the desired attitude by readily admitting the mistakes he makes, then taking quick action to correct them.

Carefully Define the Project Organization

The software project organization is the only means the software manager has to delegate responsibility downward to accomplish the many tasks of the development project. Often the requirement to define the organization with care is taken lightly, and the organizational structure becomes confused and unclear as responsibilities change and resources are reallocated to reflect project realities for development requirements.

The software organization must be clearly understood by all members of the staff, and individual responsibilities and project expectations must be clearly defined and documented at all times in order to avoid charter problems and project misunderstandings. A block diagram identifying the structure, roles, responsibilities, and personnel assignments must be visible, current, and available to all project personnel throughout the period of the development. As organizational changes are made, the block diagram identifying this structure to the staff must be updated, and these updates must be brought to the attention of the project, higher management, and, if necessary, the customer representatives. A clear set of responsibilities for each block on the organizational chart should be defined, and these responsibilities should be desseminated throughout the project. Everyone should be aware of what they are responsible for and how their responsibilities overlap with those of other staff members and with project and program areas. The transition of roles, responsibilities, and resources should be clearly identified and supported by the manager. Problems between organizational segments of the project or in the communications among these elements should be quickly dealt with, and modifications to the project structure should be made to alleviate them if required.

The software manager should review the effectiveness and viability of the project organization on a regular basis throughout the implementation period to assess its support to the productive development of software. Where necessary, the organization may require refinement in order to correct observed deficiencies. When this refining is required, it should be accomplished with deliberateness and speed so as to minimize productivity impact.

Make Timely Decisions

A common weakness of software managers is an inability to make and enforce decisions when adequate data are not available to back up the decision or to describe the problem. In a software development environment, many project conditions develop that demand timely decisions if the project is to proceed. In most of these cases, there is an individual or project group that will benefit if one decision is made and a second that will be adversely affected. The software manager is placed in a difficult position, for when he is forced to stand in the middle of these project factions and decide a course of action that will impact performance, application of resources, or project direction, he may feel in a "no-win" position. No matter which decision is made, he may be thought of negatively by the losing party and looked on, at least in the short term, as a negative influence on project success. The negative reaction may be vocal, and the manager will be painted as incompetent, insensitive, and not having the best interests of the project at heart.

In this situation, the software manager has many rationales on which he may defer the decision-making process. These include:

1. There are insufficient data on which to decide.
2. I do not have time to study the problem.
3. I will form a task force to analyze my options.
4. There are too many factors to consider at this time.
5. I must wait until this related analysis is complete.

By deferring a decision, the manager may feel that he has exercised prudent judgment, when, in fact, the manager has significantly impacted the project productivity and damaged his own credibility as well. When decisions that affect project progress are deferred, one of two possible actions results. Either all activities affected by the lack of a decision are stopped until the manager commits to a course of action, or the decision is made by the strongest faction of the staff, and the project moves ahead without the manager. In either case, the manager has lost credibility with the staff and is well on the way to losing control of the project. Morale will be low, because the only person vested with the authority for leading the project is not leading it, and the staff will be confused on what to do next and whose direction to follow.

The manager must quickly recognize the need for a decision and evaluate the impact on all areas of the project. He should involve the technical staff as much as possible in the decision-making process. The manager is not giving up any management prerogative or delegating decision-making responsibility to lower levels of the project. Within the organizational structure, however, feedback mechanisms provide the manager accurate information concerning the true feelings of the software staff on any significant project issues.

After the alternatives are weighed, the decision must be announced firmly and confidently, along with the reason for the decision. If decisions are consistently made after involving those whose work is affected and are clearly motivated by consideration for the well-being of the total project, the staff will respect the manager as well as his decisions, even if they do not always agree with the decisions.

Provide Timely Feedback on Employee Performance

In order to provide feedback, it is necessary for the software manager to take the time to evaluate the work that was performed. Personnel enjoy getting feedback on their work, but only if it is given by someone who has a true understanding of what is involved in the work. Nothing is less valid to an employee than a formal performance review from a manager who has not been involved in assigning and reviewing his work. This review is the only time many managers check the quality of their staff's work.

It is easy to praise excellent work, and it should be done in order to encourage more of the same. If the manager has made a determination that praise is not warranted, he should analyze the reasons. Was it just an average job? Perhaps no comment is necessary. If the employee has been a star performer, however, average output is noteworthy. If a job was not satisfactory, then feedback is clearly in order. Many managers are reluctant to provide feedback other than praise. It may be easy to ignore this duty, but it is not fair to the employee. If a person's work is judged by the software manager as unsatisfactory, the employee has no way of knowing unless he is told, and no way of improving unless the areas that need improvement are specifically pointed out. Criticism will be of no value unless it is constructive. The manager must stress that he is concerned with the employee's growth and is trying to help by offering feedback.

Exude Enthusiasm in All Project Dealings

The software manager must be enthusiastic about the project and should continually reflect these feelings when dealing with the staff. Enthusiasm has a way of becoming contagious, and every software project can use an epidemic of this nature.

The effective software manager is the visible center of the project to whom all project staff personnel, higher management, and customer representives turn for an assessment of the integrity of the software development effort. Software managers who are consistently complacent about the project and do not present a positive, upbeat image about progress and project potential will have a rapid and significant demoralizing effect on the staff and will project a negative impression of the software development throughout the company and customer environment.

When dealing with anyone regarding the software progress or project integrity, the software manager should consistently exude enthusiasm and confidence in order to provide a general feeling of well-being to anyone affected by or affecting the software implementation. The impression presented by the software manager should not be inaccurate and should represent the true state of the project; however, it should emphasize the positive aspects of the development environment rather than stress the negative.

Promote Visibility Throughout the Project

The software manager must ensure that all personnel assigned to the project have upward access through their management chain to the software management staff and that the project in turn has upward access and visibility throughtou the higher management and customer chains.

The software manager must be visible throughout the project, being frequently seen by even the lowest level technical personnel and exhibiting real concern and interest in their work, problems, and long-term needs, requirements, and desires. Everyone on the project needs to know that they have upward access to at least two levels of management above them and that when problems are presented through the chain, there will be quick action to resolve them. Personnel are reluctant to make sacrifices and deal with significant inconvenience when they feel that the management staff does not care or is not interested in how they perform. For this reason, managers should have frequent personal contact downward throughout the organization at least two levels. This contact should be characterized by listening and understanding, and should result in management actions to correct perceived project problems and situations.

Involve the Staff in Planning and Scheduling After the Initial Plans and Schedules Are Established

Production schedules should be negotiated with those who will do the work. If workers have committed themselves to meet a schedule based on their own feelings of how long the work should take, they are more likely to work harder to meet them. If dates are decreed from those above them, the workers are not as likely to support the deadlines.

Likewise, plans for the work to be done can be made with the cooperation of those who will be doing the work. Often, better ways to do things are recognized only by those whose work is immediately involved. If encouraged to offer suggestions, the staff can help the manager shape a better, more efficient environment.

Be Sensitive to the Differences in Staff Skills, Motivations, and Problems

The manager must recognize the differences that exist among personnel assigned to the staff and must act accordingly. There are two main categories of performers requiring different types of challenges and actions to motivate them. The first type are the "fast trackers." These individuals push the project along and provide innovative solutions to the technical and project problems, resulting in a productive software development effort. They are typically more goal oriented than are others on the project and need the freedom to act and to choose approaches. Their actions are typified by innovative approaches to problems, and they often question the basic premises on which decisions are made and technical solutions are derived. They must be heard by the manager and given sufficient authority to match or exceed the responsibilities they are assigned. The degree to which the software manager motivates the fast trackers on the project measures how successful the project will be in the long run.

The second category of personnel are the average staff, who make up the bulk of the software project. These individuals are more task oriented, requiring strong direction and motivation to perform effectively. In the main, they require a structured environment with limited prerogatives and freedom to perform.

Balance Concern for Production With Concern for People

The software manager must balance his concern for the project with common sense and concern for the staff. He must recognize that there are times when extra effort is required of all personnel assigned to the project to meet schedule and budget commitments and make clear that it will be expected when required. However, if the staff must continually work overtime in order to meet deadlines, something is wrong. Perhaps the original estimates on which the schedules are based were unrealistic. Perhaps there have been changes that dramatically increased the scope of work, but the schedules have not been adjusted accordingly. Perhaps the staff is not giving 100% daily but is procrastinating until each deadline draws near. Each of these situations can be addressed by the software manager. When overtime becomes a way of life, productivity, performance, and enthusiasm quickly diminish.

Know When to be Flexible and When to Stand Firm

The software manager has the responsibility for interfacing with higher manager and customer personnel and directing project personnel. In this capacity, the manager must always be willing to deal aggressively when protecting the integrity of the technical, administrative, or resource baselines of the software project. Frequently, for short-term expediency or to meet a critical milestone, the software manager is pressured by higher management, the customer, or by other groups within the project to compromise the long-term integrity of the project structure. Frequent acquiescence to these requests will indicate that the manager is dealing with short-term crises, forgetting the longer-term, more critical requirements to deliver a working piece of software.

There are times, however, when the external requirements are overriding and must supersede, even though supporting them will impact the software project and productivity. A second case where the manager must yield is when he recognizes the problems associated with short-term support but cannot convince responsible managment or technical personnel of the impact. The manager has the responsibility to pursue his concerns, but there is a point after which the only way to keep the project moving is to yield and modify schedules, budgets, and technical activities accordingly. In order to answer the integrity of software budgets and schedules after each of these modifications, the manager must identify the impact on the cost, schedule, and technical project integrity.

Staff the Job Efficiently and Carefully

Staffing a project is a critical, risky, and difficult task that must be done in a timely fashion. It is almost impossible to know how a person will perform within the project atmosphere until he is on the job, and mistakes in staffing can be costly. Careful attention must be paid to the staffing process in order to maximize project productivity.

The first step in intelligent staffing is to define the organization of the project in detail and identify the number of people needed, when they will be needed, the responsibilities of each position, and the skills necessary for each position. This process has been discussed in previous chapters of this book.

The second critical step in the process is to interview selectively and carefully. Staffing from within the company or on the recommendation of a respected friend or acquaintance involves the least risk, for the employee's work history is a known quantity, and the references obtained are usually more honest than those given by strangers. Even if the prospective staff member comes highly recommended from a close friend, he should be interviewed carefully. Selecting appropriate resumes from the outside should be done with care and is a much easier job if the manager knows exactly what positions he must fill.

Interviews are held for the express purpose of filling a particular job with the right candidate. They should never be allowed to be a waste of time for the manager or the prospective employee. If possible, the candidate should be briefed on the nature of the job and asked key questions before the interview is scheduled. Then, if there is definitely no interest on either part, the interview need not be held.

The manager should make every effort to present the best aspect of the company and the project, just as the employee is trying to make a favorable impression. The manager should schedule the interview as a priority matter, never allowing a last-minute crisis or hastily called meeting to interfere. He should be prepared for the interview, having studied the resume and determined what information requires expansion. He should greet the applicant on time and allow no interruptions during the interview. The applicant deserves the manager's total attention during this time.

If the manager wants to have this applicant talk to others in the project or in the company, he should contact these people well in advance so that they can adjust their schedules and be prepared for the interviewee. Staff members should be expected to treat the interview as seriously as the manager. They should never be caught off guard or asked to interview an employee when they do not know the requirements of the job he is to fill. Staff members should never be requested to interview an applicant at the last minute for the purpose of "entertaining" him while the manager does something else.

The manager should always ensure that an applicant whose work will be directed by another staff member is interviewed by that staff member. Besides being a common courtesy to both the current and future employee, this procedure allows the current staff member to accept the responsibility that goes with his charter of directing others—choosing the people who will be working under his direction. If a manager suddenly brings in and introduces a new employee to his supervisor, the manager is saying to the staff member that his responsibility clearly exceeds his authority and that the manager wants to hold on to authority that should have been delegated.

The purpose of the interview, clearly, should be to exchange information in order to determine if there is a good match between the requirements of the job and the skills and attitudes of the applicant. The manager should try to put the applicant at ease and maintain a casual yet businesslike atmosphere during the interview. He should ask specific questions regarding the candidate's experience and from these questions should be able to determine whether the candidate's previous experience is easily transferable. If there is no previous directly related experience, the manager must make the more difficult determination of whether the candidate is able to learn the required skills quickly, and whether he indeed has the aptitude for acquiring those skills. It is certainly appropriate, but rarely done, for the manager to request samples of the employee's work. Typists are routinely given tests in order to evaluate their skills. Too often, such objective information is not used in filling software positions, and the results can be painful for all concerned.

The interview is a time for honesty. The manager must describe the duties and skills required in as much detail as possible so that the applicant has enough information to determine if he or she will fit into the job. The project atmosphere should be described, and the manager should present his basic management philosophies. If the employee does not seem to be one who will adjust to the structured, teamwork-oriented environment, he should not be considered for the job. Any dead-end interviews should be terminated quickly and politely.

Although the positive aspects of the job should be stressed if the applicant seems desirable, the problems and headaches of the job should also be pointed out. This is no time for pure salesmanship. It is better for an employee who will not be happy in a job to determine this before rather than after he is hired, for turnover and disgruntled employees are not good for the project and are not good for the company's reputation.

Another important aspect of the interview is the evaluation of whether the employee's personality will fit into the group with which he will be working. If possible, the applicant should be allowed to chat informally with group members (again, the group members should be notified in advance of this event), perhaps even at lunch or during a coffee break. The confident manager of a well-run project is not afraid that the employees will "spill the beans" and realizes that the more information the applicant has about the job, the better it is for all concerned. The group should be consulted informally for their reactions, and their opinions should be considered in deciding whether to extend an offer to the candidate.

The software manager should take great care in matching the qualifications and interests of the applicant to the particular job. Software managers often make the mistake of attempting to staff each position with the most qualified individual he can find, hoping that the enhanced experience will give the project an "edge" when it needs extra support to meet milestones or to solve difficult technical problems. This approach frequently backfires, however, when the overqualified staff finds that they are performing tasks that do not challenge or motivate them. Another common management error is to staff the project with personnel who have less experience than required or anticipated to do the job. The rationale here is that by staffing the project with more junior personnel, additional funds will be available to apply to more pressing or higher-risk areas of the project. There is also a common belief that software engineers will rise to the challenge when required to accomplish tasks outside their experience level. Unfortunately, this is not always the case, and the software manager who staffs on the basis of this assumption runs the risk of having a key position staffed by someone who cannot do the job.

It is important that the manager keep the project staffed at the levels he has determined are necessary. The amount of work to be done will not change, and if the project is understaffed, current personnel will have to absorb the extra work, causing productivity and morale to suffer. On the other hand, gross overstaffing is also a mistake and will lead to personnel having nothing to do. Lack of work can be more damaging to the project than overwork.

Staffing at the proper levels is not easy, and the manager who is having difficulty finding staff should explore every alternative. The manager should elicit the help of the company's personnel department to explore resources within the company, advertise for outside candidates, and deal with agencies and those who work on a contract basis.

Have Faith in Your People and Assume the Best, But do Not Hesitate to Take Action if Proven Wrong

A maxim that is often quoted and well worth remembering is that the manager's most valuable resource is his staff. The manager is entrusting the success of the project for which he is directly responsible to his personnel. The manager should assign each staff member the job he is confident that person can perform, give the person as much control over his work as the person can handle, and have faith in his decisions and execution of the job.

Expectations of good work most often turn out to be self-fulfilling prophecies. People who feel that the manager believes they will do a good job will tend to go all out to prove him right.

If the manager does not have confidence in his people, he is constantly looking over their shoulders to make sure they are doing things correctly. The employees quickly recognize and resent the lack of trust. If the manager routinely reverses decisions made by an employee that are clearly within the employee's purview, he is saying, in effect, that the employee cannot do his job. It is very demoralizing and will cause an employee to greatly limit his own potential. The employee will be afraid to make a decision and will begin to take every small problem to the manager, feeling that the manager must approve his every move.

Sometimes managers are so protective of the project that they try to intercept all the mistakes their employees might make. A wise manager allows his people to make mistakes, knowing that it is the only way they will grow and that it ultimately will make his own job easier.

The manager must always show support for the employees' decisions, even in the most critical situation, assuming the best until he has a chance to talk to the employee. If an employee has indeed made a rash decision, or one unacceptable because of its adverse effects on the project, the manager must reverse the decision, but in a way that will permit the employee to save face at all costs. The employee must understand clearly the reasons the manager cannot support this particular decision or action, and the employee should be given the chance to reverse the decision himself. The worst case of nonsupport occurs when the manager criticizes an employee in front of other people. This outright humiliation should be avoided. If criticism is in order, the manager should speak to the employee in private at a later time.

Although optimism should be the manager's first reaction with regard to the staff, it must be tempered by good judgment. There are times when an employee's work or actions are clearly not acceptable. Unacceptable work should be brought to the employee's attention via constructive criticism aimed at helping him improve. If an employee is clearly not performing at the level required of the job, even after receiving help from the manager, further management action is required. The employee may need to be given a different kind of task, one that he can perform satisfactorily. He may need some extra training and supervision from a more experienced employee.

If an employee's work fails to improve, and he cannot perform any job within the project or does not want to accept a new assignment, the employee must be taken off the project. Someone else will have to perform the work the employee is responsible for, whether he stays or leaves.

If the employee stays, he is getting paid for services that are not being rendered. If the employee leaves, at least funds are freed with which to hire another person. It is better for the employee also, if possible, to be placed in another position or project within the company in which he fits the job.

If an employee causes disruption to the project because of behavior or negative attitude, after being given every chance to change, he must be taken off the project. Unprofessional behavior or negativism can have a more damaging effect on the project than does inferior work.

By tolerating poor performance, nonperformance, or belligerence the manager is not only harming the project but also giving the impression that he has no standards for project performance or behavior. It is also unfair to those who work hard to ignore or condone unacceptable behavior or performance.

Do Not Yield to the Temptation to Perform Technical Duties in Times of Distress

When schedules begin to slip, the manager is sometimes tempted to perform some segment of the technical task. For the first-time manager, this temptation may come early, when it proves difficult to adjust to the new role and seems more comfortable to undertake a familiar task that is easily executed. The manager must realize that the management task is a full-time job, one depending on his coordinating and supervising all the tasks carried on in the project. He must also realize that the technical task is a full-time job. If the manager chooses one job, the other is neglected. If he chooses the technical task, not only is he not performing his assigned job but also, more disastrously, no one is performing it.

When the manager suddenly begins to perform technical tasks, the staff is confused, because the organization of the project is muddled, the leader of the project now becomes a peer, and the only person to whom they can turn with problems, with priority conflicts, and for direction is too busy to deal with them.

The manager should recognize the inherent conflict of interest that arises when he chooses to perform technical tasks. For example, the manager, who supposedly supports the principle of peer review, becomes one of the staff but may not allow his work to be reviewed. If he allows the review, the staff will be reluctant to be totally honest, realizing that the performer is also the boss. In either case, the value of the activity is compromised.

During the time that the manager is performing a technical task, all the structure that has been achieved is likely to disintegrate, as it requires constant, careful attention to maintain.

The only sound actions a manager can take when the project is understaffed or behind schedule is to find personnel who can perform the extra work as quickly as possible, perhaps add resources, or, as a last resort, slip the schedule. Performing technical duties himself should simply not be considered an option if the project is to succeed.

Learn to Set Priorities Quickly

The manager's daily job is driven by a few tasks that are planned, and many more tasks which arise suddenly and require action. In order to keep the project going, it is important for the efficient manager to decide quickly the priority of a problem as it arises. Direct customer requests will probably be placed in the first priority. Requests from higher management will logically be high on the list. Any other problems that will dramatically affect the schedule should in most cases supersede both customer and higher management requests.

If a problem that logically should be handled by a particular staff member is brought to the manager, the person bringing the problem should be advised that this kind of matter is to be handled by the staff member concerned. If these same kinds of problems continue to be brought to the manager, he should talk to the responsible staff member to see why people are not taking the problems to him. Perhaps that person has had difficulty in handling them. Advise the staff member, and help him to learn to handle these problems.

If a problem that can be handled by the person bringing the problem is brought to the manager, the manager should encourage that person to make the decision himself. Many people are reluctant to make decisions until it is made clear that they have the authority to do so and will be supported in their decisions.

Personnel problems are of critical importance, but even their priorities must be weighed. No personnel problem should be ignored, no matter what urgent problem is currently being attacked. If the manager is unable to deal with a personnel problem of lesser magnitude at the moment it occurs, he must explain the urgency of the current situation, schedule a time to meet with the staff member or members, and then honor the commitment.

Perspectives on the Management Process

The manager's job is not easy. No one can follow the preceding guidelines all of the time. The kind of organization, commitment to the project, and concern for people needed to be able to follow these guidelines should be considered goals toward which the manager strives. The manager must remember at all times that his attitudes influence those of the staff members.

If the manager successfully implements the structured environment, personnel will quickly begin to appreciate the benefits of the controls and formalization of procedure. As personnel become used to the efficiencies the controls and procedures provide, they begin to support them wholeheartedly, offer suggestions for improved procedures, and often even request that stricter controls be applied. They begin to enjoy working with others on a common goal and prefer this atmosphere to one in which they must constantly contend with others in order to do their jobs, which often occurs in the disorganized, chaotic environment.

Although the software development business will always have its headaches, hassles, and frustrations, the controls and procedures advocated in this book put into place an efficient way of dealing with them as they arise, instead of allowing them to reach crisis proportions. Consequently, the headaches are fewer and less severe than they otherwise would be. Most people will welcome the relief that the structured environment brings to their jobs.

11 Summary

The management of a productive software development project requires careful planning, rigorous enforcement of management discipline, and an absolute personal commitment for success.

The successful production of quality software, as described in this book, is as much a function of planning, project control, and management effectiveness as it is of the technical project experience, staff quality, or resource availability. Managers of software projects are faced with a most difficult challenge. In order to succeed in a project, they must be effective from the very beginning of the project, when costs, schedules, and technical requirements are defined, and maintain the same degree of management competence, commitment, and experience throughout the development period.

A common characteristic of software projects is that they start with a flourish with such pronouncements as "This time we'll do it right" or "I will learn from my mistakes on that project," which seem to set an optimistic tone for the development. Unfortunately, these optimistic pronouncements often turn into protestations, such as "If only I had adequate, qualified labor and enough money, I could meet that ridiculous schedule," or "The lack of that interface has set back my development six weeks."

There is no recognition on the part of the software manager of the early project confusion and poor productivity that wasted a significant percentage of the available resources and demotivated the staff, or of the early planning not accomplished that if done would have minimized the effects of such development crises as hardware slips.

Why do software projects travel this well-worn path so frequently?

> One reason lies in the complexity of the techniques and the difficulties management and programmers face in implementing them. As with modern management practices, modern programming practices are intangibles that have to be disseminated by "soft" means such as education and training.

The techniques described in this book are complex and require insight, experience, and understanding if they are to be effectively applied to a project.

The manager is too frequently assigned responsibility directly from the technical ranks, quickly bogging down in the morass of poor requirements, missed milestones, or overrun budgets. There is a tendency to monitor project performance rather than to manage the project and direct its progress. There is a disastrous temptation by the managers to retreat to the safety of the management reports and projections, away from the unpleasant, day-to-day management and decision-making processes essential for success.

There is a way out of this quagmire. Books such as this one, Brook's *The Mythical Man-Month,* Weinberg's *The Psychology of Computer Programming* and others, coupled with a wealth of papers, articles, and conference proceedings assist the new manager.

Training courses designed to take the new manager through a sample project in the controlled atmosphere of the classroom rather than in the chaotic, unforgiving world of an actual project will pave the road, and a program of management apprenticeship will provide the environment to train in the skills essential for effective software management.

The effective software manager, as any manager, must realize that he is responsible and accountable for the project, can only focus, direct, and control the activities of the project, and will succeed only to the degree that he can organize and motivate others.

The manager must perform well all the jobs discussed in this book, not just some, and must be sufficiently realistic to recognize when something is not working well. There can be no crisis or reactive management. Rather there must be a continuous, smooth, planned transition of roles, responsibility, and data, and a project organization characterized by effective action to deal with project crises when they occur.

The manager must be a decision maker, with decisions being made in the context of a firm, planned project structure and based on an understanding of the actual state of the project.

Most importantly, the manager must be the visible source of project control. The techniques described in this book will provide the manager with the tools of the trade, which when applied effectively, will establish within the project the often-missing project center. By retaining control, the software manager can focus the activities toward a clear set of objectives consistent with the actual requirements of the project.

Successful management of software development is an acquired set of seemingly unrelated disciplines that must be planned, accepted by project personnel, and tailored to the characteristics of the development. Failure to manage is the common denominator in a significant number of disastrous or nonproductive software projects.

References

Baker, F. T. "Chief Programmer Team Management of Production Programming," *IBM Systems Journal,* vol. II, no. 1 (1972), pp. 56–73.

Bersoff, E. H., V. D. Henderson, and S. G. Siegel. *Software Configuration Management: An Investment in Product Integrity.* Englewood Cliffs, N.J.: Prentice-Hall, 1980.

Boehm, Barry W. "Software and Its Impact: A Quantitative Assessment," *Datamation,* May 1973, pp. 48–59.

Boehm, B. W., J. R. Brown, and M. Lipow. "Quantitative Evaluation of Software Quality." *Proceedings of the Second International Conference on Software Engineering,* October 1976, pp. 592–605.

Boehm, Barry W., Charles L. Holmes, Gene R. Ratkus, James P. Ramanos, Robert C. McHenry, and E. Kent Gorden. "Structured Programming Quantitative Assessment," *Computer,* June 1975, pp. 38–54.

Brandon, D. H. *Data Processing Organization and Manpower Planning.* New York: Petrocelli, 1974.

Brooks, Frederick, P., Jr. *The Mythical Man-Month: Essays on Software Engineering.* Reading, Mass.: Addison-Wesley, 1974.

Brown, J. R., and M. Lipow, "Testing for Software Reliability," *Proceedings of 1975 International Conference on Reliable Software,* April 1975, pp. 132–138.

Caine, Stephen H., and E. Kent Gordon. "PDL—A Tool for Software Design, Proceedings, National Computer Conference, 1975, pp. 271–276.

Cartwright, D., and D. Zander, eds. *Group Dynamics: Research and Theory,* 3rd ed. New York: Harper & Row, 1968.

Cougar, J. D., and R. A. Zawacki. *Motivating and Managing Computer Personnel.* New York: Wiley-Interscience, 1980.

Dahl, O. J., E. W. Dijkstra, and C. A. R. Hoare. *Structured Programming.* New York: Academic Press, 1972.

Daly, E. B. "Management of Software Development," *IEEE Transactions on Software Engineering,* May 1977, pp. 230–242.

Dalkey, Norman, et al. "The Delphi Method IV: Effect of Percentile Feedback and Feedin of Relevant Facts," Rand Corporation, March 1970.

Donelson, William S. "Project Planning and Control," *Datamation,* June 1976, pp. 62–65.

De Rose, B. C., and T. H. Nyman. "The Software Life Cycle: A Management and Technological Challenge in the Department of Defense." *IEEE Transactions on Software Engineering,* July 1978, pp. 309–318.

Drucker, P. F. *Management: Tasks, Responsibilities, and Practices.* New York: Harper & Row, 1974.

French, N. "Programmer Productivity Rising Too Slowly: Tanaka," *Computerworld,* 1977.

Gildersleeve, T. R. *Data Processing Project Management.* New York: Van Nostrand Reinhold, 1974.

Griffin, Edward L. "Real Time Estimating," *Datamation,* June 1980, pp. 188–197.

Holton, John B. "Are the New Programming Techniques Being Used?" *Datamation,* July 1977, pp. 97–103.

Hughes, Joan K., and Jay I. Michtom. *A Structured Approach to Programming.* Englewood Cliffs, N.J.: Prentice-Hall, 1977 (reviewed in *Computer,* November 1977, p. 110).

"Improved Programming Technologies Management Overview," IBM Data Processing Division, August 1973.

Jeffrey, Seymour, and T. A. Linden. "Software Engineering Is Engineering," *IEEE Computer Society Software Engineering Technical Committee Newsletter,* September 1977, pp. 5–6.

Jensen, R. W., and C. C. Tonies, eds. *Software Engineering,* Englewood Cliffs, N.J.: Prentice-Hall, 1979.

Johnson, James R. "A Working Measure of Productivity," *Datamation,* February 1977, pp. 106–112.

Kernighan, B. W., and P. J. Plauger. *The Elements of Programming Style.* New York: McGraw-Hill, 1974.

Kieder, Stephen P. "Why Projects Fail," *Datamation,* December 1974, pp. 35–37.

Koontz, H., and C. O'Donnell. *Principles of Management: An Analysis of Managerial Functions.* New York: McGraw-Hill, 1972.

Kuhn, William W. "A Software Life Cycle Case Study Using the Price Model." *Proceedings of National Aerospace Electronics Conference, 1982,* pp. 165–170.

Liskov, B. H. "A Design Methodology for Reliable Software Systems," Proceedings, American Federation of Information Processing Societies, 1972, Vol. 41, Part 1, pp. 191–200.

McClure, Robert M. "Software—The Next Five Years," *Digest of Papers, COMPCON,* Spring 1976, pp. 6–7.

McGregor, D. *The Human Side of Enterprise,* New York: McGraw-Hill, 1960.

Metzger, P. W. *Managing a Programming Project,* 2nd ed., Englewood Cliffs, N.J.: Prentice-Hall, 1981.

Myers, G. J. *Reliable Software through Composite Design.* New York: Petrocelli/Charter, 1975.

Mills, H. D. "The Complexity of Programs," in *Program Test Methods,* ed. W. C. Hetzel. Englewood Cliffs, N.J.: Prentice-Hall, 1973.

Mills, Harlan D. "Chief Programmer Teams, Principles, and Procedures," IBM Federal Systems Division Report FSC 71–5108, Gaithersburg, Md., 1971.

Mills, Harlan D. "Software Development," *IEEE Transactions on Software Engineering,* December 1976, pp. 265–273.

Mills, Harlan D. "Top-Down Programming in Large Systems," in *Debugging Techniques in Large Systems,* ed. R. Rustin, pp. 41–55. Englewood Cliffs, N.J.: Prentice-Hall, 1971.

Parnas, D. S., "On The Criteria To Be Used in Decomposing Systems into Modules," Communications of the ACM, December 1972, pp. 1053–1058.

Perlis, A., F. Sayward, and M. Shaw, *Software Metrics: An Analysis and Evaluation.* Cambridge, Mass.: The MIT Press, 1981.

Pooch, U. W., et al. "Computer Science and Computer Engineering Education in the 80's," *Computer,* vol. 11, no. 9, September 1978, pp. 60–83.

Procurement Associates, Inc., *Business Management: Project Managers Handbook,* vol. 2, Covina, Calif. (1979).

Pullen, Edward W., and Robert G. Simko. "Our Changing Industry," *Datamation,* January 1977, pp. 49–55.

Putnam, L. H., and A. Fitzsimmons. "Estimating Software Costs," *Datamation,* September 1979, pp. 189–198.

Ramanos, J. P. "ICEPAC Functional Description, Integrated Computer Engineering," P.O. Box 356, Cupertino, Calif. 94015, September 1982.

Rogers, E.M., and R. Agarwala-Rogers. *Communication in Organizations.* New York: Free Press, 1976.

Ross, Douglas T., and Kenneth E. Schoman, Jr. "An Introduction to SADT, Structure Analysis and Design Technique," Waltham, Mass.: SoftTech Inc., January 1977.

Scott, Randall F., and Dick B. Simmons. "Programmer Productivity and the Delphi Technique," New York: *Datamation,* May 1974.

Semprevivo, P. C. *Teams in Informations Systems Development.* New York: Yourdon Press, 1980.

Shneiderman, B. *Software Psychology.* Winthrop, 1980.

Spirer, H. F., and D. J. Reifer. *Successful Management of Software Projects.* The MGI Management Institute, Los Angeles, Calif: 1980.

"Structured Walk Throughs: A Project Management Tool," IBM Data Processing Division, August 1973.

Teichrow, D., and E. A. Hershey III. "PSL/PSA: A Computer Aided Structured Documentation and Analysis of Information Processing Systems," *IEEE Transactions on Software Engineering,* January 1977.

Thomsett, R. *People and Project Management.* Yourdon Press, New York: 1980.

Van Leer, P. "Top-Down Development Using a Program Design Language," *IBM Systems Journal,* vol. 15, no. 2 (1976), pp. 155–170.

Walston, C. E., and C. P. Felix. "A Method of Programming Measurement and Estimation," *IBM Systems Journal,* vol. 16, no. 1 (1977).

Wasserman, Anthony I. "On the Meaning of Discipline in Software Design and Development," in *Software Engineering Techniques,* ed. D. Bates. Infotech International, San Francisco, Calif.: 1976.

Wolverton, Ray W. "The Cost of Developing Large-Scale Software," TRW SS-7201, March 1972.

Weinberg, G. *The Psychology of Computer Programming.* New York: Van Nostrand Reinhold, 1971.

Yourdon, E. *How to Manage Structured Programming.* Yourdon Press, New York: 1976.

Yourdon, E. *Managing the Structured Technique.* Englewood Cliffs, N.J.: Prentice-Hall, 1976.

Yourdon, E., and L. Constantine. *Structured Design.* Englewood Cliffs, N.J.: Prentice-Hall, 1977.

Yourdon, E. *Structured Walkthroughs.* Englewood Cliffs, N.J.: Prentice-Hall, 1979.

Index